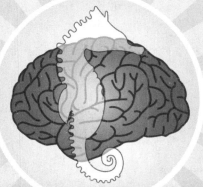

THE BRAIN
TRAINING
REVOLUTION

A PROVEN WORKOUT FOR HEALTHY BRAIN AGING

PAUL E. BENDHEIM, MD

Contributions by
Richard Samuels, PhD; Edward Wein, PhD; Tracy Hafen, MS

Published by Sourcebooks, Inc.
P.O. Box 4410, Naperville, Illinois 60567-4410
(630) 961-3900
Fax: (630) 961-2168
www.sourcebooks.com

Library of Congress Cataloging-in-Publication Data

Bendheim, Paul E.
   The brain training revolution : a proven workout for healthy brain aging / by Paul E. Bendheim.
      p. cm.
   Includes bibliographical references and index.
   1. Mental health--Popular works. 2. Brain--Aging--Prevention--Popular works. I. Title.
   RA790.B437 2009
   612.8'25--dc22

                         2009030720

Printed and bound in the United States of America.
     SB 10 9 8 7 6 5 4 3 2 1

CONTENTS

"I am a brain, Watson. The rest of me is a mere appendix. Therefore, it is the brain I must consider." —SIR ARTHUR CONAN DOYLE

ACKNOWLEDGMENTS

"Life without memory is no life at all."

In its essence, this is a book about making and preserving memories.
It is dedicated to my late father and to all the remembrances of him
that continue to speak gently yet clearly of love, generosity, intellectual
curiosity, motivation, and good deeds.

This book and BrainSavers would not have happened without the help of
many people in various ways. I have a deep sense of gratitude to all.

Traditionally, the most important inspirational sources are listed
last in the acknowledgment section, but then in sparkling terms. If a
few "someones" are so important, they deserve top billing. So right up-
front, I acknowledge and honor my late father and my still incredibly
vigorous 89-year-old, "living the brain-healthy life" mother. Together
their influences and support over my lifetime are inestimable.

My fascinating wife Judith Amiel, through her presence and patience,
her critiquing, her true companionship and loving care, has made this
sometimes trying effort much more palatable.

My daughter, Jessica, has been a truly terrific supporter and contrib-
utor—the thought of her brings a smile to my face and warmth to my
heart. My son, Daniel, is mature beyond his years and the best young fly-
fishing partner a father could imagine. Both enrich my life in wonderful
ways and make all the hard work and long travels worthwhile.

Thanks to Frank Nightingale, the first to proclaim the raison d'être for this book, and to my persevering agent Bridget Wagner at Sagalyn for finding Sourcebooks—just the right home for it.

My intent was to write a book explaining the revolutionary and exciting good-news discoveries about the aging brain in common language, not the highly technical language used in medical and scientific journals. Numerous individuals have aided me in this quest. Their diligent reviewing and editing of the drafts have made it a much more readable book. A special soul-felt thank-you to Shana Drehs, senior editor at Sourcebooks, for her commitment. Her instructive and informative comments were critical every step of the way. This book is immeasurably better because of Shana, Sara Appino, and the rest of the Sourcebooks team who believed in the need for such a book and worked long and hard to bring it to you, my readers. Francine Hardaway edited early drafts—her sense of direction, literary touch, and commonsense approach greatly improved the book's direction and style. I alone am responsible for any errors or oversights.

Rebecca Durnin is a talented and serious young artist whose drawings first impressed me at Pomona College's senior-year exhibit in the spring of 2006. Becca's creative and original illustrations add incalculable zest to the book's intent and delivery of its message. Our many and long discussions regarding the content of her illustrations were creative refreshments for me.

I have a real indebtedness to my scientific colleagues at BrainSavers—Rich Samuels, Ed Wein, and Tracy Hafen. They contributed expertise in cognitive psychology, nutrition, and physical exercise, respectively. Ed's encyclopedic knowledge of nutritional sciences gained over thirty years in food science, nutrition, and biotechnology aided me considerably—they do not teach enough nutrition in medical school! Tracy's talents are many; she is tireless and never ceases to amaze me with her creativity in physical exercise programming and much, much more. Rich, in addition to his friendship, intellectual insights, and "level 7" contributions to brain reserve, CQ, and other aspects of the World Brain Gym, was the maestro in planning and producing the DVD. Additionally, he teamed with Chris Bohnsack of Bohnsack Design, a creative puzzle designer, to develop the color and the black and white brain exercises in the book.

The majority of the tasty recipes were the creative work of Executive Chef Jim Perko and Theresa Healy at Discover Nutrition 365, with additional contributions by Melanie Albert, Sarah Cahill, and Dorothy Turner. Theresa and Romina Yee developed the menus, which along with additional recipes, can be found on the website www.brainsavers.com.

Doug Barrett, my medical school classmate, lifelong friend, and colleague in neurology, was gracious with his time in reviewing chapter drafts. Numerous other colleagues deserve mention. Foremost among them are Steven Ferris, Art Kramer, Howard Fillit, Flint Beal, Daniel Chain, Ed McAuley, John Eckstein, and Keith Mansford.

I am fortunate to have benefitted from interactions with many talented neurologists and scientists during my medical school, residency, and fellowship years, and beyond. My future career as a neurologist and investigator was nurtured early on by Bill Sibley and Bill Buchsbaum, and also by Doug Stuart, William Dantzler, Marshall Denowitz, Jay Smith, Phil Krutzsch, and John Palmer at the University of Arizona, College of Medicine. Yechiel Becker at the Hebrew University of Jerusalem truly launched me in the research lab during my medical school "sabbatical," encouraged my intuition that the brain was a formidable yet exciting frontier in medical science, and became a lifelong friend. Dave Bolton, John Caronna, Bill Schwartz , Ken Johnson, Hill Panitch, Ben Podemski, Jim Schmidley, David Chad, David Greenberg, Bob Fishman, Lewis Rowland, Gareth Parry, Henry Wisniewski, Pankesh Mehta, Richard Carp, Yuval Herishanu, Eric Reiman, Pierre Tariot, Audrey Penn, Neil Raskin, Roger Simon, Bob Layzer, Michael Aminoff, Ivan Diamond, Howard Fields, Stanley Prusiner, Dick Barringer, Michael Charness, Marshall Elzinga, Ivan Leiberburg, and Neil Cashman taught, inspired, and influenced me in important and various ways during my professional life.

Guidance, advice, support, and camaraderie have come in various doses and combinations from family, especially sisters Margo and Vicki; brother Fred; cousins Paul and Flo Eckstein, John and Diane Eckstein, and Peter and Alice Buseck; and friends John Schmidt, Jim Leonhard, Jim Wirth, Stephen Meadow, Hazel Richards, Julia Rosen, Nate Summer, Lynda Samuels, Patsy Lowry, Claudia Gilburd, Ziva Yavin, Petrie Wilson, Judith Kristen, David Jerman, Bill Joost, and Joe Moore.

At BrainSavers, I have worked with an incredible, motivated, and committed team, including Bobbie Danielson, Tom Curzon, Steve Seiler, Len Schutzman, Larry Luke, Tom Meites, Jay Geer, Jeff Wilson, Shelley DiGiacomo, Jonathan Ariano, Raj Gangadean, Vicky Sweeney, Lynn Staub, Bobby Scott, Toni Gehm, André Early, Leslie Haston, Tom Gladfelter, and John Nimsky.

Deserving mention are Robert Hing at the Scottsdale Resort and Athletic Club, Bill Lavidge and Tim Trull at the Lavidge Company, Tyler Quinn at Hoisted Sail Productions, and Curtis Kurowski. Permission from the law firm of Osborn Maledon to reproduce two cognitive exercises is appreciated.

The early-morning coffee crew of Lance, Jake, and Megan, at Hava Java in Phoenix, always had a fresh cup of French roast ready when I needed it.

Finally, the positive influence of others too numerous to name here deserve mention: my many teachers, professors, clinical mentors, medical and scientific colleagues, students and house staff, research assistants, and patients who over the years continued my education, kept my imagination stimulated, and certainly contributed to my personal brain reserve.

To anyone I have inadvertently omitted: my apologies. It's the people in one's life that count—my heartfelt thanks go out to all.

INTRODUCTION—
YOU ARE YOUR BRAIN

"There is no doubt, those of us who expand our minds, exercise our brains and our bodies, and give them good food, feel better, perform better, remain independent longer. We age better."—LINDA, SCOTTSDALE RESIDENT, AGE 70

Ed and Linda are a retired American couple living in Scottsdale, Arizona, a colorful, cactus-studded desert community near Phoenix. Ed is 81 and Linda is 70. When I first met them in 2007, they had concerns that are familiar to almost everyone older than 50. They had noticed that, as they aged, their minds seemed to work less quickly than before, and they sometimes had trouble remembering names or facts. They certainly did not have dementia—a progressive disease process that seriously affects one's ability to remember, think, name and use objects, use language fluently, and behave "normally"—but they had become aware that their brains and minds had slowed down.

Ed and Linda began to take part in the brain-healthy lifestyle program that this book is based on. After participating for just two months, the couple reported that their minds were sharper and that their mental activities seemed to happen more easily. "Now, I can remember five numbers in an account sequence when writing checks," Linda said. She also reported remembering passwords more quickly and more accurately, and feeling as if she could better retain more information in general. Ed says he also now remembers names better than before.

Ed and Linda have continued their brain-healthy lifestyle for more than two years. They do it right: physical exercise (regular walking, yoga, and moderate exercise in the swimming pool), mental exercise (lots of reading, crossword puzzles, socializing with friends, participating in an Italian language discussion group, and computer-based mind-stimulating activities), and a brain-healthy diet (vegetables, fruits, salads, olive oil, red wine, chicken for Linda, fish for Ed, and natural snacks).

"We are not couch potatoes," Ed says. "We enjoy life more since we are keeping active—both our brains and bodies."

Addressing declines in mental performance, like that which Ed and Linda experienced, is a rapidly growing issue for older Americans.

- By 2020, the number of Americans age 50 and up will soar by 31 million, to 118 million.

- About two-thirds of Americans older than 50 complain of memory problems.

- Aging Americans fear memory loss and Alzheimer's disease more than they fear cancer, heart disease, and even death.

This book is about how to fight off memory loss, age-associated brain slowdown, and Alzheimer's disease. It's about what you can do to blunt the assaults of aging and to perform at a high level in your sixties, seventies, and beyond. It's about training your brain to be better.

WHAT WE KNOW ABOUT THE BRAIN

President George H. W. Bush declared the 1990s the Decade of the Brain. It was in that decade and the early years of this century that brain research revealed some incredibly exciting things that previously seemed part of the realm of science fiction. That research, some of which will be presented in the following chapters, has resulted in two unexpected and fundamentally important principles about the hidden potential in each of our brains.

1. **Your aging brain is plastic.** Scientists have determined that the brain is more flexible, or plastic, than previously believed. That means that the brain is malleable and changeable—it can actually generate new cells and new connections even later in life. It is not hardwired from birth and then frozen that way. The idea that the brain can rewire and reshape itself has revolutionized the way we look at the aging brain.

2. **You can build a fortress against brain enemies.** By using your brain every day in mentally challenging activities you build *brain reserve*, a personal insurance policy for a fortified brain. Exercising your brain makes use of its plastic quality (helping you create new brain cells and new connections) and provides ongoing strength building for the brain you've spent your life educating and loading with knowledge and wisdom. The result is a brain that is used to thinking, remembering, and performing at the top of its game. Keeping your brain "in shape" protects you against age-associated memory loss, Alzheimer's disease, and other assaults on the brain. It is this protection, this brain reserve, that I'll refer to often throughout this book.

Doctors and scientists now know, contrary to centuries of previous beliefs, that the aging brain can change itself, restructure for better performance, and become stronger. That's right! We can regain, retrain, and maintain our brains. Just like we expect some loss of heart, lung, joint, muscle, and sexual functioning with age, some loss of brain cells and mental efficiency is a normal part of healthy aging. But there are crucial things you can do to maintain efficiency:

- Because the brain is changeable and plastic, loss of brain cells is not something you have to just accept—your 50-, 60-, 70-, and even 80-year-old brain creates and sustains new cells when you give it the opportunity to grow.

- Loss of connections between brain cells is not a one-way street— giving your brain regular workouts creates new, active, and protective connections. This is brain reserve, which reduces your risk of memory loss and Alzheimer's disease.

• You can fight off memory loss—your memory can remain strong and even become more robust as you age, if you live a brain-healthy lifestyle. That is what the Brain Training Revolution is all about.

Given the recent breakthroughs in the science of the aging brain, it now seems reasonable to predict that we can reduce and perhaps largely eliminate much "normal" age-associated memory impairment—the No. 1 health concern of Americans over the age of 50. More important, the terrifying risk and reality of Alzheimer's disease might be greatly reduced over the next several decades by applying these new discoveries coupled with emerging biomedical-based preventive and therapeutic strategies.

How is this possible? A brain-healthy lifestyle is a large part of the answer.

CogniByte
In 2007 the Centers for Disease Control and Prevention, in conjunction with the National Alzheimer's Association, published *The Healthy Brain Initiative: A National Public Health Road Map to Maintaining Cognitive Health.*

After reviewing the evidence, the National Alzheimer's Association (the leading not-for-profit, non-governmental agency devoted to research and to assisting victims and caregivers of Alzheimer's disease) announced in 2005 that if each and every one of us got involved, we could eliminate Alzheimer's disease in the future.

This announcement was two years after I had started BrainSavers—a company dedicated to promoting programs and products for a brain-healthy lifestyle—whose mission "is to help maintain healthy minds, reducing the impact of age-related memory impairment and the risk of developing Alzheimer's disease."

Make some brain-healthy lifestyle changes. Get involved in improving your brain. Come join the Brain Training Revolution.

YOU ARE YOUR BRAIN

The biochemist and famous science-fiction author Isaac Asimov called it "the three-pound universe," the most complicated organization of matter known to mankind.

William F. Allman, author of *Apprentices of Wonder: Inside the Neural Network Revolution*, called it "a monstrous, beautiful mess... a tangled web that displays cognitive powers far exceeding any of the silicon machines we have built to mimic it."

And the American humorist Will Rogers said, "It needs as much exercise as your body does—maybe more."

"It" is the human brain—the most amazing, elegant, and complex structure in the universe—the reason we have the Bible, the Giza Pyramids, the Greek Parthenon, the Code of Hammurabi, the many inventions of ancient China, the music of Mozart and Beethoven, the plays of Shakespeare, the novels of Faulkner, the paintings of Monet, the oeuvre of Marcel Duchamp, the U.S. Declaration of Independence and Constitution, computers and the Internet, artificial hearts, the Martian rover, the human genome sequenced, and nanotechnology, just to name a few.

The brain, the critical organ that resides in and is protected by your skull, is the core of your self. It defines your identity. It is the essence of your uniqueness and the planning and control center of your body. There are thousands, if not tens of thousands, of other people in this world right now who have bodies much like yours—similar eye, skin, and hair colors; similar height, weight, and other defining physical features—not to mention the millions of people who have preceded you. But out of the almost seven billion fellow humans who currently inhabit the earth, there isn't one who has a brain that remotely resembles your own.

Of course, I am speaking not of the anatomy of your brain, for all our brains appear nearly identical. I am referring to the intangibles of your brain: your personality, intelligence, value system, humor, language and speech patterns, eating preferences—all this and much, much more are contained within your brain and no other. Each brain does a one-of-a-kind job analyzing new information, which is why no two people perceive, describe, or remember a sensory experience in identical ways.

You might undergo a heart transplant, but you would be the same lover. Similarly, you might replace your kidneys, liver, and lungs but with little effect on your personality. Your irreplaceable brain makes you the person everyone knows as you. That's why when someone's brain begins to fail, family members often say to the doctor, "She's just not herself."

OBSTACLES TO OPTIMUM BRAIN FUNCTION

The brain is like every other organ in your body: it suffers from wear and tear over time. Some changes that result are unwelcome and can be truly worrisome. It's important to realize that there are some brain-aging realities.

Just as you're aware of the risk of heart disease and cancer, and the steps you can take to reduce them, you should also be aware that with age comes increased risk for significant memory loss. (I'm guessing you already know this, and that's why you picked up this book!) My mission is to help you minimize those risks through science-based interventions that you can easily and enjoyably make part of your everyday lifestyle.

Think of it this way: All machines need maintenance. Parts wear out, oil needs changing, components become dull. From the simplest mechanical tool to the most complex electronic-gadget-laden fighter jet, without regular maintenance, efficiency decreases and the machine eventually stops working.

The brain is no exception. Starting at about the age of 40, the brain begins to shrink moderately. The debris from old and dying cells and their worn-out connecting cables accumulates between cells and results in some loss of function.

The challenge is to minimize wear and tear, and to maintain, strengthen, and repair those cells and connections to the best of our abilities, so that the essential memory, learning, and creative activities of the brain stay strong. If we do this, these critically important brain functions (e.g., decision making, complex task execution, thinking, memory formation) will remain highly functional and the source of our greatest joys as we age. The goal is to prolong our mental and physical independence as long as we possibly can. As President John F. Kennedy once said, "The time to fix the roof is when the sun is shining."

BRAIN DISEASE

In addition to Alzheimer's disease, there are a number of relatively common brain diseases and conditions that are associated with aging and result in the loss of memory, the abilities to use spoken and written language correctly, to reason and judge soundly, to plan and execute complicated tasks, and to think abstractly. Vascular dementia and stroke—or the death of brain areas ranging in size from that of a pinhead to almost an entire hemisphere of the brain—result, for example, when the blood vessels transporting vital oxygen, sugars, and other essential nutrients become blocked from fatty deposits or rupture as a result of high blood pressure. Parkinson's disease, characterized by tremors and rigidity, is sometimes accompanied by memory and thinking problems. Parkinson's results from a deficiency of dopamine, one of the key messenger chemicals in the brain. Other age-associated brain diseases that are less common but that affect memory, thinking, and/or behavior include Creutzfeldt-Jakob disease and other degenerative disorders, normal pressure hydrocephalus, vitamin B_{12} and other deficiencies, thyroid disorders and other metabolic conditions, and some toxins.

But the greatest scourge of the aging brain is Alzheimer's disease. It is a tragedy that more than five million Americans suffer from Alzheimer's disease today, and that number is estimated to reach about sixteen million by 2050, portending a truly catastrophic health and cost-of-care crisis. The single greatest risk factor for Alzheimer's disease is advancing age; the older you are, the greater is your risk.

According to current statistics, in the United States, Alzheimer's disease affects:

- One of every six women who live to be at least 55

- One of every ten men who live to be at least 55

- 13 percent of all Americans over the age of 65

- Almost 40 percent of Americans who live beyond the age of 80

- 5.3 million Americans in total, including 200,000 who are younger than 65

Here are some other facts about Alzheimer's:

- An American is diagnosed with Alzheimer's every 70 seconds.

- As many as 10 million Americans have mild cognitive impairment, which often progresses to Alzheimer's or another type of dementia (brain disease characterized by loss of memory, language ability, thinking skills, and behavioral problems).

- About 14 million baby boomers (born between 1946 and 1964) will develop dementia, and 10 million will develop Alzheimer's.

- There will be 500,000 new Alzheimer's diagnoses in 2010, 600,000 in 2030, and almost 1 million in 2050.

- Medicare will spend $160 billion on treatment for Alzheimer's and other types of dementia in 2010.

- About 10 million family members, friends, and volunteers provide unpaid Alzheimer's care each year.

- The U.S. government spent about $650 million on Alzheimer's and dementia research in 2008.

Those figures are staggering. It's time to take a look at how we're going to fight back.

WHAT IS THE BRAIN TRAINING REVOLUTION?

At its core, the Brain Training Revolution is a detailed but easy-to-follow lifestyle program to help you maintain and enhance normal brain function during midlife and beyond. It's a medical doctor's prescription for healthy brain aging for folks who are 45 and older.

The Brain Training Revolution is designed to strengthen your brain's inherent abilities to perceive your world; process, remember, and recall it better; and use these abilities to react, learn, think, and create more easily. It does this by guiding you to live a brain-healthy life, which incorporates brain-healthy eating, modest physical exercise, stress management, a good night's sleep, and mental exercises for the most important "muscle" you have. When healthy food and physical exercise properly nourish your brain, and when fun and engaging mental exercises stimulate it, your brain will grow new cells and connections. It will become stronger. You can grow your brain and help protect it from the relentless aging process. Although the Brain Training Revolution is all about brain health and a brain-healthy lifestyle, it is also a prescription for an overall healthy lifestyle.

I salute the pioneering work of Dr. Dean Ornish and others who have proved that changes in lifestyle can reverse heart disease. But where Dr. Ornish developed a heart-healthy lifestyle with emphasis on reversing already-existing heart disease, my colleagues and I have designed a healthy lifestyle for brains, for people who want to do everything possible to avoid having an unhealthy brain, people who want to minimize the risk of age-associated memory loss and terrible diseases like Alzheimer's and stroke.

The foundation of my program is this: a brain-healthy diet in combination with regular, modest physical exercise and invigorating mental challenges can maintain and improve brain health. Following the Brain Training Revolution will result in better brain function: better memory, better learning ability, better decision making, and a reduced incidence of Alzheimer's disease and dementia.

What's more, a brain-healthy lifestyle not only protects the aging brain from future assaults but also may reverse some of the specific changes associated with Alzheimer's disease. For example, in an aging brain at risk for Alzheimer's, the buildup of toxic beta-amyloid protein begins years before the memory loss and other signs of Alzheimer's disease appear in clinical tests. Early evidence from research laboratories suggests some reversal of this marker of Alzheimer's can occur from lifestyle interventions. Stay tuned for more developments on this front.

Thousands of talented scientists, physicians, psychologists, philosophers, ethicists, and other professionals have investigated brain aging and reached encouraging insights and, in many cases, sound recommendations. This book and the Brain Training Revolution program are based on research in human and animal studies published in peer-reviewed journals by the world's leading experts across many medical and scientific disciplines.

When you look at the body of research that has been produced, one thing is striking: we have rediscovered what the ancients knew and practiced! The Industrial Revolution, the biomedical revolution, and the technological revolution of the past few decades all have given scientists powerful tools with which to measure the biological and chemical processes in the body and the intricate workings of the brain. But to an incredibly large extent, they have also confirmed what ancient observers analyzed, interpreted, and endorsed. Going back to biblical times, various authorities have recommended some of the same lifestyle components that together comprise the Brain Training Revolution equation for health.

So, there is no silver bullet—a crossword puzzle a day, a dietary supplement, or single food or exercise—to cure all your ills. But there is solid evidence that physical exercise, brain exercise, and a diet of natural foods make up the triumvirate of brain health. The commonsense basis of this book is a formula that has worked from biblical times up through today. It has stood the test of time. The challenge is to get these healthy habits back into our lifestyle, to change even in relatively small ways the cycle of our days.

My goal is to present—in understandable language—a handbook that showcases the best evidence for healthy brain aging: a guide to brain-building lifestyle changes you can adopt to the degree that they are suitable for you. In the resources section, you'll find many recent books that delve into the science of the aging brain. But here I aim to provide the actual ingredients for a brain-healthy lifestyle: a complete, easy, and fun plan of realistic physical, mental, and dietary activities. This program does not make it difficult to live well day after day, month after month, or year after year; it is a prescription that you can take in baby steps to fit your own comfort level, knowing all along that each step you take is in the right direction.

It's impossible to prevent aging. Dr. Andrew Weil writes in his popular book *Healthy Aging* that he does not believe that aging is reversible. I agree that anti-aging medicine is bunk. Aging is as much a part of the cycle of life as any other biological rhythm. It should be welcomed, as it can be a beautiful, productive, and creative time—one that brings, among other things, great maturity of the mind. And while our brains at 70 may not be as quick as when we were 50, they can remain active, complex, and wonderfully imaginative nevertheless.

WHAT YOU'LL GET OUT OF THIS BOOK

Considerable evidence shows that modifying your behavior to create a brain-healthy lifestyle can substantially improve functioning of your brain at any age while also reducing the risk of age-related brain impairment. Although biological processes take a modest toll on our brains as we age, you have the ultimate control. We all experience, to some degree, age-associated memory lapses (or senior moments) and the slowing down of some mental processes, but we also have the power to minimize their severity. Even more important, we can take positive steps to reduce our chances of developing Alzheimer's disease.

If you control the things you can control—your response to stress, the food you consume, the restfulness of your sleep, and your care for your body—you can greatly influence the vitality of your brain. Your challenge is to focus on everything you can control so that you can take care of your mind and memory and build a brain reserve to guard against Alzheimer's disease and stroke.

It is never too late to start the Brain Training Revolution, and the scientific evidence is clear—you will feel better and your body and brain will benefit. As you read this book, you'll gain valuable insights into what it takes to make that happen. Here are some of the things you'll discover:

- The features of the brain's anatomy and functionality that are critical to healthy brain aging

- What you can expect to experience as your brain gets older

- How to boost your brain's performance in midlife and beyond while combating normal age-associated memory loss

- How to protect and strengthen the "memory maker" in your brain, the small sea horse–shaped structure called the hippocampus

- How modest lifestyle adjustments related to diet and exercise can make a huge difference in maintaining a healthy brain and body

- The importance of brain reserve and how you can build more of it starting at any age

- How the Brain Training Revolution can work on not just your brain but also your heart, lungs, muscles, attitude, and enjoyment of life to its fullest

- Simple things you can do every day to keep your brain healthy and functioning at its peak as you age

The overarching principle of this book is to inform you of your choices. You can be your own healthy brain doctor. You can age well and enjoy the golden years. And in the plainest terms possible, I will show you how.

BE SMART ABOUT YOUR BRAIN

Not all experts are credible. While there is a tremendous amount of scientific and medical research in the field of brain aging, not everybody offers a scientifically based program or product. Beware of those who promote anti-aging remedies as cure-alls for age-related problems, such as hormone therapies, unproven nutraceuticals, exotic medicines, and supplements unsupported by scientific evidence. Always remember that the person trying to sell you a product is never objective about its effectiveness. Your medical doctor is the best person to help you understand and navigate your options. Trust only your doctor—and yourself—with your life, your brain, and your memories.

HOW THIS BOOK WORKS

This book is organized in three basic sections. Part 1 provides an overview of the brain and, more specifically, the aging brain. You will become familiar with the basic anatomy and physiology of the brain—the support elements, the workhorses and "sea horses," and how it has all been woven together over millions of years of evolution into the most incredible seeing, hearing, remembering, learning, thinking, controlling, interacting, imagining, and creating object in the universe. You will learn how your brain forms and stores memories in the hippocampus, and how stress, sleep, diet, exercise, and intellectual curiosity and "mind work" affect this critical structure and other parts of the brain. Understanding the differences, both anatomical and functional, between young brains and old brains sets the stage for part 2.

Part 2 is the core of the book—the Brain Training Revolution lifestyle program designed for you. If you understand and follow the prescriptions in part 2, your brain, your whole body, and all those you cherish and who cherish you will thank you. The first chapter in this section, chapter 4, reviews some of the recent human research that provides the scientific basis for the Brain Training Revolution. As with any complicated system, the better the fuel, the better the performance. So, chapter 5, Food for Thinking, deals with the critical diet and nutritional elements to power your brain.

Next comes chapter 6, a detailed but modest physical exercise plan so that no matter what shape you are in, you can build new brain cells while increasing your stamina, strengthening muscles, and increasing balance and flexibility—all critical elements for warding off the effects of aging and for maximizing physical independence.

Because Gray Matters, chapter 7, is next in part 2. Here you'll read about some mental activities that are crucial for toning and maintaining brain strength and for building brain reserve, and I'll introduce you to the Cognitive Quotient method for tracking your brain strengthening exercises. All of this is accompanied by fun and challenging mental exercises designed to build brain reserve while sharpening your senses, memory, and other key cognitive activities. Some of the exercises are in full color, designed to stimulate your brain in ways that black text on a white page just can't. Chapter 8, on stress, summarizes the good and bad of this unavoidable element in our everyday lives. You will learn beneficial ways to keep unhealthy stress at bay and protect your brain from the ravages of unmanaged stress. Finally, part 2 concludes as you conclude each day, with sleep, in chapter 9. Sleep is critical to memory formation and learning at any age, and the Brain Training Revolution provides a prescription to help you sleep well.

Part 3 contains resources for those readers interested in more in-depth materials about brain health, a lively assortment of books on numerous aspects of the brain, informative and authoritative websites, and my notes. Also in this section are nutritional quotient scorecards for the Jump-Start method of the Brain Training Revolution nutritional plan, the answers to the Chapter 7 cognitive exercises, and a starter set of tasty brain-healthy recipes. The BrainSavers website www.brainsavers.com has even more content: additional recipes, menus, a glossary of brain terms, a description of the twenty "muscles" of the brain, and an extensive bibliography, including academic books and journal references that provide the scientific basis for this book.

BONUS DVD!

Accompanying this book is an interactive DVD featuring examples of cognitive exercises that build brain reserve, physical exercises good for brain and body, an introduction to the Brain Training Revolution nutritional plan, and a discussion of other aspects of a brain-healthy lifestyle. I recommend watching the first part of the DVD before reading the book, and then trying the exercises included on the DVD after you have completed the book.

WHY SHOULD YOU LISTEN TO ME?

You might ask, "Why should I listen to you?" The answer? I have had a long career as a neurologist, and I have devoted almost three decades to dealing personally and directly with various aspects of Alzheimer's and other degenerative brain disorders. I completed a postdoctoral research fellowship in what was then known as slow-virus diseases of the brain, now known as prion diseases or transmissible spongiform encephalopathies, but often popularly referred to as "mad-cow disease," which contributed to Nobel Prize–winning findings. I have been privileged to interact with numerous truly great and groundbreaking clinicians and research scientists in various aspects of neuroscience.

My eureka moment came at the end of 2003, when I realized that brain science had advanced to the point that one could propose brain-healthy living without being accused of science-fiction-based medicine. In 2009, brain health is where heart health was thirty years ago. Back then, the medical community was only beginning to teach, preach, and practice the nutritional, physical exercise, smoking cessation, and stress reduction components of a heart-healthy lifestyle. We have come a long way—today, many schoolchildren can recite at least a partial list of heart-healthy habits. Within ten years I hope that most adults will know what a brain-healthy lifestyle is, and within twenty years, that this will have trickled down to students.

In 2007, after stints in academia, in pharmaceutical and biotechnology companies, and in helping to start a state-of-the-art Alzheimer's center at one of the largest community hospitals in Phoenix, I chose to devote all of my professional energies and time to a rather unusual path for a mainstream neurology doctor: a brain-health company, BrainSavers, which I had founded in 2004. First, I recruited a small but eminent group of scientific advisers and, over time, built a development team, then a management team. BrainSavers has evolved into a small but growing company committed to bringing evidence-based programs and products to aging adults who are concerned with maximizing brain health.

My BrainSavers colleagues and I conducted a trial in a health club of a prototype of the healthy brain-aging program we developed, and participants received it tremendously well. The results demonstrated that memory and other cognitive skills improved. This and other evidence convinced me the time was right for the Brain Training Revolution.

I hope you will keep an open mind to my recommendations, as they're meant to help you, to guide you, and to clarify for you the sometimes-confusing maze of medical and scientific information related to health.

That said, herein you'll find my opinions, and I encourage you to seek additional information from your own doctor, following his or her advice in combination with the brain-healthy lifestyle program here. After all, the field is moving ahead quickly. This book will stay the same after it's printed, but medical science will march on. So it behooves you to keep up with the most current perspectives. Use the Internet, read newspapers and weekly news magazines, attend seminars, ask your friends, and ask your doctor.

In writing this book and in working out the details of the Brain Training Revolution "prescription," several experts have ably assisted me; foremost among them Richard Samuels, PhD in psychology, who has worked with memory-impaired individuals for thirty years; Edward Wein, PhD in biochemical engineering with expertise in food science; and Tracy Hafen, MS in exercise physiology and an expert in fitness program design. I also relied on the voluminous published results of other doctors and scientists from a wide range of disciplines. So a team developed this program—and we invite you to join our team.

In the chapters that follow, you will read about the brain's sea horse, tiny worms, mice, songbirds, monkey fingers, man's best friend, and London taxi drivers. While you now may not understand how these things are relevant, by the time you finish this book, you'll have a basic understanding as to how they have contributed to the exciting science of healthy aging brains and how you can keep your own brain healthy over time.

The answers are out there, at least in large part, and they are yours for the taking.

PART 1

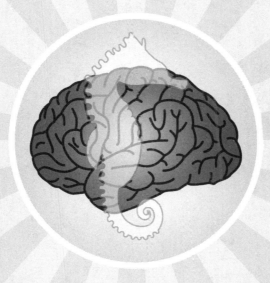

GETTING UP TO SPEED ON
YOUR AGING BRAIN

THE THREE-POUND UNIVERSE

"The brain is wider than the sky."—EMILY DICKINSON

"Even though it is common knowledge, it never ceases to amaze me that all the richness of our mental life—all our feelings, our emotions, our thoughts, our ambitions, our love lives, our religious sentiments, and even what each of us regards as his or her own intimate private self–is simply the activity of these little specks of jelly in our heads, in our brains. There is nothing else."—V. S. RAMACHANDRAN, MD, PHD

WHAT IS THE BRAIN?

How is it possible that 1,350 grams—or about three pounds of tissue—control every thought, feeling, emotion, personality trait, dream, muscle movement, beat of your heart, and breath that you take?

Yet that is the average weight of the human brain (about the size of a small cantaloupe). A dolphin's brain is slightly heavier, but an elephant's brain is three times heavier, and a sperm whale's brain is more than five times heavier.

As the author and psychologist Susan Blackmore once said, "Compared to other animals, our brains are way out of proportion to our body mass. This huge organ is dangerous and painful to give birth to, expensive to build, and, in a resting human, uses about 20 percent of the body's energy even though it is just 2 percent of the body's weight. There must be some reason for all this evolutionary expense."

Indeed, there is. The human brain far exceeds in capacity and ability any other species' brain. And boy, is it complicated! The human brain is the single most amazing, complex, and mysterious object in the known universe. Subatomic physics, the thirty thousand genes that make up our genetic code, the intricacies of ecological relationships, even the vastness of galaxies are orders of magnitude less complex than the wirings and work-ings of this three-pound mass of gray and white matter.

The fully developed human brain is the result of about six hundred mil-lion years of evolution. The result is about one hundred billion (that's 100,000,000,000!) brain cells (or neurons, as neuroscientists call them), which are supported by up to one trillion (1,000,000,000,000) glial cells (*glia* means "glue"; these cells provide a supporting scaffold and house-keeping chores for neurons). Neurons communicate with other neurons at an estimated one quadrillion (1,000,000,000,000,000) intersections (synapses). The past several decades have witnessed an explosion in the biochemical, genetic, and molecular understanding of the brain—from dis-coveries about its formation and development, which DNA sequences of the genetic code control, to its subcellular and molecular anatomy as deci-phered by electron microscopy and other advanced imaging technologies, as well as the intricacies of communications transmitted initially via an electrical impulse within one cell through to synapses (connecting points), where the cell conveys information to its neighbors by neurotransmitters, or specialized "talking" chemicals.

This knowledge explosion has enabled incredible advances in our under-standing of both normal aging brains and brains ravaged by Alzheimer's and other diseases. The results are better treatments, an understanding of how we make and store memories, and notions of the unique human attributes of consciousness and self-understanding. Before I explore how the new discov-eries can benefit you, let's take a look at what's going on in your own head.

YOUR BRAIN ON BOOKS

The increase in brain research has opened our minds to insightful scientific descriptions and evidence in ways barely fathomable only a few decades ago. Today there are books for the general reader that explore virtually every cultural, social, and political aspect of our lives and how those aspects relate to the brain. *Your Brain on Cubs* even gets into the minds of sports fans. In Part 3, you'll find lists of suggested reading, but here are a few of my favorites to give you a taste of the range of exciting and varied reaches of twenty-first-century brain science:

An Alchemy of Mind, by Diane Ackerman

A Brief Tour of Human Consciousness, by V. S. Ramachandran

The Executive Brain: Frontal Lobes and the Civilized Mind,
     by Elkohonon Goldberg

Freedom and Neurobiology, by John Searle

Human: The Science Behind What Makes Us Unique,
     by Michael Gazzaniga

The Political Brain: The Role of Emotion in Deciding the Fate of the
     Nation, by Drew Westen

Proust Was a Neuroscientist, by Jonah Lehrer

Spark: The Revolutionary New Science of Exercise and the Brain,
     by John Ratey

Synaptic Self: How Our Brains Became Who We Are,
     by Joseph LeDoux

The Man Who Mistook His Wife for a Hat, by Oliver Sacks

This Is Your Brain on Music, by Daniel Levitin

Why Zebras Don't Get Ulcers, by Robert Sapolsky

FROM THE OUTSIDE LOOKING IN

Let's start with a brief tour of the major physical characteristics of the brain and its bony home. As did all other organs, the brain, spinal cord, and other nervous system components began with our prehistoric ancestors and evolved through countless mutations. Over hundreds of millions of years, the evolutionary process selected the hardiest mutations, and the result is the human brain as it is today.

The Skull: Nature's Protective Custody

Just as the tight security of Fort Knox protects the gold of the U.S. Treasury, as the hood of a car protects the engine, and as a durable case protects your computer, the skull has evolved as a fortress to keep your brain safe while you work and play and sleep in what is often a dangerous world.

The thick, bony skull serves as a barrier against inadvertent, in-your-face walls and dashboards; falling, flying, or swinging objects; punches; hail; and untold other potential assaults of daily living. But the skull does have its limitations, which is why we wear protective helmets when playing football and riding bicycles, and why boxers suffer brain injuries at an alarming frequency.

CogniByte
The early English word *skulle* is from the Nordic precedents *skal* and *skul,* which mean "bowl." It appears to be related to the Nordic toast "Skoal," which may have originated from the ancient use of a skull to serve ceremonial drinks.

The Cerebral Hemispheres: Your Real Crown Jewels

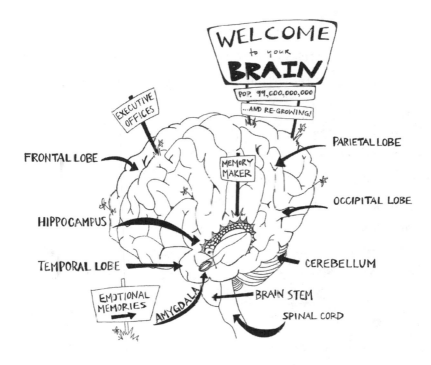

"The great sins of the world take place in the brain: but it is in the brain that everything takes place...It is in the brain that the poppy is red, that the apple is odorous, that the skylark sings."—OSCAR WILDE

The two approximately equal halves of the brain are the right and left cerebral hemispheres. These are the largest divisions of the brain and are further subdivided into frontal, parietal, temporal, and occipital lobes. The cortex (which means "bark" or "rind") is an outer surface of gray matter that entirely cloaks the hemispheres. Beneath the cortex in the cerebral hemispheres are subsurface white matter and deeper collections of brain cells (nuclei and ganglia) with fascinating names like *indusium griseum* and *amygdala* and specialized functions. These deep nuclei, in conjunction with the cortex and other evolutionarily older parts of the brain beneath them, are involved in virtually every aspect of the brain's incredible workings: memory, emotions, language, hunger and thirst, a host of conscious activities, control and coordination of motor movements and posture, processing of the endless barrage of sensory information from your internal and external environments, hormonal secretions, temperature regulation, metabolic rate, hydration, and all the other unconscious and reflexive activities necessary for life.

The subcortical white matter comprises dense bundles of impressively long (up to three feet) cablelike extensions of neurons that connect every nook and cranny of the brain. The corpus callosum, a glistening white superhighway of hundreds of millions of microscopic cables, connects the two hemispheres. In this bidirectional communications network, too many bits of information to count travel in milliseconds so that the left hand knows what the right hand is doing and so all the thoughts and plans that originate from diverse areas of either side of the brain are coordinated, cohesive, and consistent.

The cerebral hemispheres are the control and processing modules for their respective opposite sides of the body: The left hemisphere processes incoming visual, tactile, and other sensations from the right side of the body and sends commands to move the muscles of the right side of the body. The right hemisphere does the same for the left side of the body. Although certain traits or functions such as language, musical ability, logical thinking, mathematical ability, and analytical processing tend to be unevenly distributed in the two hemispheres in most people, full performance in most every aspect of human endeavor requires that both hemispheres work together. For example, artists do not draw only using their right hemisphere; the left hemisphere contributes for the full expression of artistic talent.

The Cerebral Cortex: Because Gray Matters

Compared to the brains of our primate ancestors, most of the increased weight of our brains occurs because we have much larger frontal lobes, with their massive cortex. The size of these parts of the brain is what truly distinguishes human brains from those of all other species in terms of anatomy. Even our closest evolutionary relatives, chimps and bonobos, have much smaller frontal lobes and much less cortical volume. This difference is obvious when you compare the shape of their forehead with our own: our skull has been pushed forward to accommodate the expansion of the brain.

The cortex looks much like a walnut or a map of the moon, with crevices, mounds, and folds. All of those crevices, mounds, and folds allow the cortex to occupy a much smaller container (your skull) than if it were all flattened out (it would cover a modest-sized desk!). The cortex packs in about thirty billion nerve cells organized in layers and columns and joined together by trillions of synaptic connections. The total surface area of the entire brain's billions of nerve cells is about four football fields!

The Frontal Lobes: The Chief Executive Officer

Somerset Maugham noted, "The highest activities of consciousness have their origins in physical occurrences of the brain." These highest activities—making big decisions, planning, remembering critical long-term information, and executing complex actions—all originate in your frontal lobes. Modern-day neuroscience has even borrowed a phrase from the business world to describe the unique activities of the frontal lobes—*executive functions*. Your frontal lobes are the chair of the board, the chief executive officer, and even the head of business development of your privately owned, personal company. The parietal, temporal, and occipital lobes make up the other members of senior management.

Without proper functioning in the frontal lobes, the personality of your company changes: its leadership ability, its decision making and planning abilities, its vibrancy, its efficiency in directing operations, and its productivity. The frontal lobes are particularly vulnerable to aging processes and can shrink dramatically in advanced Alzheimer's disease. Profoundly disturbing behaviors, including socially inappropriate language and actions, irritability, and hostility, often present in Alzheimer's patients, are attributable in large part to frontal lobe impairment.

OUR FRONTAL LOBES, OURSELVES

The crucial role of the frontal lobes in defining personality traits and behavior, our individual psychological makeup, was first appreciated more than 150 years ago. Phineas Gage, of Vermont, was a foreman on a railroad construction crew. In 1848, an explosion sent a metal rod through his facial bones and skull, destroying a large part of the left frontal lobe and some of the right lobe. Although he lived and suffered no paralysis, loss of memory, thinking, or speech impediment, "Gage was no longer Gage," according to his friends. His social skills were compromised, his behavior was erratic, and he could no longer direct his work gang.

Gage had an accidental lobotomy! About a hundred years later, from the 1930s to the 1960s, before the development of the first antipsychotic drugs to successfully treat severe psychiatric disorders, the neurosurgical procedure of prefrontal lobotomy was used to treat some cases of schizophrenia and incapacitating depression. The surgery severs the underlying white matter to disconnect the most anterior parts of the frontal lobes from the rest of the brain, much as what had happened to Gage. A common outcome was a pronounced change in the individual's personality.

No company can function at the top of its game with an impaired leader, hence the need to nourish and maintain your frontal lobes. Just as the superachievers of Fortune 500 companies are constantly educating themselves, analyzing the competition, and exploring opportunities, your frontal lobes need to be constantly stimulated, educated, and updated so that the rest of the brain receives the best possible high-level commands. (Part 2 of this book is a training manual for your frontal lobes, your hippocampus, and other brain structures.)

Parietal Lobes: The Tracking and Receiving Department

The parietal lobes are your tracking and receiving department. This is where much of the sensory information from the world around you ends up for final processing, analysis, comparisons with previously received signals, and integration into a comprehensive and comprehensible scheme of the world around you. Your ability to navigate and become oriented in your environment are functions of the parietal lobes.

If the parietal lobes are impaired, you will have a tough time moving efficiently from place to place. Your perception of space becomes distorted, and you may even ignore space altogether! Likewise, objects in space can seem distorted or unrecognizable. Damage to your parietal lobes can have effects such as not being able to distinguish your right side from your left side.

The Occipital Lobes: Eyes in the Back of Your Head

The central role of the occipital lobes is the processing of visual information; without functioning occipital lobes, you would lose visual awareness. Much of what we learn depends on sensory information that reaches our brains from the retina, located at the back of each eye. In fact, most of us use and trust our eyes, our visual interpretation of the facts, more than we trust any other of the primary senses. "Seeing is believing," "eyewitness," "a picture is worth a thousand words," and "the mind's eye" are all phrases that are testimony to the centrality of vision in our mental representation of our world. The health of the occipital lobes and their complex connections to other parts of the brain are critical for memories and for learning from visual information sources.

For example, when you look at a map and form a working memory of a travel route you have planned, the first step is the processing of millions of visible light "hits" that react with the photoreceptors on your retinal cells. The information is then passed to the occipital lobes, processed, and immediately transmitted to the hippocampus, where it becomes a working memory. That is how you remember the name of your destination and recall it as you progress in your journey.

Thus, we actually see with our brains, not with our eyes. Our eyes sense changes in light, but it is our brain that sees, for example, the flower. In fact, Paul Bach-y-Rita, a great pioneer of neuroplasticity (the brain's ability to change itself depending on its experiences), explains that a blind man who feels the structure of the sidewalk, the features of a room, or the side of a building through the mechanical impulses that the tip of his cane transmits up through his hand, arm, and spinal cord to his brain actually visualizes those structures. That is the brain's ability to see.

The Temporal Lobes: Hearing, Listening, and Remembering

The temporal lobes are critical for memory formation (more about this in Chapter 2), language function, and the processing of auditory sensations, from basic noises to the complex sounds of language, music, and nature. The ability to consciously recognize and attach meaning to sounds depends on an amazingly intricate, interwoven number of neural subsystems that are widely distributed throughout the brain. The same is true of the other primary sensations of touch, taste, smell, and sight.

The Cerebellum: Smoothing Out the Bumps

The cerebellum is located at the back base of the brain and is primarily involved in complex motor activities. The cerebellar white matter has a beautiful treelike shape and is named the arbor vitae (which means "tree of life"). Think of the entire cerebellum as a fine-tuner. When it is damaged, muscle strength is not lost but fine coordination and motor control

THE HIPPOCAMPUS: THE MEMORY-MAKING SEA HORSE IN YOUR BRAIN

Embedded in the temporal lobe of each half of the brain is the sea horse–shaped hippocampus (which means "sea horse" in Greek), a structure that is critical to memory making.

The hippocampus is central to mental life. With a damaged hippocampus, you can form fewer memories. Without a hippocampus, you could not form memories for a single event in your life! The hippocampus's emotional partner is the amygdala, an almond-shaped structure that is essential in terms of the emotional content of memories. We will explore the hippocampus in much more detail throughout this book.

is affected. Individuals with cerebellar problems may appear drunk because they have lost motor control.

The motor output and movement producing systems of the brain and body, instructed by the frontal lobe, lose their efficiency when disease injures or impairs the cerebellum. In contrast, it has been claimed that athletes who excel at the most demanding motor activities that require coordination, such as hitting a baseball hurled at 100 miles per hour, have cerebellums that function more robustly than that of the average person. This makes sense and there are a few studies that support this conclusion. The cerebellum is also involved in paying attention and in integrating and processing complex sensory inputs such as music and spoken language. It also seems to have a role in regulating emotional responses and in the learning and recall of movements—motor memory.

THE BRAIN STEM: KEEPING THE LIGHTS ON

If the hemispheres are the executive office suites of your personal company, the brain stem is the operations center. The compact but essential neuronal structures in the brain stem keep the lights on and maintain the internal environment. Because the brain stem connects the brain with the spinal cord, all instructions from your brain pass through here to reach the muscles you want to move. Likewise, all sensations from your body travel up through the brain stem to reach the brain, where you become aware of them. The brain stem is also the origin of the cranial nerves, which regulate many basic bodily functions; convey sight, sound, taste, smell, and tactile sensations; and direct movements of your face, mouth, and tongue (basically everything from the neck up). The next time someone tells you to say "cheese" for a photo, the cranial nerves enable you to smile.

The brain stem is so tightly packed with critical structures that control breathing, heart rate, alertness, consciousness, and countless other functions that even the smallest of lesions can be devastating. Lesions here can result in decreased alertness and even a comatose state.

The Spinal Cord: Communications with the Field

Communications up and down the chain of command are critical for success in a complex technology company. Executives make decisions that direct the production and distribution of goods; employees in the field report on their sales and marketing activities, the demands of purchasers, and the competition. The communications between the frontal lobes and other lobes of the brain reach the producers—muscles and glands—via the spinal cord, which stretches from the brain stem to the lower part of your back. The spinal cord contains sensory cables that carry inputs up to the decision makers in the brain and motor cables that carry input down to the muscles that execute instructions. The entire spectrum of sensations that your fingers feel—whether hot or cold, rough or smooth—are transmitted to the spinal cord and then to the brain. So, in a sense the spinal cord is the receiving department of your company. The spinal cord also ships directions to move your muscles and operate your many organs along the nerves that reach the most distant reaches of your body, to the tips of your fingers and toes, to your glands, heart, and intestines (and everywhere else in between).

The Neurons

The simplest thought or command that the brain makes is the result of the cumulative effort of tens and hundreds of millions of neurons, which are supported by billions of glial cells.

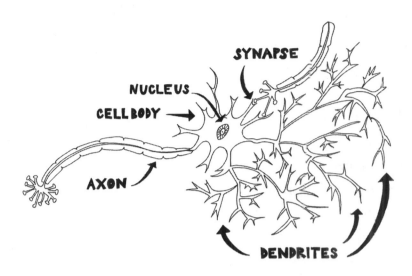

A neuron is the most awesome functional object in nature. It is the smallest unit of the human brain and the pinnacle of biological evolution. Each tiny neuron consists of three basic parts: a cell body, an axon, and a dendrite. The cell body stores information in DNA and RNA, and it manufactures proteins needed for structure and function and chemicals for sending messages. The axon is a long, cablelike extension leading away from the cell. Dendrites (from the Greek for "tree") are the many shorter cables mostly on the side of the cell body opposite the axon. Dendrites are the receiving ends of nerve cells. On each dendrite five thousand to ten thousand axons (but sometimes up to two hundred thousand) form synaptic connections and relay their signals. Synapses enable neurons to form vast interconnected circuits that are crucial to perception, memory formation, storage, recall, learning, and thought. They also enable the nervous system to control, either directly via nerves or indirectly via hormones, every

CogniByte

The word *synapse* comes from *synaptein*, which was coined from the Greek prefix *syn–*, which means "together," and *haptein*, which means "to clasp." The synaptic connection is actually a gap between the partnering dendrite and axon, about one-millionth of an inch wide.

other system of the body. Both axons and dendrites are jam-packed with complex molecules and submicroscopic structures, and the total length of all the axons and dendrites in the human brain is estimated at 2.5 million miles!

Your brain's mass of connected neurons—all one hundred billion of them—is masterfully orchestrated and performs indescribably complex activities in fractions of a second. This aesthetically pleasing orchestration has its visual counterpart in the anatomy of the brain under the microscope, with lacelike intricacies of neurons that are every bit as breathtaking as the night sky in all its twinkling magnificence.

MINISCULE LIGHTNING BOLTS AND TALKING CHEMICALS

Most life experiences begin with external signals in the form of energy packets reaching sensitive receptors in your eyes, ears, nose, tongue, and skin. Nerves instantaneously translate the energy packets into messages in the form of electrical charges and chemical signals (neurotransmitters). Together these electrical charges and neurotransmitters constitute the physical-chemical language of the brain. Synapses relay the information using neurotransmitters that either excite or depress the cells further down the line. Acetylcholine, dopamine, serotonin, and adrenaline are some examples of neurotransmitters.

This dual messenger system of mini-lightning bolts and talking chemicals allows information to zip around in milliseconds to destinations in the brain, one of which is the hippocampus where critical information is bundled together as a discrete memory. All this complex processing happens without you being aware, but in that blink of an eye, your remarkable brain creates a conscious image—and a memory.

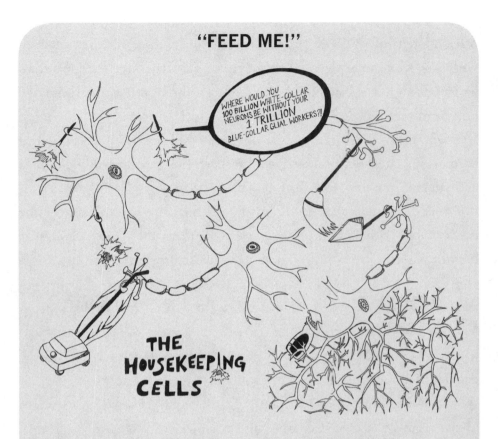

Like any living thing, a nerve cell needs energy and support. Most of the behind-the-scenes duties (like sustenance, maintenance, and repair) are performed by various types of glia, which crowd around the neurons they serve. For example, specialized glia interface tightly with the thousands of miles of tiny blood vessels that enter every nook and cranny of the brain to supply it with oxygen, simple sugar, and the building blocks of proteins and complex fats necessary for the highest human intellectual functions and the most mundane housekeeping chores. The removal of waste products is accomplished by other glia working with blood exiting the brain and with cerebrospinal fluid, which is the water-based irrigation system that bathes the inside and outside of the brain. In Part 2, we will explore the nutritional needs for optimal brain function and how best to get them.

Wiring It All Together

Nerve cells have evolved into various sizes and shapes to let your brain perform all kinds of special functions. Thus, the brain contains separate but connected systems for muscle control, hearing, touch, taste, and smell; a wonderfully complex visual system; attention systems; memory networks; and a multitude of other complex organizations built from neurons and their synapses.

Images of the dense network of axons and dendrites, which are visible under a microscope after the cells are stained with silver or other special chemicals, look like a Jackson Pollock painting, a scramble of lines without direction. However, there are specific addresses to the paths that connect axons and dendrites. That life experiences can change those paths, and the connections among them—even in brains of older adults—is one of the major neuroscien-

tific principles underlying the Brain Training Revolution. As a founding father of neurophysiology and Nobel laureate, Sir Charles Sherrington described: "The human brain is an enchanted loom where millions of flashing shuttles weave a dissolving pattern, always a meaningful pattern, though never an abiding one, a shifting harmony of sub-patterns. It is as if the Milky Way entered upon some cosmic dance."

Walking, dancing, speaking, hearing, tasting, feeling, seeing, thinking, calculating, praying, playing, arguing, loving, caring—no matter what activity you engage in, the intricacies of your brain make it all possible and make your personal way of accomplishing these acts distinct.

ADDING IT ALL UP: THE WHOLE IS GREATER THAN THE SUM OF ITS PARTS

Think of the frontal, parietal, temporal, and occipital lobes as separate but connected components of your mental firepower. The components are conceptually equivalent to the major muscle groups in your body below: each major area of the brain contains countless smaller "muscles," or neural networks performing perceptual and cognitive functions.

When you put it all together, you've got quite a lot packed into that skull.

Chapter 2

MAKING MEMORIES

"My father leans against the mantelpiece and begins to load his pipe with tobacco whose aroma bestows a presence on thirty vanished years. That aroma and the smell of the smoke that follows it are to me the quintessence of memory."—BERYL MARKHAM, *WEST WITH THE NIGHT*

WHAT'S A MEMORY?

Surveys in the past several years have found that almost two-thirds of we Americans over the age of 40 admit that our memory function is worse than it was ten years earlier (I believe some of the rest are slightly less than fully truthful). In any case, upward of one hundred million Americans have senior moments, cognitive coughs, or memory misfires.

So what is memory and how important is it? The famous surrealist filmmaker Luis Buñuel described the centrality of memories to the meaning of our lives as follows: "You have to begin to lose your memory, if only in bits and pieces, to realize that memory is what makes our lives. Life without memory is no life at all. Our memory is our coherence, our reason, our feeling, even our action. Without it, we are nothing."

Memories underlay our uniquely human abilities to experience our environment and then, from those experiences, remember, learn, and create. The brain receives information, stores it for moments, days, or decades, and later recalls it when needed. Memory is that mental process of bringing the past back into the present.

For example, think of an apple. If you are looking at an apple, the eye sends messages from the reflected light through a chain of precisely connected neurons to the occipital lobes of the brain. You can close your eyes and visualize what an apple looks like because your eyes have previously sent messages based on the light reflected from a real apple, your tongue has tasted the sweetness of an apple, and your ears have heard the crunch when you take a bite. All of that sensory information and more has been stored and restored, modified and modified again (in a largely "unconscious" process), to create a detailed memory of an apple that might include its red color outside and white color inside, its smoothness, coolness, crunchiness, pie worthiness, and other qualities.

You can visualize an apple in your mind even if the last time you actually saw, picked up, tasted, or smelled an apple was months or years ago. Hundreds of thousands—and probably millions—of neurons connected by tens of millions of synapses store various aspects of "apple" throughout your cortex. To create a single representation of an apple in your mind, the brain's individual perceptive and cognitive systems process all the information so that when you think *apple*, even with your eyes closed, all of those characteristics are pulled from their long-term-memory storage places in the cortex. Every time you see, smell, taste, or hear the crunching of an apple—or think about an apple—synaptic connections are changed and the memory of an apple is reinforced and altered to a greater or lesser extent.

Within a fraction of a second of reading the word *apple* in the previous sentences, groups of cells scattered throughout your brain fired together and brought forth a mental picture of an apple, a rich descriptive memory unique to your brain. So, a memory is the result of that conscious mental process by which we recall, or "re-member," an earlier experience, thought, or feeling.

All told, memory is a deeply complex biological, emotional, and intellectual process. Until relatively recently, people who made the brain their business didn't really have a clue as to where we make and store memories. In fact, no less than the genius-inventor-scientist Thomas Edison completely missed the mark in describing how we form and recall memories. In his diaries, Edison wrote, "We do not remember. A certain group of our little people do this for us. They live in that part of the brain which has become known as the 'fold of Broca'…There may be twelve or fifteen shifts that change about and are on duty at different times like men in a factory…Therefore it seems likely that remembering a thing is all a matter of getting in touch with the shift that was on duty when the recording was done."

Although numerous details remain to be discovered and described at the dawn of the twenty-first century, memory science has advanced by leaps and bounds during the past few decades. The greatest single advance in memory science is attributed to the case of one unfortunate individual, H.M., the man who could not remember.

PATIENT H.M.

The tragic but remarkably informative story of the most famous patient in the history of neurology is widely chronicled. Until his death in 2008, neurologists and memory researchers knew the patient not by his full name, Henry Gustav Molaison, but simply as patient H.M. H.M. had suffered since childhood from progressively severe epileptic seizures. In an effort to help him lead a more normal life, Dr. William Beecher Scoville, a Harvard-trained neurosurgeon on staff at the Hartford Hospital, in Connecticut, operated and removed a small portion of the temporal lobes, which included a good part of the hippocampus, on both sides of H.M.'s brain. H.M.'s seizures decreased according to plan. Unfortunately, there was an unexpected complication: H.M. was not able to form lasting memories after the surgery. Nothing!

Dr. Brenda Milner is the brain researcher who, along with Scoville, first described H.M.'s postsurgical loss of memory-forming ability in a landmark 1957 paper. Subsequently, she and other investigators met with H.M. numerous times to conduct additional clinical research. Over the years, he was introduced again and again to Milner and a host of others as they studied his memory, intelligence, and many other aspects of his brain's functions. Each time he met Milner, H.M. could immediately repeat her name, but if she left the room and returned a few minutes later, H.M. had absolutely no memory of her face, her name, or any detail of the previous meeting. Each meeting was a completely new experience for him. H.M. could retain new information, or create instantaneous memories, for a few moments if he concentrated, but once he was distracted, all that information disappeared.

Apart from H.M.'s inability to make a lasting memory, nothing else was wrong with him—his personality; intelligence; old memories as a child, a teenager, and a young adult; and his motor-memory skills, such as learning to manipulate a simple mechanical object, were all intact. He was able to recall memories from up until about two years before surgery: fishing adventures with his father, emotional events from his childhood, and his old girlfriends Beverly and Mildred.

With the partial removal of his hippocampus and some nearby cortex, H.M.'s brain camera had no film and his brain's diary never had another biographical entry, not for the fifty-five years after his surgery until the time he died.

The study of Henry Molaison broke the ice in memory research. We now have a detailed understanding of where memories are formed in the brain, where they are stored initially and subsequently, the centrality of short-term or "working" memory and long-term memory to our mental health and ability to function as social creatures, and the importance of forgetting. We know how crucial restful, sufficient sleep is to memory and that the reduction of long-term stress in our frenetic lives positively affects memory.

Perhaps most important for the tens of millions of Americans over the age of 45 is that modern brain science has discovered that, no matter how old we are, there are simple daily habits, physical and mental activities, that enhance our ability to make memories and ensure that those memories last and that we remember and recall them easily. We can take charge of protecting our brain to a considerable degree from what previously was thought to be inevitable age-associated memory loss and, much worse, the development of Alzheimer's disease.

CogniByte

If I forget thee, O Jerusalem,
let my right hand forget her cunning.
If I do not remember thee,
let my tongue cleave to the roof of my
     mouth;
if I prefer not Jerusalem above my chief
     joy.

—Psalm 137

Reflecting the importance of memory to religion and to all aspects of civilization, the words *remember* and *remembering* occur hundreds of times in the Old Testament alone.

HIPPOCAMPUS AND AMYGDALA

The hippocampus, which was introduced in chapter 1, is critical for the creation of memories, including working memories, those that enable us to function from moment to moment and to concentrate on the tasks at hand.

Let's think about the apple again. Just as you're about to reach for an apple, you hear the phone ring in the other room. You leave the kitchen, walk to the living room, and answer the phone. It is your working memory in the hippocampus that allows for the short-term storage of this information (the plan to eat an apple) while you have a five-minute conversation with a friend. After you hang up the phone, you remember that you were going to eat the apple, and your working memory enables you to return to that task.

Most working memories like this are discarded within a few days. But what happens when we add a little drama to the situation by stirring in emotional content to the rather unremarkable experience of eating a snack? Let's say that during the phone call someone informs you that one of your closest friends had been killed in a tragic accident. After the immediate shock wears off, you realize that you still need to eat. So you return to the kitchen and force yourself to eat an apple. It's a relatively safe bet that for years to come, maybe even for an entire lifetime, every time you see or think of an apple you will also remember your friend.

What happened in your brain? Right next to the hippocampus is the amygdala (which means "almond" in Greek). The amygdala is the emotional meter of your brain. So, when you heard the tragic news of your friend, the amygdala went into high gear and gave your hippocampus what was essentially a big kick in the rear in the form of an electrical shock and an injection of chemicals. It shouted to the hippocampus, "This one needs to be permanently saved!" The result is an emotionally tagged memory that is on its way to long-term storage, much like when you save to the hard drive on your computer.

That a onetime emotional experience often becomes a permanent memory, recallable even decades later, is the work of this amygdala-hippocampus partnership. We often need to repeat other unemotional experiences many times for them to become a memory, and even then they do not last very long. Most of us must dial a new telephone number many times before we can recall it from memory. Even then, if we do not use it regularly, after several months we often cannot drag it out of storage.

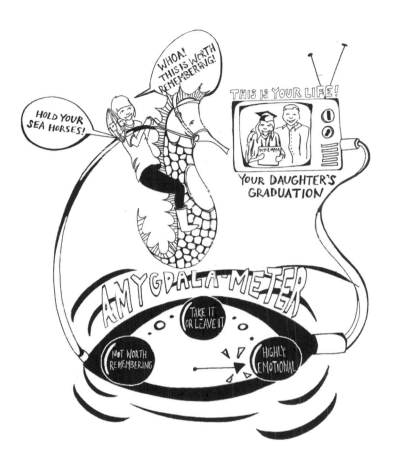

THE SEA HORSE OF A LONDON CABBIE

"The Knowledge" is an extremely rigorous examination that all London taxi drivers must pass. Dating back to 1851, the test requires would-be drivers to memorize the names and locations of nearly every street, hotel, shop, and restaurant—any place on any road—that a passenger might ask to be taken to in central London.

In a 2000 study by Dr. Eleanor Maguire and her colleagues at University College London, magnetic resonance images (MRIs) showed that the drivers who had passed the test had a larger posterior hippocampus than controls who did not drive taxis. In fact, the sizes of the cabbies' hippocampi correlated with the time spent driving their taxis. The posterior hippocampus is a critical structure for geographical memory—the ability to recall places and routes.

The study is evidence of the ability of specific areas of the brain to enlarge in response to demands, which is similar to exercised muscles! It's an illuminating real-life example of the adult brain's ability to use challenging mental workouts to reshape and rewire itself and to build brain reserve. On hearing the results of the study, David Cohen of the London Cab Drivers' Club said, "I never noticed part of my brain growing—it makes you wonder what happened to the rest of it."

What's Worth Keeping from Today?

For most people, more than 99 percent of all sensations and thoughts that could become memories never do. Here is a simple experiment to make the point: Look around the room in which you are now sitting. In turning your head 180 degrees with your eyes open, you have received thousands of specific visual sensations. How many of these can you immediately recall? How many will you remember in one hour? Not many. You will probably only remember an overall image of the room and some specifics of several of the items in it. A month later you likely will not remember the event at all. In general, we remember about 50 percent of events the next day, about 10 percent the next week, 5 percent within a month, and less than 1 percent a year or two later. Our brains simply "forget" more than 99 percent of all experiences.

THE ABSENT AND SILENT GODDESS: FORGETTING

The mechanism of forgetting is built into our brains. On the one hand, the hippocampus never records most of what we experience even as a short-term (working) memory. If everything we sensed, experienced, thought, and did became permanently etched into our brains, we would suffer from data overload. On the other hand, most of our short-term memories never make it into permanent storage; they are "forgotten." And with the passage of time, even terrible memories are softened and we are able to face another dawn.

In describing the importance of forgetting, founding father Thomas Paine said,

> Memory, like a beauty that is always present to hear itself flattered, is flattered by everyone. But the absent and silent goddess, Forgetfulness, has no votaries, and is never thought of; yet we owe her much. She is the goddess of ease, though not of pleasure. When the mind is like a room hung with black, and every corner of it crowded with the most horrid images imagination can create, this kind, speechless goddess of a maid, Forgetfulness, is following us night and day with her opium wand, and gently touching first one and then another, benumbs them into rest, and at last glides them away with the silence of a departing shadow. It is thus the tortured mind is restored to the calm condition of ease, and fitted for happiness.

How Does Your Brain Decide What to Remember?

It is the rare external sensation or internal thought that makes it from our short-term memory into long-term storage. So, how does your brain decide what to remember?

We all learned as students the time-tested method of practice makes perfect: repeating facts, numbers, or even a motor skill such as hitting a ball. Repetition helps us remember, and the more we repeat, the stronger the memory is. Focus, attention, and concentration—conscious mental decisions to commit any newly acquired information to memory—facilitate the process and sharpen your brain's effort.

Brain scientists have recently discovered that while you sleep, your hippocampus reviews the day's events and decides what goes into long-term storage and what is discarded. It's like a sea horse in a theater watching a rerun of your life that day. Warren Buffett, the esteemed business leader and investment guru, describes his brain during his dream-filled nights as "a multiplex going on in there. It's a full-time occupation."

To illustrate, let's return to our apple example. Because of the tragic emotional news linked to eating the apple, the hippocampus, having been instructed by the amygdala, decides that the apple episode will be saved permanently. The current scientific understanding is that, over time, hippocampal memories are transferred into long-term storage, primarily in the frontal cortex. This new apple memory becomes integrated with all the other apple memories previously saved in other storage areas throughout the brain. This transfer out of the hippocampus to distant cortical areas probably explains how H.M. was able to recall old memories years after he lost the capacity to form new memories.

OTHER MEMORY SYSTEMS

The brain is not the only tissue of the body capable of making memories. Muscle or motor memory is the ability, with practice, to more efficiently perform a complex motor activity such as dancing, playing golf or tennis, or playing the piano. These memories reside in specialized motor-memory networks in the brain. The immune system also has memory, although most of us do not think of it that way. When you are exposed for the first time to a pathogen such as a virus or bacteria, your white blood cells identify it as not belonging and then use a molecular memory system, which is unrelated to the brain's memory systems, to store the information and coordinate an attack to eliminate the pathogen now and even years later. In fact, the immune system can react to and form memories of millions of foreign substances. Several Nobel Prizes have been awarded for work on the special memory mechanisms of the immune system.

REMEMBER WHEN YOU WERE 10? THAT WAS FIFTY YEARS AGO!

Let's fast-forward to twenty-five years after the day you received the phone call with the news of your friend's death. Your children are grown, have families of their own, and your daughter visits with her husband and their children. It's the Thanksgiving holiday weekend, and, on the Saturday after the feast, you all visit a local farmers' market. Your four-year-old granddaughter sees a basket of apples, picks one out, and hands it to you. Suddenly the "apple episode" from twenty-five years ago, when you were about to eat an apple and then heard about your friend's death, comes back in full living color in your mind.

What happened? Your granddaughter triggered the recall of this long-forgotten apple memory. All the bits and pieces of sight, taste, smell, and feel were pulled out of storage and reassembled into a cohesive, powerful memory. The synapses of millions of cells orchestrated and coordinated this unique memory by speaking an electrical and chemical language to one another.

External or internal signals can trigger memories from ten, twenty-five, or even fifty years earlier. Remember being kissed fifty years ago when you were a teenager? What about your school's fight song? Your first car? Those memories have all been patiently waiting to be called back into consciousness. It takes just a trigger, and voilà, they reappear in your mind with real-life colors, sounds, tastes, and feelings.

MEMORY AND AGING

All memory, learning, language, mental creativity, and other higher cortical functions that humans are capable of depend on healthy neurons, organized in clusters and networks and connected by synapses. The normal wear and tear of aging slows down and reduces the efficiency of memory recall, which is considered normal, "age-associated memory loss." It's a nuisance but it is not disruptive of a normal life. Severe memory problems result from neurological diseases such as vascular dementia from strokes and Alzheimer's disease. In these diseases critical brain structures are severely damaged and their electrical-chemical communications impaired. These are disruptive of a normal life. Each of us must do all within our capabilities to minimize the risks of these memory-robbing diseases.

Chapter 3

NEW THINKING ON THINKING: THE YOUNG BRAIN, THE OLD BRAIN, AND THE BETTER BRAIN

"Whenever a new discovery is reported to the scientific world, they say first, 'It is probably not true.' Thereafter, when the truth of the proposition has been demonstrated beyond question, they say, 'Yes, it may be true, but it is not important.' Finally, when sufficient time has elapsed to fully evidence its importance, they say, 'Yes, surely it is important, but it is no longer new.'"—MICHEL DE MONTAIGNE (1533–1592)

MASTER OF YOUR DESTINY

Before the revolutionary discoveries of the late twentieth century that underlie this book, it was widely believed and taught that mental function after the age of 40 was a one-way, downhill path. In fact, the late distinguished chair and professor emeritus of Columbia University's Neurological Institute, H. Houston Merritt, once told a group of medical students gathered around him, "One of the unfortunate experiences of growing old is sitting in my favorite chair and listening to my Betz cells commit suicide by diving into the ventricular lakes" (Betz cells are large pyramidal nerve cells in the frontal cortex, and ventricles are the fluid-filled cavities in the brain). This statement struck me, for a neurological "giant" and revered teacher delivered it with a tinge of sadness and resignation. I have never forgotten those words.

Today we know better. If you challenge your brain through novel experiences, by socializing regularly, analyzing, thinking, remembering, imagining, and creating—in short, by engaging in a rich mental life full of stimulating brain exercises—even over periods as brief as a few months, you will change your brain's wiring and other architectural elements, enlarge its capacity, and better it with respect to the abilities and directions that you select.

A number of renowned neuroscientists are the pathfinders who pushed the boundaries of brain science in the past several decades with their work on adult brain plasticity. Let's review some of the evidence.

A Snippet of Plasticity History

Paul Bach-y-Rita, one of the pioneers of brain plasticity, had his mind's eye open and his frontal cortex humming in thought from observations he made about his father, the poet and professor of Spanish Pedro Bach-y-Rita. In the late 1950s, Pedro had a major stroke, at age 65, which left him paralyzed on one side and unable to speak. His treating physicians concluded that the severe neurological deficit was permanent and that there was no hope for a meaningful recovery. Paul's brother George, a medical student at the time, refused to accept this verdict. He moved in with his father and "forced" him to use his paralyzed limbs—thus Pedro actually retraced the developmental path taken by toddlers in learning to ambulate, first crawling, then standing, and finally walking. It took a year, but Pedro made a complete recovery and resumed his scholarly pursuits. Years later he died from a heart attack while hiking at 9,000 feet in the mountains of Columbia. His father's recovery led Paul Bach-y-Rita to conclude that even a fully mature older human brain had an intrinsic capability to change in rather dramatic fashion through relearning, retraining, and actual reorganization of its "wiring." He then spent the next forty plus years, mostly at the University of Wisconsin, pursuing the scientific basis of plasticity.

Worms That Smell

"As the worm turns" is the basic observation that Cori Bargmann, a neurobiologist at Rockefeller University, uses in her revealing experiments of the tiny, 1-millimeter-long roundworm *C. elegans*. Given *C. elegans*'s huge contribution to understanding our brain's wiring (the 2002 Nobel Prize in Physiology or Medicine was awarded to three scientists for their research on this lowly creature), let's rename it Sir Elegans. Sir Elegans, affectionately the "bloodhound of invertebrates," has only 302 brain cells connected at about 7,000 synapses. (Remember, you and I each have about one hundred billion neurons—ten billion in the frontal cortex alone—and trillions of synapses.) There are thousands of bacteria in the dirt where Sir Elegans lives. Some are nutritious table food, but others contain dangerous, lethal toxins. Sir Elegans uses thirty-two cells—10 percent of his entire brain—to smell the difference between food and foe. Using his primitive brain, Sir Elegans explores, analyzes, and learns to distinguish between the good odors of nourishing foods and the bad smells of toxins. Sir Elegans's brain remembers its environment and turns toward food and away from danger—and he has only 302 neurons!

Sir Elegans is an informative example of brain plasticity. What Bargmann and her colleagues have begun to clarify are some of the basic mechanisms that underlie plasticity in a primitive nervous system. It is plasticity that underlies memory and learning in the human brain. Sir Elegans, the lowly roundworm, is providing a road map toward understanding how our complex brains are wired and rewired.

Mice That Remember, and Forget

Mice have long been a popular experimental species in the laboratories of brain scientists. Numerous studies have focused on mice memories, and the modeling and remodeling that occurs in the hippocampus as memories are initiated and then made permanent. Mice that learn how to find a submerged platform while swimming show changes in the synaptic structure of the hippocampus—it seems appropriate that their personal sea horse would grow from water-based brain challenges. It is even possible to model forgetting in mice—the selective erasure of unpleasant memories was reported in 2008. It's a brave new world for understanding how brains do what only they can do!

The changeability of other adult brain components also has been demonstrated in mice. In one set of experiments, Mriganka Sur and his colleagues at MIT's Center for Learning and Memory have produced rewired mice that respond to a flashing light by using brain cells in an area of the cortex that is genetically evolved for hearing, not vision. Creating new brain pathways for novel learning is another demonstration of the adult mouse brain's capacity to adapt and to remodel when challenged. Nature determines the initial wiring of brains but nurture rewires it. As is the norm for progression of discoveries in medical science, findings made in laboratory animals sometimes are later replicated in humans, so stay tuned for further developments in this rapidly evolving field of brain plasticity.

Monkey Fingers

A few years after Bach-y-Rita's seminal observation, future Nobel laureates David Hubel and Torsten Wiesel demonstrated that when they sewed one eye of a kitten shut, the cortical area designed to process vision from that eye received visual input from the other eye, "as though the brain didn't want to waste any 'cortical real estate' and had found a way to rewire itself." These unexpected observations opened the door for other trailblazers in brain plasticity.

Michael Merzenich and his colleagues at the Universities of Wisconsin and later at the University of California, San Francisco, used monkeys in exploring additional features of the brain's plastic nature. When the nerves to a primate's fingers are cut and then grow back, sometimes the wires (axons) are crossed. Feelings from a thumb might travel along fibers originally serving the index or middle finger, for example. The result is that sensory input ends up in a different spot in the cortex than where it was received before the wires crossed. But Merzenich found that the cortex had rewired itself: the brain's map of the fingers and hand had changed to interpret the sensory data from the monkey's fingers correctly.

We now know that the brain constantly changes and reshapes itself as a result of the daily input it receives from internal processing and thinking, and from the body's novel sensory and learning inputs. The constant rewiring, strengthening, and building of new synaptic connections among the thirty billion neurons in the cortex occurs because our brains are sponges for experiences, and for remembering and learning based on those experiences. Just ask the birds...

Songbirds that Babble

Ever heard someone called a birdbrain? Well, birds' brains are nothing to scoff at. Forty years ago, Fernando Nottebohm at Rockefeller University in New York City pioneered the study of songbirds as a model for language development in the human brain. There are about four thousand identified species of songbirds—Georgia's state bird, the brown thrasher, can sing up to three thousand different tunes. Avian brains are a fertile resource for studying not only plasticity at the cellular and regional level but also changes in neurotransmitters and the influence of the environment on the constantly changing brain.

Eliot Brenowitz at the University of Washington observed, "Young birds go through an initial 'babbling' stage when they first begin to sing, in a manner very similar to human infants when they start speaking." Some songbirds continue to learn new tunes as they age, and their brains demonstrate changes that correlate with this learning. Canaries, great reed warblers, swamp sparrows, and zebra finches have specific neuronal populations that regulate song learning. The songs are sometimes tied to the reproductive cycle. During the breeding season, when males croon under the influence of testosterone, and females respond under the influence of estrogen, some brain areas involved with song become larger than in birds that aren't breeding because new brain cells are incorporated into them.

The music that songbirds learn to sing to one another is a real-world demonstration of the plastic nature of the brain and how the environment influences it. Birds' brains change when they produce song and our brains change when we listen. In the words of the neuroscientist, musician, and author Daniel Levitin, "Who among us hasn't sat and listened to a songbird on a spring morning and found the beauty, the melody, the structure of it enticing?"

Old Dogs Can Learn New Tricks: A Lesson for Their Masters

Did you know that dogs' brains age too? Old dogs suffer age-related changes similar to those in humans and can be an instructive model for human brain aging. In 2005, Norton Milgram at the University of Toronto, Carl Cotman at the University of California, Irvine, and their colleagues hypothesized that the mental ability of aged beagles might increase if they received more mental stimulation, along with more physical exercise and a diet of fruits and vegetables rich in antioxidants. After a year living a behaviorally enriched life, the old beagles had better learning ability. The results were even greater after two years in the experiment. In February 2009, Stump, a 10-year-old Sussex spaniel (70-years in human time), was named top dog by the prestigious Westminster Kennel Club. But as the author and dog trainer Jack Volhard commented to the *New York Times*, "I wonder how many 70-year-olds consider themselves 'old'?" The lessons for our aging brains seem clear.

THE YOUNG BRAIN

Now that we've looked at some examples of how brains can change, let's take a look at how they form and develop. The fundamental instructions used to build your brain come from about twenty thousand genes, which dictate the basic structure of your brain and how its fundamental wiring and architectural elements develop over the first twenty years of your life. The mental explorations that you are exposed to and engage in starting at birth—the countless sensory experiences and their processing; your continuing formal and informal education; the remembering, thinking, and learning that you do over a lifetime—refine and change your brain.

Let's briefly explore how your brain develops. This will set the stage for the Brain Training Revolution: the changes in lifestyle you can make in your middle age and beyond to strengthen your memories and overall brain function while reducing your risk for Alzheimer's disease and stroke.

The brain starts to form early in gestation, growing at a prodigious clip through early childhood. Up until the age of 2, about 250,000 new cells are added every minute, 15 million an hour, and 360 million a day. And then the rate of new cell production decreases, although the brain keeps growing, mainly by constructing new synapses—all driven by the input of new information, which in turn drives memory formation and learning.

The brain continues increasing in size until about the age of 20. That's when it is the big kahuna, the heavyweight. Over the course of a lifetime, the brain receives billions of sensory stimuli from the environment. From early to middle adulthood, the sensory functions of taste, smell, hearing, touch, and vision are at their peak performance. Our abilities to distinguish nuances of flavor in the foods we eat, subtle variations in the

CogniByte

The brain is like a sponge: it likes to soak up material. It soaks up sensory experiences from the environment (such as reading this book); stores them as memories; learns from them; and subsequently uses them to produce knowledge, wisdom, judgment, creative acts, and other unique mental abilities.

The young brain soaks up new information without limits. My daughter, Jessica, amazed me when, at the age of 2, she began speaking Hebrew within a few days after beginning preschool in Israel. We had arrived there on my sabbatical about a month before her second birthday, she was already quite fluent in English for her age, and within a few weeks, she was speaking only Hebrew with her new playmates.

pitch of our favorite music, the keenness of our sight, the discriminatory ability of our fingertips are all at their maximum. Our fine motor and athletic skills controlled by the motor systems of the brain are also at peak performance in young adulthood.

Meanwhile, throughout our lives, some cells that have reached the end of their genetically programmed life spans (or are not being sufficiently used) are eliminated along with their synapses, a process that continues throughout our years but, to some extent, is compensated for by the birth of new cells and fresh synapses. As we will explore later, you can partly control and significantly enhance the manufacturing of new brain cells and synapses depending on the lifestyle you choose.

THE OLD BRAIN

Even after months of studying, my brain did not come close to my daughter Jessica's in mastering Hebrew. That's because I had an older brain. The older brain is stiffer than a young brain, like a well-used sponge. It is not quite as absorbent as it once was, and it often needs a bit of gentle (or not-so-gentle) squeezing to start soaking up again. The older brain has collected considerable bits of chemical rust (amyloid, phosphorylated tau, lipofuscin, and some "misfolded" proteins). These various old-brain molecules can appear red, yellow, green, and silver when viewed with special microscopic techniques. One in particular, the amyloid of Alzheimer's disease, even demonstrates a chameleon-like red-green switching under polarized light. It has been determined that most, if not all, of those molecules are actually by-products of brain metabolism.

Your aging brain, like every other organ, is undergoing a predictable process of wear and tear. Part of this is the moderate decrease in white matter, which is primarily composed of the fatty substance myelin (which insulates the long axons that speed signals along your brain's informational pathways). The decrease in white matter might account for some of the slowdown in brain processing experienced in normal aging. Also contributing to the decrease is a slight decrease in blood flow to the brain and a moderate decrease in the total number of neurons. As a result, "Doc, it just takes me longer than it used to" is a frequent expression of the frustration that many aging people feel.

Wear and tear also takes place in gray matter cells. Brain cells contain miniature power plants called mitochondria. During mitochondrial metabolism, free radicals are produced. Free radicals wreak havoc and are little devils. To neutralize free radicals and to keep the system in balance and operating at peak performance, all cells both produce antioxidants and recruit them from foods. Antioxidant molecules essentially put dangerous free radicals into tight bear hugs, which prevents them from damaging cells. As we age, the balance changes; our cells produce less energy, more free radicals, and fewer antioxidants. Increasing evidence points to these as age-related factors in the decrease of many brain and body functions.

By the age of 40 most of us begin to feel the initial symptoms that aging, free radicals, and hormonal changes cause on brain and body parts. The earliest sign of aging, which often causes worries, is frequently mildly decreased perceptive abilities, or the sensitivity of our senses. (I'm not counting going gray and hair loss.) We may first notice a decrease in our ability to hear high-frequency sounds or difficulty reading small print (especially in dim light) around the age of 40 or 50. Somewhat later, we might notice that foods taste blander than we remember them. Such decreases in sensory sharpness are components of normal aging, and we can compensate by being more attentive, using hearing aids and reading glasses, and increasing our use of spices.

It is important to recognize that generally older brains are not as nimble as younger brains. Just as most of us cannot compete at the same physical level against someone who is twenty or thirty years younger, so our older brains usually cannot compete in skills measured only by time or efficiency.

But we all know exceptions and most of these exceptions have their basis in constantly challenging and training our bodies and our brains.

A 5-year-old's brain is normally quicker than a 30-year-old's brain when it comes to learning a new language, for example, and a 30-year-old's brain usually can memorize a longer list of objects, process new information more efficiently, and perform simultaneous multiple tasks better than a 70-year-old's brain. In fact, as we age, we lose about 1 cortical neuron each second, or 85,000 a day and 31 million each year. Because each neuron has around ten thousand connections, the connectors are disappearing at the rate of almost one billion per day. Scientists, neurologists, and other physicians and psychologists who study brain function have made it abundantly clear that such changes, none of which interferes with living a rich and full life, are part of normal brain aging.

Don't worry. We're going to explore how you can grow more cells, connect them, and make your brain sharper at any age.

CogniByte

Other critical activities that the brain controls, such as the basic drives for eating, sleeping, and sex, also undergo more or less predictable changes with aging. What is normal is relative, so each of us must determine with the advice of our physician whether a decrease in appetite or sexual performance or changed sleep patterns requires more intervention than reassurance.

Like a Good Bottle of Wine

Most of us would like to freeze in time our peak performance, whether with vision, hearing, muscular strength and agility, sexual performance, or mental abilities. But the brain is the only organ that in many ways can increase its performance with time. And the mind reveals those increases: older brains are wiser in ways we all cherish and admire. And you are in control of building and maintaining your brain.

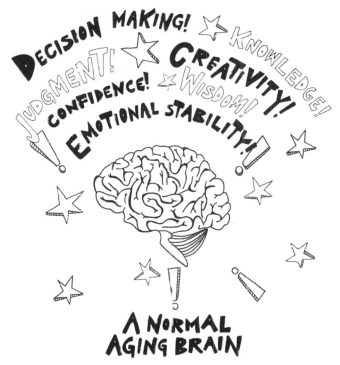

DECISION MAKING! ☆ KNOWLEDGE! JUDGMENT! ☆ CREATIVITY! CONFIDENCE! ☆ WISDOM! EMOTIONAL STABILITY!

A NORMAL AGING BRAIN

My 89-year-old mother is a great example. Life's experiences have enriched her brain and mind, and because of this, she possesses emotional stability, wisdom, insight, and judgment that are rare in younger people. She handles mental stress in ways that younger folks simply cannot because their brains have not matured. And she refuses to give in to aging. She is always on the go—doing ceramics on her potter's wheel, cooking, walking, exercising at the gym, playing bridge, or attending concerts, book clubs, and other social activities. She even recently acquired a few egg-laying hens in her yard. I feel tired just watching her!

SIZE DOES MATTER—SOMEWHAT

As you get older, your brain gets smaller. There is no contradicting that evidence. But brain size may not mean much. Albert Einstein's brain was below average in weight. In fact, geniuses have brains that are no bigger than the brains of the rest of us.

The Boskops were humans who inhabited the southern African landscape between ten and thirty thousand years ago. Paleontologists estimate that their brains weighed, on average, four pounds, which is 30 percent heavier than the brains of *Homo sapiens*—you and me. The Boskops are long gone.

The point? No matter how big your brain, it's how you use it that matters.

Many cultures around the world hold their elderly in the deepest respect because they know that they carry great knowledge. Think of all the esteemed professionals in many areas who continue to use their brains far beyond middle age and make major contributions to society while living a full life.

The greatest athletic coaches are well into their middle and even senior years—despite the reality that their physical skills peaked in their twenties. That's because as athletes age, they store in their brains complex experiences: tactics, strategy, know-how, and techniques they have learned over many years.

Along with wisdom and knowledge, certain brain functions improve with age: vocabulary, use of antonyms and synonyms, and even the size of our factual database. Expert knowledge, or how to do complicated work- or hobby-related activities, is also age resistant. As we keep experiencing life and practicing our professions or other stimulating mental activities, we learn more, which improves our problem-solving ability.

I am not writing about the type of problems from standardized tests or the ones used in book after book of mental puzzles. Doing these is beneficial, but our goal is to deal with real-world problems from our daily lives: interpersonal relationships, family finances, business operations, and a social club's functioning. It is these activities that we lose sleep about when our brains seem to have difficulty sorting, remembering, analyzing, and solving.

In general, older brains solve these types of problems better than younger brains—not faster, but better. And if you had to choose between faster or better when making truly important decisions, I think it's a no-brainer.

Think about this: At the time of writing this book, the average age of U.S. Supreme Court justices is 69 years, the average age of U.S. senators is 60, and U.S. presidents take office, on average, at the age of 55. The median age for a chief executive officer of a Fortune 500 company is 55, but there are numerous examples of top-notch visionary leaders beyond the age of 70—individuals like Warren Buffett, T. Boone Pickens, and many more.

So, what matters is not age but motivation, energy, and wisdom.

THE BETTER BRAIN

You can think about your brain like your leg muscles. If you've been at a desk job for twenty years and your only exercise has been walking from your car to your office and occasional light yard work on the weekends, you probably will not feel comfortable in a 5K or 10K walkathon.

However, if you begin a physical fitness program and gradually increase muscular strength and cardiovascular endurance, in six months you will be able to do a 5K walk with ease, and after six more months a 10K walk with confidence. And if you keep at it, you will soon be speed walking or even jogging.

During training, your leg muscles demand more energy for the work they are doing. So blood flow increases to deliver more oxygen and nutrients to your muscles, and they enlarge and grow new muscle fibers. If you have exercised for a long time, during continued training you may not be able to dramatically decrease your times for swimming, walking, or running, but you continue to build and maintain physical reserve.

Brain reserve works in the same way. One of the most exciting recent developments in brain research is the use of molecular biology to genetically engineer mice so that they are born with one or two human genes mixed in with their thousands of normal mouse genes. Because the human genes transfer to following generations of mice, they are labeled "transgenic." Transgenic mice have been used to study Alzheimer's disease, and they provide new insights into memory, thinking, and behavioral problems in humans. Mice with one or more specific Alzheimer's-associated genes active in their brains "lose their minds" in a sense and develop memory and behavioral problems. Anatomically, their brains show microscopic changes that mimic the devastating destruction seen in human victims of Alzheimer's, including the telltale amyloid plaques—dense collections of protein junk. In humans and mice with Alzheimer's, the total amount of amyloid in the brain correlates with disease severity.

The study of these engineered mice has led to novel therapeutic approaches to solving Alzheimer's disease. In cleverly designed experiments led by Sangram Sisodia's team at the University of Chicago, genetically engineered mice destined to develop the mouse equivalent of Alzheimer's were placed in an "enriched" environment in which they had running wheels, toys, and various materials to explore. This is not your standard laboratory habitat but the mouse equivalent of living in a five-star, exclusive, active-adult community. The mice were encouraged to exercise their brains in new ways even though the genetic deck was stacked against them. Paul Alard and Carl Cotman at the University of California, Irvine, tested, in other transgenic mice, whether voluntary physical exercise alone would affect Alzheimer's and its development (a free membership in a mouse fitness center!). Both groups of researchers independently demonstrated that the brains of the mice that were able to exercise their brains by playing and exploring and their bodies by running had significantly less Alzheimer's-associated microscopic changes, and they performed better on memory tests. As D. Stephen Snyder, director of the etiology of Alzheimer's program in the National Institute of Aging's Neuroscience and Neuropsychology of Aging Program commented, "Both of these studies are exciting because they offer insight into one of the pathways through which exercise and environment might promote resistance to development of cognitive changes that come with aging and Alzheimer's disease."

How does this relate to what's happening in your head? You can choose and sculpt how your ever-changing brain will work from this day forward. You can reshape your brain's architecture by living a full, active (mentally, socially, and physically), exploring, and learning life. These, along with healthy eating, are the core components of a total brain health regimen, just as aerobics, strength, balance, and flexibility are components of a complete physical exercise regimen. Exercising your brain changes it so that new, strong parts are formed; with this fortification comes added protection against age-related changes. William James, one of the founders of modern psychology, predicted more than one hundred years ago what twenty-first-century neuroscience has now proved: "The greatest discovery of my generation is that a human being can alter his life by altering his attitudes of mind."

BRAIN RESERVE

The anatomical changes you trigger in your brain by staying mentally and physically active underlie the idea of brain reserve. Think of it as the brain equivalent to the body's physical reserve. Consistent, moderate physical exercise over months and years protects your body from age-related conditions and diseases. Folks who are in shape from regular exercise have the physical reserve to meet all sorts of physical challenges and the staying power required to remain independent and physically active even in old age. Literally thousands of studies document that regular physical exercise prolongs healthy life and improves mood; it reduces the risk of heart disease, stroke, diabetes, depression and other mental illnesses, osteoporosis, and falls and resultant fractures.

Consistent, invigorating mental exercise builds brain strength and reserve and protects your aging brain. As the American anthropologist

George Dorsey put it, "The more you use your brain, the more brain you will have to use."

With respect to our brain reserve, just like most of us scale down our participation in physical exercise after the age of 40 or so (and pay the price), many of us do less learning and fewer brain-strengthening activities after we finish college and have settled into a career. But each of us needs to keep at it—the more you engage your brain with stimulating leisure activities that exercise its memory and other cognitive systems, the more you renew and fortify this marvelous "muscle," and the more brain reserve you build to protect you down the road.

PART 2

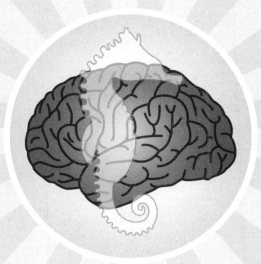

A BRAIN-HEALTHY LIFESTYLE

Chapter 4

THE BRAIN TRAINING REVOLUTION

"If you make brain-healthy lifestyle changes and take action by getting involved, we could realize a future without Alzheimer's disease."
—NATIONAL ALZHEIMER'S ASSOCIATION

Part 1 of this book provided a background understanding of how your brain is built; how it perceives the world, learns, and remembers; and how it ages. Now it's time to dive headfirst into the your Brain Training Revolution program. A brain-healthy lifestyle is truly a revolutionary concept. This chapter briefly reviews the much-studied lifestyle components that have been proven to benefit the aging brain. If you can't wait to get started, skip this chapter and go immediately to the next.

Think of brain training as the broad, steely shoulders of Atlas, on which stand better memory, better overall cognitive functioning, repairs to the damage from normal use and aging, and reduced future risks for Alzheimer's disease and stroke. Brain training uses the brain's inherent plasticity to build brain reserve, a concept you'll remember from chapter 3. Brain training means a life full of activities that stimulate the birth of new neurons; nourish and protect them; connect them to one another and to their preexisting neuronal cousins; and strengthen their communicating, learning, remembering, and creative abilities.

Sound complicated? It's not. Following the Brain Training Revolution program is an invigorating way to use mental and physical exercise and a natural, nutritious, brain-healthy diet to improve your life. We'll review each of these briefly now, and then you'll find separate chapters devoted to each component followed by chapters on stress and sleep, both important issues for your brain as well.

A BRAIN-HEALTHY LIFESTYLE
Walk the Talk: Why Physical Exercise Grows Your Brain

> *"Lack of activity destroys the good condition of every human being, while movement and methodical physical exercise save it and preserve it."*
> —PLATO, CIRCA 370 B.C.

> *"It is exercise alone that supports the spirits, and keeps the mind in vigor."*
> —MARCUS TULLIUS CICERO, CIRCA 65 B.C.

The positive relationship between physical exercise and overall health and longevity has been touted for more than two thousand years. Modern scientific research methods have proven over and over again what the ancients knew. In a landmark 1986 study of almost seventeen thousand Harvard graduates, Dr. Ralph Paffenbarger and his colleagues found that participants who consistently burned approximately 300 calories a day from physical exercise, the amount of calories that the body uses to walk briskly for 45–60 minutes—reduced their likelihood of death from all types of causes (primarily heart, vascular, and lung diseases) by an extraordinary 28 percent.

The toll on your body from not exercising is about the same as the terribly frightening toll that smoking takes. Most people nowadays are too sensible to consider ravaging their health by smoking. Unfortunately, many of the same people fail to recognize the extraordinary benefits of exercise in preventing and treating medical problems. Regular physical exercise decreases your risk of premature death, heart and vascular disease, cancer, stroke, diabetes, obesity, high blood pressure, osteoporosis, bone fractures, anxiety, and depression. Exercise also decreases your overall health-care costs. Thousands of exercise-based research studies published over the past thirty years add up to one inescapable conclusion: exercise = preventive medicine.

Happiness is more difficult to measure, but as the second U.S. president, John Adams, declared: "Exercise invigorates and enlivens all the faculties of body and of mind. It spreads a gladness and satisfaction over our minds and qualifies us for every sort of business, and every sort of pleasure."

What about exercise and the brain, though? Just as you can bulk up a specific muscle through exercise, you can enlarge and strengthen specific regions of your brain through exercise. Sound crazy? Moderate physical exercise, such as walking for at least 30 minutes three or more times a week, increases blood flow to the brain, enlarges your frontal lobes, and adds new memory-recording neurons in your hippocampus. Through exercise you can replenish some of the cells lost in the aging process. Moderate aerobic physical exercise, the type that makes you breathe faster and increases your heart rate, is the most powerful trigger of new cell production in the brain.

Art Kramer is an expert in the cognitive effects of physical exercise. Kramer and his research group at the University of Illinois at Urbana-Champaign have published several enlightening studies over the years. In one they showed that moderate, regular stamina-building (aerobic) exercise led to improved memory and other cognitive abilities in aged healthy individuals.

More recently, Kramer and his colleagues have documented larger brains in aging adults who began exercising and continued to do so for six months. The study examined healthy but sedentary seniors, aged 60 to 79 years old. Half of the participants began a walking program—as walking is an everyday activity central to overall good health and to maintaining independence with advancing age—of just 15 minutes three times a week. Over the next six months, the group gradually increased the walks to 45 to 60 minutes three times per week. That's all! They walked for up to an hour three times a week! During the same time period, the other half of participants did non-stamina building exercises, such as stretching and toning, in which they did not increase their heart and breathing rates as much as the other group did. MRI scans of participants' brains at the end of the study demonstrated that only those who were in the stamina-building program showed significant enlargement in the frontal and temporal lobe areas essential for executive functions and memory.

CogniByte

"Fitness training improves neuronal efficiency and performance...Older brains are a lot more flexible and plastic than we have been led to believe."—ART KRAMER

In 2004, two studies published in *Journal of the American Medical Association* hit on this same topic. The first found that "long-term regular physical activity, including walking, is associated with significantly better cognitive function and less cognitive decline in older women." The second study concluded that, in men who walk two or more miles each day, "walking is associated with a reduced risk of dementia." That's about 40 minutes of walking. No pain, lots of gain!

What about brains that may already be on that slippery slope to Alzheimer's or another form of dementia? A 2006 study by Eric Larson and colleagues in Seattle examined more than 1,700 individuals over age 65 and concluded that "regular voluntary physical exercise is associated with a delay in onset of dementia and Alzheimer's disease, further supporting its value for elderly persons." In 2008, Nicola Lautenschlager and colleagues in Australia demonstrated for the first time that the rate of progression of some memory and other cognitive impairments can be slowed down and that moderate physical exercise actually improves some impaired function—in this case, only about 30 minutes per day, five days a week.

Does exercise help *you* remember and think better? Does exercise protect *your* brain from those moments when you can't remember someone's name or where you left your car keys? Yes! Hot off the press is a 2009 study that concludes: "Our results clearly indicate that higher levels of aerobic fitness are associated with increased hippocampal volumes in older humans, which translates to better memory function."

Use It or Lose It: Exercising above the Shoulders

"Retirement is no excuse for an idle brain. If you're not active, then you're more susceptible to the onslaught of Alzheimer's."—P. MURALI DORAISWAMY, MD, DUKE UNIVERSITY

"You're building a reserve of brain cells when you're active."—MARILYN ALBERT, PHD, JOHNS HOPKINS UNIVERSITY AND SPOKESPERSON FOR THE ALZHEIMER'S ASSOCIATION

People who are in shape are better able to react to life's physical challenges, whether a mild flu or surgery or a heart attack. Physical reserve helps you bounce back more quickly from an illness or an injury. Brain reserve works the same way. The greater your brain reserve, the less likely you are to be affected by Alzheimer's. Remember those London cabbies who enlarged their hippocampi by learning the roads and shoppes of central London? They built brain reserve.

Joe Verghese and colleagues, as part of the Einstein Aging Study, set out to determine whether leisure activities can reduce the risk of illnesses like Alzheimer's disease. They tracked 469 people older than the age of 75 for more than ten years. The stunning results were published in the prestigious *New England Journal of Medicine*. Healthy elderly people who engaged in leisure activities like board games, reading, playing a musical instrument, doing crossword puzzles, writing, and participating in group discussions had much lower risk of developing Alzheimer's disease and other dementias. The more participants used their intellectual capacity, the less they lost it!

Can a healthy 70-year-old do mental exercises to actually offset and reverse the mental effects of aging? The Advanced Cognitive Training for Independent and Vital Elderly (ACTIVE) study, sponsored by the National Institute of Aging at the National Institutes of Health, demonstrated that two years after completion of a ten-session cognitive training program, participants remembered things more clearly, processed new information more speedily, and reasoned more efficiently, to the equivalent of knocking off seven to fourteen years from their brain age. A 2006 follow-up report demonstrated some benefits persisted even five years later. These results have caused a buzz in the brain aging arena.

What's more, Michael Valenzuela and Perminder Sachdev from the University of New South Wales collected and analyzed data from twenty-two studies involving 29,000 individuals. Their conclusion from this massive analysis is unambiguous; "...complex patterns of mental activity in the early, mid- and late-life stages is associated with a significant reduction in dementia incidence." "Use it or lose it," long a descriptive for below the neck functions, has moved up inside your head.

Having Alzheimer's but Not Acting Like It

Today Alzheimer's can be diagnosed definitively only by an autopsy. However, autopsies also show that some people who did not show signs of severe memory loss or Alzheimer's disease during life have brains full of the amyloid protein prevalent in Alzheimer's. How is it that some people have pathological evidence of Alzheimer's disease but were still able to function normally while alive? Brain reserve is the answer. As Jean Marx noted in *Science* magazine, "Keeping mentally and physically active when young and middle-aged can help stave off the brain degeneration of Alzheimer's."

The Brain Needs High-Grade Natural Fuel

"Let food be your medicine and medicine your food."—HIPPOCRATES, THE FATHER OF MEDICINE, CIRCA 400 B.C.

How do healthy and unhealthy eating affect the brain? In the bombardment consumers face at the supermarkets of America, where the average supermarket stocks thirty thousand to forty thousand products—not to mention the options like natural or enhanced or enriched, spiked with vitamins and supplements, organic, natural, processed this way and that way, low carb, high carb, low saturated fat, low trans-fat, free-range, uncaged—how to choose? What is the key nutrient, the essential mineral, the silver bullet, for healthy eating? The history of American dietary habits, the unfortunate path we have traveled from "food" to "nutritionism," as the savvy writer Michael Pollan describes it—in other words, our obsession with extracting nutrients and repackaging them in processed foods—parallels the rise of heart disease, diabetes, obesity, and now Alzheimer's disease.

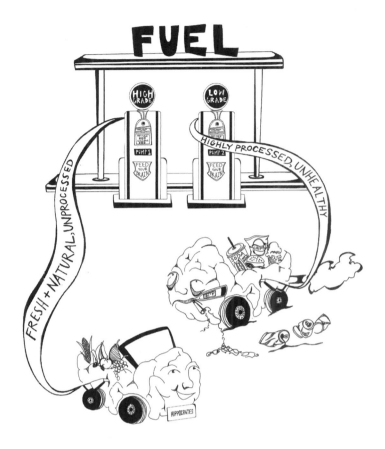

In our obsession with nutritionism, when barely a month goes by without the introduction of some new diet plan based on "modern research," the best advice on how to eat may be one of the most ancient in written history: the Bible. Most of the Bible's dietary guidelines are consistent with what the foremost twenty-first century nutritional experts recognize as brain and heart healthy. For example, in Genesis we find the verse, "Behold, I have given you every herb bearing seed, which is upon the face of all the earth, and every tree, in which is the fruit of a tree yielding seed; it shall be food for you." The Bible mentions foods like wheat, barley, wine, figs, pomegranates, olive oil, fish, and honey. You'll read more about these foods in chapter 5, where I'll talk about a nutritious and tasty diet for maintaining brain health and reducing your risk for Alzheimer's disease.

The closer our diet is to what nature provides in an unadulterated state, the better it is for our overall health and for our brain. Let's take a look at some of the evidence in support of this claim.

Two studies from 2002, both published in the *Journal of the American Medical Association*, looked at the eating habits of healthy aging adults in Chicago and the Netherlands, respectively. Both studies came to the same conclusion: healthy aging individuals who consumed diets rich in natural vitamin E (that found in natural foods, not supplements) had a markedly reduced risk of Alzheimer's disease. In another study, published in the *Annals of Neurology*, doctors at Harvard Medical School found that total vegetable intake was associated with less cognitive decline in aging women. The combinations of natural nutrients available in fruits and vegetables had greater benefits than isolated nutrients in vitamin supplements.

Vitamins, minerals, omega-3 fatty acids, and other essential micronutrients are more effective when you consume them in their natural state—in real food rather than isolated, purified, or synthesized as supplements in capsules or tablets. Natural food, or what I call "food for thinking," is what our brains (and our bodies) evolved to make use of over millions years; not the unnatural, highly processed products that some food technology and supplement companies so cleverly market.

The diet of people in the Mediterranean region resembles in key aspects that which the Bible recommends. The Mediterranean diet is characterized by fruits, vegetables, olive oil, grains, seeds, nuts, modest amounts of alcohol (usually red wine), fish, legumes, and less high-fat dairy, meat, and other sources of highly saturated fats. This diet has long been associated with less heart disease. A recent study at Columbia University found that people who consistently followed a Mediterranean-style diet reduced the risk of developing Alzheimer's by 40 percent. Other studies have found that eating more vegetables, fruits (especially berries), and juices reduces the risk of developing Alzheimer's by up to 70 percent.

And finally, a flurry of reviews and new studies published in the past two years led to the inescapable conclusion that a brain–healthy diet can significantly reduce age-associated memory problems and the risk of dementia and Alzheimer's disease.

SO, WHAT DOES IT ALL MEAN?

The brain can change at any age—with a proper diet, you arm it with nutritional ammunition; with physical exercise, it can grow new neurons; with cognitive stimulation, it can reorganize the connections among neurons to create new functional capabilities. The next three chapters delineate specific recommendations for each of the big three of healthy brain aging. These are followed by chapters dealing with the importance of stress management and healthy sleep. How robust the changes in your brain are depends on you taking charge of your brain's health. That is, it's up to you to get involved. It's time to join the team and to start putting into action what you have learned.

Chapter 5

FOOD FOR THINKING

"Eat right, exercise some. Break free of the chains of obesity, return to the virtues of our ancient dietary heritage, take the time to enjoy a good meal, and the time to enjoy the active life that meal makes possible. These are some of the most powerful things you can do to unleash the amazing potential of your brain."—JEFF VICTOROFF, MD, UNIVERSITY OF SOUTHERN CALIFORNIA

WHAT YOU EAT AFFECTS HOW YOU THINK AND REMEMBER

Have you ever noticed that when you miss a meal, you feel a bit fuzzy upstairs? Maybe you have difficulty concentrating and remembering, or perhaps you become irritable and grouchy. This is your brain's warning light: it's telling you that, while it's still running, its fuel gauge is nearing empty.

A constant supply of simple sugar (or glucose) is the rock-bottom fuel requirement to keep you awake, alert, and able to think and remember. But keeping your brain at peak health requires more than just basic fuel. It involves daily nutritional maintenance and tune-ups in the form

CogniBite

What is brain-healthy food? Food that you find in gardens, fields, orchards, rivers, and seas. The less processed it is, the better it is for you.

of essential fats, amino acids (the building blocks of proteins), vitamins, minerals, and the antioxidants contained in fruits and vegetables (which are vital for health and healthy aging).

It looks like a simple grocery list, but the relationships among the ingredients are complex, and the science behind it all is sophisticated. But scientists do know what the brain needs and where we can find it.

For example, some studies document that the energy boost provided by a hearty dose of sugar enables the brain to perform at a higher level for an hour or two. Other studies have reported similar results for stimulants such as coffee, tea, or caffeinated soft drinks, which can also boost brain performance over the short run. But I'm not suggesting you eat more candy and chug more cola! Downing a sugar-fueled energy boost is not the same as nourishing yourself. For optimal, long-term brain functioning and health, simple sugars and coffee won't cut it.

The way to achieve your best brain performance every day and all day to live to age 90 and beyond is to eat balanced meals that consist of healthful, real foods in moderation. Our brains evolved over millions of years to use the nutrients as provided by nature. If you take any message from this chapter, make it this one principle, adapted from Michael Pollan: Eat real food in moderation. This means mostly fruits, vegetables, whole grains, and fish. The lower it is on the food chain, the better; and the less processed it is, the better. That is all you need to remember! Forget the deluge of marketing hype about processed foods and supplements. Good nutrition is not complex.

In this chapter, we'll first explore the brain-healthy nutrients that natural, real foods offer. Then we'll dive right into an easy-to-follow nutritional plan that will provide your brain and body with the daily nutrient balance they need to function optimally for a lifetime.

With the Brain Training Revolution, there are two ways for you to reach your goal of feeding your brain well. First, with the Slow and Steady plan, you modify your current diet week by week (or month by month, if that is more comfortable for you) by adding brain-healthy foods one category at a time. Second, you can adopt the Three-Level Jump-Start plan, in which you start on day 1 with level 1: a plateful of delectables from the eight major categories of brain-healthy foods. You'll move through levels 2 and 3 as you progress toward eating the optimum number of daily servings from each category. Both approaches will get you to the goal of eating well day in and day out to fortify your brain and body against the wear and tear of aging.

> **CogniBite**
>
> The term *Mediterranean diet* became popular starting in 1993 and is based on the traditional diets of peoples living around the Mediterranean Sea. Fifty years ago, such people had life expectancies among the highest in the world, with rates of heart and other chronic diseases among the lowest, even though access to advanced medicines and other medical interventions was limited. The Brain Training Revolution nutritional plan is based on the Mediterranean diet, which has similarities to the Biblical recommendations on eating mentioned in chapter 4.

Look all around America and you will see the results of sugary, high-fat, and processed foods: a society full of overweight, under-exercised individuals and epidemics of childhood and adult obesity, diabetes, cancer, heart disease, stroke, various metabolic syndromes, and Alzheimer's disease. Compelling evidence shows that every one of these diseases and conditions is attributable, in considerable part, to our unnatural eating habits. The Brain Training Revolution nutritional plan is all about brain health and a brain-healthy diet. However, what's nutritionally best from the neck up is also terrific for the rest of you.

The Greedy, Selective Brain

The brain is the most demanding organ in your body when it comes to energy requirements. Each of the billions of cells in your brain is a small factory, and like any factory, each cell requires fuel to keep it going.

The brain's primary fuel, as noted earlier, is glucose. But your brain needs many other nutrients as well to function optimally and not just chug along. The brain has evolved to use nutrients found in nature as building blocks to construct and repair the cells it needs to run. Here is a partial list of the nutrients that are central to brain health and to a brain-healthy lifestyle:

- Glucose

- Fiber

- Amino acids

- Fats such as essential omega-3 and omega-6 fatty acids

- Vitamins—such as E, C, B_6, B_{12}, thiamin, and folate

- Minerals such as calcium, sodium, potassium, iron, copper, manganese, magnesium, and selenium

- Antioxidants from vegetables and fruits

- Special molecules like choline from foods for building neurotransmitters

Large proteins and complex fats cannot gain entrance to the brain, nor can large complex sugar molecules (carbohydrates). These must be broken down by our digestive system and transported through the blood to the brain, where they are used to power the mind and direct the body.

As modern nutritional scientists explore the metabolic mysteries of the brain, they discover over and over that nature's plan is best; nutrients are more effective when they come from real foods rather than as isolated supplements. In the words of Alzheimer's disease expert Marwan Sabbagh, "If it's the choice between a carrot and a beta-carotene capsule, go with the carrot."

Our endless tinkering and processing in the manufacture of foods (such as adding of trans-fats and high-fructose corn syrup) have created a big problem for our brains, our entire bodies, and our society. In only about sixty years, we have made the rapid transition from eating well with long-standing natural and ethnic food traditions to consuming highly processed foods.

> **CogniBite**
>
> Vitamin E, as it is found naturally in nuts and vegetables, is more effective in protecting the aging brain from Alzheimer's disease than when it is consumed as a supplement in capsules. Vitamin E is not one molecule but eight related compounds. In foods like almonds, sunflower seeds, red bell peppers, and wheat germ, vitamin E and its related compounds come in the correct ratio and are "packaged" by mother nature along with thousands of other nutrient molecules, some of which aid in its absorption, availability, and function.

WHAT YOUR BRAIN NEEDS TO FUNCTION
Sugar: Sweet and Necessary

As I've hinted already, sugar is by far the most important energy source for your brain. Glucose provides energy for the hippocampus memory factory, its emotional sidekick the amygdala, and all the other working parts of your brain. It is a ready-to-burn fuel, so essential that you will lose consciousness if the level in your blood falls below a critical concentration. But you don't need to eat simple sugars to get all the glucose your brain needs. Fruits, vegetables, and grains are a much healthier source of glucose than are candy, cola, and processed foods.

Sugars are the basic building blocks of all carbohydrates, and therein lies the key. All carbohydrates are not created equal! When you link three or more simple sugars together, you get complex carbohydrates, like those found in whole grains, vegetables, and fruit. These are a healthier source of energy because the body must break them down into simple forms that cells can burn more easily. This digestive process takes time because of the presence of fiber in the grains and vegetables. The result is a slow but steady supply of glucose entering the blood to provide a constant fuel source for the brain and other organs. When you have a simple sugar, without fiber, flying solo down the digestive tract, you get rapid entry from the gut into your bloodstream and a burst of energy rushes to the brain, giving you a quick high followed by a crash.

CARBOHYDRATES AND YOUR BRAIN

Sugars are simple carbohydrates that contain just one or two molecules. The names of such sugars usually end in —ose: glucose (your brain's main fuel); fructose (in fruits and corn); lactose (in milk products); sucrose (table sugar); maltose (in vegetables); and honey, which is actually a mixture of simple sugars. The best way to eat most of the carbohydrates you need for energy is not as sucrose and fructose but as complex carbohydrates.

Starches are complex carbohydrates and should provide most of the sugars in our diet. They are abundant in whole grains and vegetables. The controlled breakdown of dietary starches in the presence of dietary fiber is a healthy way to provide a constant energy-rich supply of glucose to your brain and keep your glycemic index low. The most common sources of starch are rice, wheat, potatoes, sweet potatoes, corn, beans, peas, lentils, and other vegetables.

Fiber is the indigestible part of all plant foods. Cellulose is the best-known example of dietary fiber. It differs from the sugars or starches because it passes through your system largely without being digested and provides only minimal calories as a result of a bit of "chewing" by bacteria in your gut. It does, however, contribute to health as it plays a significant role in maintaining optimal intestinal functioning, regulating the digestion process, reducing the risk of colon cancer, and lowering cholesterol uptake—important for your brain. Good sources of fiber include vegetables, fruits, legumes, and whole grains.

Amino Acids: Building Blocks for Proteins

Proteins control and direct all brain activities and are the major structural parts of brain cells and their synaptic connections. Each protein is constructed by a special class of proteins called enzymes, which link amino acids together one after another in linear chains containing less than ten to up to hundreds of amino acids in precise sequence. Nerve cells talk to one another via neurotransmitters in an intricate process with hundreds of proteins supporting and regulating these absolutely essential internal communications. When nerve cells decide to join together in new synapses to help make permanent a memory or newly learned task, proteins do the joining. Nothing happens in your brain without proteins doing the work.

Cells can manufacture many amino acids, but some are what nutritional scientists and biochemists label "essential." These essential amino acids cannot be synthesized by our cells and so must be obtained from food. Meat, fish, dairy products, and combinations of plant foods are protein-rich sources of amino acids.

Water: The Brain Is Loaded with It and Floating in It

Like oxygen, water is required for survival. Seventy percent of the brain's weight is water. In this aqueous environment, many of the thousands of chemicals inside and outside the nerve cells float around, bumping into other compounds until the right partner is found. They then interact to do the cell's work. The brain is also bathed externally in shock-absorbing cerebrospinal fluid, which is derived from blood plasma and is more than 90 percent water. Each of us needs to drink several quarts of water per day for optimal health.

Fats: *Fat Head* Is a Medically Accurate Term

Many people have been led to believe that dietary fats are bad. However, certain fats obtained from food are critical for optimal brain health. Your brain cells depend on fats for construction, repair, and ongoing communications. Dietary fats are critical components of the outer walls of brain cells and the insulating sheaths of nerves, allowing the lightning-fast transmission of signals back and forth from the brain to the far reaches of the body. When you add it all up, your brain is about two-thirds fat! So a reasonable goal is to have a fat brain and lean body!

All fats and oils (liquid fats), also known as lipids, are not the same, however. Essential fatty acids are those fats that must be obtained from the diet because the body cannot synthesize them. Among the most important of these are the unsaturated omega-3 and omega-6 fatty acids. Cholesterol is not an essential fat as your body can synthesize all it needs. Remarkably, 20 percent of the dry weight of the brain consists of one omega-3 fatty acid, docosahexaenoic acid (DHA).

We do not need to worry about getting enough omega-6 fatty acids. The American diet provides more than ten times the needed amount of omega-6s primarily through the fats found in most processed foods and common cooking oils such as sunflower, corn, safflower, cottonseed, and soybean. But we do need to worry about insufficient consumption of omega-3s. Nutritional experts have determined that we should be eating omega-3s and omega-6s in a ratio of about 1:4. But the average American diet now has ten to twenty or more times the amount of omega-6s in it than omega-3s.

With an excess ratio of omega-6 to omega-3 in your diet and an excess in your body of so-called bad fats, like some forms of cholesterol and triglycerides, you are at higher risk of heart disease, vascular disease, and stroke. "Vascular dementia" from blood vessel disease and stroke is responsible for 15 to 30 percent of all cases of dementia, second only to Alzheimer's disease.

We need to restore the balance of omega-6 to omega-3 fatty acids in our diets. Don't get me wrong—every once in a while a juicy steak, a cheeseburger, or a slice of chocolate cake à la mode is okay, but choose healthier and equally tasty options most of the time.

FISHING FOR OMEGA-3S

Foods rich in omega-3 fatty acids include salmon, sardines, herring, anchovies, tuna, mackerel, and other cold-water fish; walnuts and walnut oil; flaxseeds and flaxseed oil; and canola oil. Make these a regular part of your brain-healthy diet.

Foods rich in omega-6 fatty acids include nuts, legumes, and most vegetable oils. Eat these in moderation. Avoid eating more than an infrequent serving of high-fat red meats and dairy products, and many processed foods, as these contain saturated and/or trans-fats that can harm your body and brain.

Diets rich in fish, with their omega-3 fatty acids, reduce the risk of stroke, vascular disease, and heart disease. Eha Nurk and her Norwegian and British colleagues have reviewed the data from earlier studies and investigated a new group of 2,031 aging adults in Norway. Their 2007 findings are consistent with earlier results: fish eaters do better on cognitive performance than do non-fish eaters.

There is also exciting new evidence that increasing the consumption of fish and omega-3s may reduce the risk of Alzheimer's disease. The U.S. Department of Health and Human Services concluded in 2005 that "fish consumption was associated with a reduced risk of Alzheimer's dementia." Although fish oils and fish oil supplements may have similar benefits, the results are not nearly as certain. Some studies have found that only fish but not fish oil supplements are effective. When in doubt, eat real fish, not extracted oils or supplements.

There's no question that brain and body health are at risk if you consume too much of the wrong kinds of fats or not enough of the right kind! Meals consistently providing essential fatty acids, especially omega-3s, are what you need for your healthy aging brain.

ABCs and Es of Vitamins

Vitamins play many critical roles in brain cells. Think of them as uniquely specialized technicians in a sophisticated factory, responsible for critical details of a complex manufacturing process. Among the most important vitamins for brain health are the B series (including thiamin and folate), C, and E. Because the body does not make vitamins, we have to get them from the foods we eat. A well-balanced diet plentiful with fruits, vegetables, grains, nuts, seeds, fish, and modest amounts of meat and dairy products will supply you with all the vitamins your brain and body needs.

Minerals

Each of the essential minerals does a specific job—or in fact, many jobs—and some of them do extra work, in teams, to keep our neurons and all the other body's cells healthy. Calcium in bones and teeth and iron in blood and muscle are widely known examples, but at least a dozen other minerals are essential for life, including copper, iodine, iron, magnesium, manganese, sodium, potassium, selenium, and zinc. Sodium, potassium, and calcium participate in literally millions of brain and nerve activities each minute. Our bodies cannot make minerals. They come from the earth's soils and seas and are incorporated into the plants and animals that we eat.

Antioxidants

I wrote a bit about antioxidants and free radicals earlier. Increasingly, scientists are finding that oxidative damage caused by free radicals is responsible for much aging of the brain and other parts of your body. Free radicals pollute the cell's environment and damage its various parts, so the body has evolved a defense system that can clean up and neutralize these villains. Antioxidants are molecules of various sizes and shapes that protect brain and body cells from free radicals and the oxidative damage they cause.

It is estimated that in every brain cell, ten thousand interactions occur each day between free radicals and DNA. Fortunately, much of this potential damage can be averted by dietary antioxidants, and the brain itself also manufactures other antioxidants—but only when supplied with the necessary nutrients. There are perhaps twenty thousand compounds in foods that have antioxidant properties—another compelling reason to take what nature has provided.

Vitamins E and C are critical vitamins, and they also function as two potent antioxidants. It's best to consume these vitamins from real foods instead of supplements. "A significant number of studies have shown that fruits and vegetables promote health, while antioxidant supplements do not," according to Michael Ristow from the Institute of Nutrition at the University of Jena, Germany. In 2009, he and his colleagues found that supplemental vitamins C and E given in combination as antioxidants actually prevented some health-promoting effects of physical exercise in humans.

The Brain Training Revolution nutritional plan does not address the issue of supplements in detail. Unless you have a specific deficiency, there is no scientific evidence supporting their use. They are simply unnecessary. Virtually every substance that is now marketed as a pill or capsule was first identified in a real food, where it exists in the presence of many other compounds, some of which are critical for absorption and biological activity. In a supplement all the supporting actors have been removed. When you consider buying a supplement that is advertised as coming from a specific fruit, vegetable, or fish, remember the words of integrative medicine expert Andrew Weil: "I have seen bottles in health food stores that have a photo of a bunch of broccoli on the label, and the implication is that this is broccoli in a pill. It's not broccoli in a pill. It's sulphurophane in a pill, and that's one element of an incredibly complex plant that has all sorts of different things in it." As a nation we spend $6 billion dollars annually on these unproven substitutes and we are no better off. Some supplements can actually be detrimental to your health. But there are medical circumstances when, for example, extra vitamin B_{12}, iron, calcium, magnesium, or another supplement is important for health. If in doubt, consult your physician.

Fortunately, there is a simple and scientifically valid solution to our nutritional quandary. Numerous scientific studies (not sponsored by the processed foods and supplement industries) have documented that the consumption of a plant-rich diet is associated with reduced risks for cancer, heart disease, obesity, diabetes, and stroke. This same correlation has been demonstrated for the brain. Folks who eat a fruit- and vegetable-rich diet have better-aging brains and a reduced risk of Alzheimer's disease. Good for the brain, good for the body.

WHAT'S THE ANSWER?

Carbohydrates, amino acids, protein, water, fat, vitamins, minerals, antioxidants—that's an overwhelming list. Here's the healthy, easy and satisfying answer that wraps all of it together:

- Go back to natural foods in their native states. Unprocessed is better than processed. Slightly processed is better than highly processed. The more it looks like what you see growing in the fields and orchards, and the more it resembles the stuff for sale at the farmers' market, the better it is for you.

- No matter where you live, no matter what your racial and ethnic background, no matter what your genetic inheritance, if you eat a diet centered on fruits and vegetables, nuts, seeds, whole grains, fish, and healthy vegetable oils, and a diet with modest amounts of low-fat dairy products and wine, your brain will function optimally and you will reduce your risk of memory loss and Alzheimer's disease.

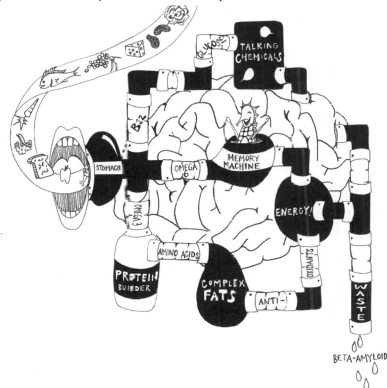

WHAT YOUR BRAIN LIKES

For optimal brain health, we want to eat foods that

- Provide the best fuel for energy in the most effective and safest form

- Do not contribute to high blood pressure, vascular disease, diabetes, or obesity, that conditions increase your risk of stroke and dementia

- Provide effective natural, antioxidants to counteract free radical damage

- Supply essential minerals, vitamins, fats, and the other building blocks of complex molecules that will fine-tune your aging brain

The food groups listed below meet the preceding criteria. Keep in mind that we are considering only foods for which there is substantial scientific evidence that they help maintain a well-functioning aging brain; contribute to improved memory and overall cognition; or decrease your risk of age-associated memory decline, Alzheimer's disease, stroke, and other less common dementias associated with aging. The following foods are actual foods that you can buy in your local grocery store, supermarket, farmers' market (if you are so lucky), or that you can grow in your own garden. All of these foods are considered must-eat foods. The fresher, the better! The less processed, the better!

Keep in mind that these are only examples. The more you vary the types of fruits and vegetables the better. Each one has a different mix of complex carbohydrates, proteins, minerals, vitamins, antioxidants, and other essential nutrients.

- Fruits and fresh fruit juices

- Nuts and seeds

- Whole grains like breads, pastas, and cereals

- Vegetables: a wide variety of sizes, shapes, and colors

- Legumes (beans and peas)

- Fish, especially those high in healthy fats

- Canola, olive, and other unsaturated vegetable oils

- Low-fat dairy and lean meats, especially poultry

- Wine (mostly red) in moderation

WHAT YOUR BRAIN DOES NOT LIKE

Foods that are not healthy for the brain tend to be highly processed; too high in salt, simple sugars, and unhealthy saturated fats and trans-fats; nutrient poor; and generative of free radicals. Processed foods often lack fiber, vitamins, minerals, and other nutrients important for health. The vitamins, omega-3s, and other critical nutrients they do contain are usually added and as such are not in their natural, more effective state.

So, for the sake of your brain (and your body) avoid the following:

- Foods high in salt: snack foods like chips, heavily salted nuts, and high-sodium canned soups

- Processed foods high in simple sugars (either table sugar or high-fructose corn syrup): cola, sweetened juices, drink mixes, candy, cookies, other high-calorie sweet snacks

- Foods high in saturated fat and cholesterol: fat-rich red meats and high-fat dairy products (keep saturated fat consumption to less than 10 percent of total caloric intake)

CogniBite

You may think that you like something, but taste can trick your brain. Over the course of its long evolution, the human brain has learned and remembered the taste of good nutrition—lots of energy in small packages with many other essential micronutrients as bonuses. The food industry learned to give you the same sweet, salty, and fatty flavors without the nutrition. But your memory for taste does not know the difference. It's a cruel trick.

- Foods high in trans-fats: any food containing the designation "partially hydrogenated," most commonly found in margarines, shortenings, fried foods, chips, and many baked goods

- Foods high in calories from fat: the U.S. Department of Agriculture and the Food and Drug Administration recommend that no more than 20 to 35 percent of total calories come from fat

TWO APPROACHES TO A BRAIN-HEALTHY DIET

Now that we have a basic understanding of food categories that are good for the brain, let's start converting this information into an action plan for brain-healthy eating at any age, but with an emphasis on starting at the age of 40.

SLOW AND STEADY OR THREE-LEVEL JUMP-START

The Brain Training Revolution offers you two approaches toward building your brain-healthy diet. Your consistent strides on either path will take you to the finish line: an optimum diet for healthy brain aging, peak mental performance, better memories, and less chance of Alzheimer's disease.

What is important isn't the minute details but the overarching nutritional principles. As diet study after diet study reveals, many of us start various diets but most fall off the bandwagon, and a frequent reason is the rigidity of the plan and our longing for foods that we are used to consuming that are not in the plan. As the *New York Times* writer William Grimes, who renamed the 2005 USDA diet recommendations the "Uncle Sam diet," described the dilemma most of us face in trying to follow highly structured dietary guidelines. "In the world of the guidelines, food is a kind of medicine that, taken in the right doses, can promote good health. In the real world, of course, people regard food and its flavors as a source of pleasure. And therein lies just one of the problems with the guidelines, which my wife took one look at before saying with a shake of her head, 'No one is ever going to eat like this.'" Grimes was right on, and I took his advice to heart (and to mind) in building the dietary recommendations here.

The Brain Training Revolution's recommendations are to gradually modify your current diet. For instance, even if you do not want to follow precisely one of the plans presented here, familiarize yourself with the eight categories of food you should be eating for better brain and body health. Then next time you are buying groceries, think about one of the categories and buy a few items. Or if you are already eating some from this category, expand your list and buy a few more than your norm. And start adding them to your meals and making them snacks occasionally, and keep building up over two or three months. If you do this you will find yourself feeling better and performing better.

The Brain Training Revolution is not a weight-loss plan; rather, it prescribes that you add healthy foods to your diet and decrease unhealthy foods. I wouldn't give up an occasional doughnut, handful of potato chips, soft drink, pastrami sandwich, lamb chop, steak, or hot-fudge sundae, and I don't expect you to either. But the operative word is *occasional*. What I do encourage is that most of the time you eat a brain-healthy diet and make those less healthy, less nutritional treats and meals the exceptions and not the rule.

Here are the two different approaches toward building your brain-healthy diet.

1. **Slow and Steady.** This approach adds brain-healthy foods category by category, one by one, week by week, or month by month. This method works best for those who like to take smaller steps and make gradual changes.

CogniBite

Nutritional guidelines are intended to point you toward better health through proper nutrition. They are not like a precise prescription for a medicine in which an exact dose must be taken at the correct times for the necessary number of days. Eating is a joy for most of us. The joy will increase as you eat regularly in a healthier fashion.

2. **Three-Level Jump-Start.** This approach gets you into high gear quickly. Some of us like to plunge right in and do a major overhaul. If this fits your personality, then it's probably the approach that is best for you. You begin from the outset with brain-healthy foods from all the categories without paying attention to number of servings per day. Then, in levels 2 and 3 you progressively increase the number of servings per category as described in detail further on.

What is important is to realize that you have complete control. I urge you to pick an approach that makes sense for you—one that you are confident in and motivated by so that you can stick with it. If you are not sure which plan makes the most sense for you personally, read the following pages in one sitting to get a flavor. Then follow your initial instinct once you have familiarized yourself with the two basic choices.

THE NUTRITIONAL QUOTIENT

Keeping score can be a powerful motivator as you make dietary changes. The Nutritional Quotient (NQ) is meant to help you in this regard: it is a simple way for you to track the number of servings of brain-healthy foods you consume each day and sum them up weekly. The goal is to earn 100 points each week, a convincing demonstration that you are doing good things for your brain by way of your mouth. If you earn more than 100 points, all the better.

Turn to page 273 for a personal NQ scorecard you can easily reproduce. This scorecard is designed to help you stay on course to reach your final goal of a complete brain-healthy diet.

SLOW AND STEADY

Think of a supermarket with eight aisles. Each week (or longer if you are more comfortable with a slower pace of change) you will go down one that you have not been down before and select some of the foods you find. In successive weeks, you will also revisit the ones you already wandered through. By the end of eight weeks you will have gone through all the aisles, and you will know what healthy foods in each aisle appeal to you the most.

You'll want to eat healthy foods each week, but don't pay attention to the number of servings, amounts, or any other measuring. Just experiment and enjoy new tastes. There's no real counting or charting here. Just keep the foods visible and make a real effort to eat them.

SLOW AND STEADY: THE GOAL

This is where you want to end up after eight weeks. The everyday meals and snacks of your brain-healthy diet should contain the following:

- Fresh vegetables in abundance, especially the leafy vegetables such as spinach and the cruciferous vegetables such as broccoli, cauliflower, Brussels sprouts, and cabbage
- Plenty of fresh fruit
- Healthy amounts of nuts, seeds (especially almonds and sunflower seeds), and legumes (peas and beans)
- Whole-grain cereals, breads, and pastas
- Frequent fish meals, especially fatty fish such as salmon, sardines, herring, and mackerel
- Healthy oils such as canola, olive, flaxseed, soybean, sunflower, peanut, corn
- Modest amounts of poultry
- Low-fat dairy products
- Moderate (one or two glasses per day) intake of alcohol (mostly red wine) with meals if you already drink

Week 1

Vegetables are your first week's assignment. This week, when you're shopping, grab a bit of whatever fresh veggies look good to you. Artichoke, asparagus, broccoli, Brussels sprouts, cabbage, carrots, cauliflower... we are barely in the "Cs"– the list is endless. Mix them up. Eat them as snacks, or sauté some for dinner in a bit of olive oil. Add lettuce, tomatoes, and sprouts to a sandwich. Have fun, be brave and experiment. The more colorful the veggies on your plate, the better it is for you. Think about various colored lettuces, spinach, onions, bell peppers, cabbage, radishes, scallions, chives, cucumbers, squash, kohlrabi, radicchio, and yams.

Salad is my favorite refreshing way to consume plenty of vegetables. Throw in a few almonds, peanuts, or sunflower seeds. Add some tuna, salmon, or chicken, and a dash of olive oil and some lemon juice. Sprinkle a dash of mixed dried herbs for more flavor or a bit of black pepper, and a pinch of salt if you must, for flavoring.

Week 2

Pay attention to fruit this week and pick out a few varieties to try with your meals or as snacks between meals: a handful of strawberries, blueberries, or other berries, oranges, tangerines, apples, pears, melons, peaches, or a mango. Buy at least seven pieces of fruit. Fresh squeezed juice counts. Try to eat one a day.

Use fruit in place of pastry, cookies, and ice cream for dessert. But if this leads to cravings you can't ignore then try a gradual reduction approach: For the first several weeks reduce the amount of ice cream, for example, by about one-third and add some cut-up fruit and perhaps a few nuts on top. Once you are okay with this smaller core of ice cream or pastry, then reduce by another one-third and increase the fruit proportionately.

Week 3

This week, substitute some whole grains—breads, pastas, cereals—for those less healthy varieties you have been eating. Try some grains you have not tasted before: quinoa, barley, wild rice, and even some special preparations of these grains like couscous. Buy whole-grain breads, wraps, or pitas for your sandwiches. Try a whole-grain pasta for dinner. Whole-grain cereals, natural granolas, and oatmeal are wonderful to start the day. Added raisins, fresh cut-up fruits, and some nuts increase the appeal for me.

Week 4

This week focus on beans, peas, and other legumes. Beans are a healthy substitution for red meat. They come in a wide variety of colorful, tasty choices, and you can add zest with spices, vegetables, bits of chicken, or cheese. A small handful of unsalted peanuts makes a tasty, hearty snack. (Be careful with peanuts—the calories can really add up!) Another option is hummus. Add a bit of olive oil and use whole-grain pita bread as an edible spoon. A few olives and you have a real Mediterranean snack, delightfully healthy.

Week 5

This week your focus is on nuts and seeds—eat them as snacks or add them to salads or vegetable dishes. The less roasted they are, the higher the nutritional value. Almonds, walnuts, and sunflower seeds are good brain-healthy choices. Try to limit these to a small handful a day because, just like dried fruit, the calories can really add up.

Week 6

This week visit the fish counter. Buy a piece or two of salmon, trout, tuna, or any fish that looks appealing to you. Broil, bake, or if you fry (which I do not recommend) be sure to use a healthy vegetable oil. Another option is BBQ—barbecued fresh fish is wonderful! Even canned fish is better than no fish, so if fresh fish is too drastic for your mind-set or taste buds as you begin this program, just pick up a couple cans of salmon, sardines, herring, or anchovies. Eat these on whole-grain crackers, in sandwiches, on salads, or mixed with pasta. But easy on the shellfish as they are fairly rich in cholesterol even though relatively low in total fats.

Week 7

This week try new healthy fats and oils. Buy a bottle of olive oil (soybean, flaxseed, sunflower, peanut, corn, and canola oil are also healthy choices). Try the oils for cooking, salad dressings, on cooked vegetables, and for dipping instead of butter or margarine.

Week 8

This week stroll down the aisle with low-fat dairy products: milk, yogurts, and cheeses. If you normally buy a gallon of whole milk, this week buy a half gallon of whole milk and a half gallon of 1 percent or skim milk. Try a low-fat natural cheese and some low-fat yogurt. Add fresh fruit, a few nuts and seeds, whole-grain cereal, or granola to yogurt for additional flavor and more of a main dish.

Red Wine

On any day, you can have a glass or two of red wine with dinner. Don't start drinking for brain health if you have not been consuming alcohol previously. If you have any questions about this part of the nutrition prescription, check with your personal physician.

Overview

Slow and Steady is for those of you most comfortable with small changes and steady progress. It is one easy way to work toward a brain-healthy diet. Once you have become accustomed to eating these brain-healthy foods, gradually increase their presence in your diet until you have made them the core of your daily eating habits and consume them frequently in sufficient amounts. When you have finished incorporating the Slow and Steady approach into your lifestyle, you will be at the same point as if you had started and completed level 1 of the Jump-Start method. To achieve the next steps, move on to level 2 of the Three-Level Jump-Start method that follows. Whether it takes you two weeks, two months, or longer to achieve the objectives of level 2, don't stress. Keep at it and you will get there. Then you can move on to level 3.

THREE-LEVEL JUMP-START

Depending on what your diet is like now, start at the appropriate level in the Three-Level Jump-Start approach. If you are already at level 1, then begin at level 2. If you are at level 2, start at level 3. If you are at level 3, congratulations! You can concentrate on the other aspects of a brain-healthy lifestyle. Here are the goals of each level:

- Level 1: Increase alertness, awareness, and attentiveness.

- Level 2: Improve cortical function.

- Level 3: Improve creativity and imagination.

As you go from level 1 to level 3, you'll get closer to the optimum diet for brain health, but you also need to spend more time and effort making your food choices. Level 3 is the ultimate diet recommendation in the Brain Training Revolution, but each level is a big step toward your brighter, brain-healthy future.

Level 1: Increase Alertness, Awareness, and Attentiveness

In level 1, you'll train your brain to remember and act on the words of our former Secretary of Health and Human Services Tommy Thompson: "You lower your calorie intake, you lower your fats, your carbs, you eat more fruits and vegetables, more whole grain, and you exercise." It's that simple! If you don't want to measure food portions or keep track of what and when you eat, Thompson's pithy advice will get you started on a brain-healthy diet.

Level 1 does not call for specific amounts or numbers of servings per day or per week. The aim here is to introduce these healthy foods into your diet, not to sweat over them. In level 1 of this approach, you select healthy foods from all eight categories instead of from just one category. Refer to the pyramid and to the descriptions of the eight categories above in the Jump-Start program. In Part 3 you will find more extensive lists of foods in each of the categories to assist you when you are shopping for level 1.

As you begin eating new foods, mixing and matching, and experimenting with them, you will find that giving your brain and body what they want, need, and deserve is an exciting journey. One way to make change easier and more exciting is to recruit your spouse, partner, or a friend. Talking about what you're shopping for and cooking with someone else builds confidence and is an engaging social activity, in itself good for the brain.

For level 1, target your daily caloric intake at 1,700 to 2,000 calories per day. To maintain your weight, the more you exercise, the higher your caloric intake can be. But a sincere word of caution: it takes a lot of exercise to burn off indulgent foods. Modest exercise for an hour only burns about 500 calories. A single slice of cheese pizza has approximately 270 calories. Decrease the fried, fast, and highly processed foods in your diet. Substitute a piece of fish, a fresh salad with cheeses and bits of meat, or a lean turkey or chicken sandwich on whole-grain bread for one or two of your usual fried food lunches or red meat dinners each week.

As for snacks that you may be used to eating in the morning, mid-afternoon, and late evening, replace chips, pretzels, or candy bars with fresh fruits; veggies such as baby carrots, celery stalks, cherry tomatoes, and sliced red peppers; unsalted nuts; a handful of granola or trail mix; or a healthy all-natural nutritional bar. If you don't feel like chopping and slicing, prepared ready-to-eat veggies can be found in the produce section of most supermarkets. Chips or other hard-to-avoid favorites can be nibbled once or twice a week, but they should be your treats, not your regular snacks. You will be happier, you'll be healthier, and you'll feel better when the diet you pursue has more "nature" and less "factory" in it.

Next, you'll see that levels 2 and 3 spell out how much of each food group you should consume, as opposed to the more general recommendations of level 1. Some of us want to follow guidelines more or less precisely. If this approach makes you more comfortable, if it will help you make brain-healthy modifications to your diet, then certainly the actual measuring, counting, weighing, and tracking of what you consume at each meal over a period of time should be part of your program. Do this as long as it takes until the diet becomes part of your gustatory memory and occupies a privileged place in your gray matter. As an additional aid, consider using a notebook or hand-held electronic device to record the types and amounts of foods you eat.

Level 2: Improve Cortical Function

1-2/DAY
3/WEEK FISH
1-2/DAY LOW-FAT DAIRY
2-3 tsp/DAY HEALTHY FATS
3-4/WEEK NUTS + SEEDS
1/DAY LEGUMES
3/DAY WHOLE GRAINS
2/DAY FRUIT
3/DAY VEGETABLES
LEVEL TWO

The major difference between level 1 and level 2 is that you will now keep track of the number of servings you eat in each major category. Use a weekly scorecard to track your progress (see page 274). This level requires more effort on your part, but you will be better nourished and feel better overall.

Eating must be fun, though, so don't sweat it. If you miss a day's vegetables, it is certainly not the end of the world. In all honesty, even I have been known to fall off the wagon now and then—a breakfast of fried eggs, potatoes, sausage, and toast; a lunch of a couple of hot dogs or a burger; and fried chicken for dinner—especially when I travel and eat out. Do I feel guilty—of course not! I jog most days and I know my lifestyle is healthy about 325 days out of the year. If you do better than me, my hat is off to you!

The key level 2 recommendations are for daily consumptions based on a diet of 2,000 calories per day (a good target for those over 40 years old).

You will find that as you achieve your daily and weekly goals of brain-healthy servings, you will willingly (sometimes unconsciously) reduce the amounts of refined sugars, refined flours, fried and fatty red meats, and high-fat dairy that you previously consumed.

Here is a list of daily serving recommendations (unless otherwise noted):

- Every day eat three servings of any varieties of vegetables. That's 1 ½ cups of salad (not much) and that's an entire day's requirement at level 2!

- Eat two servings per day of a variety of fruits and berries. One medium-sized apple or a fist-sized bunch of grapes does it—how easy!

- Eat three servings of whole grains per day (refer to the box on page 88 for serving sizes). Uncooked whole-grain cereals, breads, and pastas in many varieties are becoming increasingly available as America makes the move back to a more natural way of eating.

- Eat one serving per day of beans, peas, and other legumes.

- Eat three servings of fish per week.

- Eat one small handful of nuts and seeds every other day (three to four servings per week).

- Use 2 to 3 tablespoons of healthy fats each day.

- Eat one to two servings of low-fat dairy per day.

- You can drink one or two glasses of red wine per day. Compared to white wine and other alcoholic drinks, the best evidence is that red wine is the brain's drink of choice. Don't start drinking alcohol if you have any medical or religious reasons not to begin, or if you simply don't drink. Check with your doctor if you have any concerns.

WHAT'S A SERVING?

One serving of vegetables is

- 1 cup of raw, leafy vegetables
- ½ cup of other vegetables, cooked or raw
- ¾ cup of carrot, tomato, or other vegetable juice

One serving of fruit is

- 1 medium-sized orange, apple, pear, or banana
- ½ cup of chopped or cooked fruit
- ¾ cup of fresh orange, grapefruit, pineapple, or other juice

One serving of dairy is

- 1 cup of milk or yogurt
- 1.5 ounces of natural cheese

One serving of fish, poultry, or meat is

- 5 to 6 ounces of cooked fish, lean poultry, or meat

One serving of beans, peas, or legumes is

- 1 cup of cooked beans (the equivalent of one meat serving)

One serving of whole grains is

- 1 medium-sized (1 ounce) slice of 100 percent whole-grain bread
- 1 cup of 100 percent whole-grain, ready-to-eat cereal
- ½ cup of cooked whole-grain hot cereal, such as oatmeal
- 1 small (1 ounce) 100 percent whole-grain muffin
- ½ cup of cooked, 100 percent whole-grain pasta, brown rice, or other grain
- 1 ounce (before cooking) of whole-grain pasta, brown rice, or other grain

In level 2, you should be decreasing brain-unhealthy foods from your diet. At the completion of level 2, you should be consuming no more than half the amount of fried, highly processed foods that you were eating before you started the Brain Training Revolution. In Level 3 we will aim to reduce them to "endangered species" categorization.

Level 3: Improve Imagination and Creativity

After a month or two at level 2, you will have integrated the recommended number of servings of the eight food categories into your diet. Your brain will be better nourished and better equipped to form longer-lasting memories. In level 3, you'll take the final step—increasing the number of servings per day of these natural foods and thus the amounts consumed to give your brain all it needs day in and day out to be what only the human brain can be at its peak: imaginative and creative.

The difference between levels 2 and 3 is only the number of servings you consume of the eight categories. You may want to continue using a chart to track your progress in level 3 (see page 275). Never, ever feel guilty when you don't achieve your daily or weekly goals. The stress is worse for your brain than missing a few servings of vegetables or eating a serving of potato chips, a fast-food hamburger with chips, or scrumptious barbecued ribs once in a while.

Be imaginative and creative in your eating—as long as you adhere to the basic principles of eating naturally, include all the major categories regularly, and get physical exercise almost every day. Cooking new recipes, trying new dishes at ethnic restaurants, socializing over meals—these and other culinary activities are good for your brain.

As noted for level 2, the amounts listed below are daily servings unless otherwise noted. You will find that you no longer crave highly processed, high-salt, high-fat foods or sugary sweets such as colas, cookies, and pastries as often as you used to. But total abstinence does not work, as diet study after diet study demonstrates. So, now that you have disciplined yourself and have reached the highest level of a brain-healthy diet, treat yourself once a week or so when an irresistible craving hits. But continue to obey limits and don't allow yourself to slip back into your previously less healthy eating habits. Personal discipline is the key.

- Five to six servings of vegetables every day

- Four servings of a variety of fruits and berries

- Six servings of whole grains per day

- One serving of beans, peas, and legumes per day

- Five servings of fish per week

- One small handful of nuts and seeds every day

- 4 to 5 teaspoons of healthy fats each day (1 teaspoon of olive oil contains 40 calories)

- Two to three servings of low-fat dairy per day

- One to two glasses of red wine per day

As you get started and follow either the Slow and Steady or the Three-Level Jump-Start plan for eating your way to a healthy brain, consider what you are doing as "food for thinking." Grow into the Brain Training Revolution nutrition plan and you will supply your most valuable organ, the part of you that is truly you, with all that it needs to run in high gear. Putting all these nutrients to best use means exercising the "muscles" of your brain and your body every day. Now that your brain is primed with the right nutrients, it is ready to direct the rest of your body to get more fit along with it.

Chapter 6

BODY MOVES TO GROW AND STRENGTHEN YOUR BRAIN

"No less than two hours a day should be devoted to exercise."—THOMAS JEFFERSON

"Physical fitness is not only one of the most important keys to a healthy body, it is the basis of dynamic and creative intellectual activity."—JOHN F. KENNEDY

As I described in the previous chapters, truly unexpected, revolutionary discoveries made over the past few years have proven the mind-body connection, a connection recognized since the dawn of western civilization. Exercise physiologists, cognitive psychologists, and other brain-interested scientists have now demonstrated conclusively that your brain gets larger and functions better if you exercise your body. Regular modest physical exercise protects your brain from Alzheimer's disease and from stroke.

I am not talking about running marathons, or playing five sets of grueling tennis singles. I am not even talking about following Thomas Jefferson's advice—most of us simply don't have two hours a day for exercise. But I am talking about walking for at least a half hour three or more times a week.

The message is simple. If you are not exercising, then start. Take it easy, but stick with it. You cannot afford not to exercise—your body can't afford it, and your brain can't afford it. If you follow the program so that within six months you are exercising three to four hours a week, just thirty minutes or so each day, you have invested in building brain reserve for positive returns. Each "investment" of activity carries you further down the path to better brain and body health.

THE PHYSICAL ACTIVITY QUOTIENT

Taking full advantage of exercise's ability to build the brain requires that you participate in several types of activities, most of which you can do easily at home. Each different activity contributes to brain health in a different way and in varying degrees. The Brain Training Revolution exercise program is based on the Physical Activity Quotient, or PQ for short. The PQ is a simple way for you to track and quantify the amount of physical exercise you do to build and strengthen your brain. In the program, each activity is assigned PQ points on the basis of the estimated benefit. The goal is to earn 100 points each week, a level that provides you with substantial brain benefit from exercise.

CogniByte

If our president and other high-ranking government officials can find time to exercise almost daily in the midst of these chaotic and challenging times, so can you!

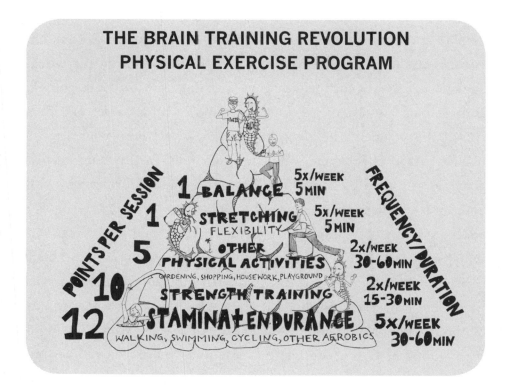

THE BRAIN TRAINING REVOLUTION
PHYSICAL EXERCISE PROGRAM

POINTS PER SESSION

FREQUENCY/DURATION

1 BALANCE 5x/WEEK 5 MIN

1 STRETCHING FLEXIBILITY 5x/WEEK 5 MIN

5 OTHER PHYSICAL ACTIVITIES
GARDENING, SHOPPING, HOUSEWORK, PLAYGROUND 2x/WEEK 30-60 MIN

10 STRENGTH TRAINING 2x/WEEK 15-30 MIN

12 STAMINA+ENDURANCE
WALKING, SWIMMING, CYCLING, OTHER AEROBICS 5x/WEEK 30-60 MIN

Stamina-building activities (also known as endurance training and aerobics) are the base of the pyramid. The bulk of the brain-building power you gain from physical exercise comes from stamina-building exercises like walking, swimming, cycling, and those fitness center-based activities such as aerobic dance, water aerobics, and spinning classes. If you're serious about maintaining your brain, you cannot skip the stamina-building exercises with their high PQ value. Just 30 minutes of it three times a week at the start directly and dramatically improves brain health, and you earn 36 points for the week—and a huge benefit for your brain, heart, muscles, and mood.

Strength training also has brain-health benefits. It lowers blood pressure by 2 to 4 percent, thereby reducing your risk for blood vessel diseases such as stroke and vascular dementia; significantly lengthens the amount of time you can remain independent; improves psychological well-being; and enhances the production of brain-growth factors. These are unique molecules that support neuronal growth. If you strength train for at least 15 minutes twice a week, you earn another 20 points.

In addition to the formal exercises of the Brain Training Revolution, you can also boost brain function by participating in informal physical activities. Activities such as gardening, playing with children, golfing, and cleaning house increase your heart and breathing rates and thus contribute to stamina building, burn calories, help keep your arteries unclogged and pliable, and stimulate your brain. Participating in such activities at least twice a week for 30 to 60 minutes provides you with another 10 points toward your goal of 100 points.

The rest of the PQ points come from balance and stretching/flexibility exercises. These exercises earn fewer PQ points because their effects on brain health are less dramatic and more indirect. Don't be fooled, however, into thinking these activities are not important. Without good balance and movement in your joints, your chances of maintaining an active lifestyle decrease and you are more likely to experience injuries that deter you from your activities or even diminish your ability to live independently.

The PQ system is based solely on completing the activities and not on how well you do them. You simply have to perform the recommended activities for certain times, as in the pyramid. If you do, you obtain a perfect score, whether or not your single-leg balance improves or the amount of weight you lift or resistance you use increases. Remember, it's not about how well you do the brain-healthy activities; it's about doing them!

THE PHYSICAL ACTIVITY PROGRAM

Let's start at the base of the activity pyramid with walking and other stamina-building exercises, the type of physical exertion that is most important for brain health. Then we'll work our way up to the top of the pyramid. After you understand the individual components of the physical activity program, this chapter continues with detailed step-by-step instructions to help you implement the program and put the individual components together into one practical plan.

Before you begin the Brain Training Revolution physical exercise program, visit your doctor and let him or her know what types of activities you will be doing. You can even bring the book with you and show it to your doctor. If you have any known injuries or conditions that physical exercise might affect, make sure you get instructions from your physician about how to modify the activities so you can do them safely.

STAMINA-BUILDING

Stamina-building or aerobic activity forms the base of brain-enhancing physical exercise. You may have heard this type of activity referred to as aerobics, cardiovascular exercise, cardiorespiratory activity, or endurance exercise. Stamina-building activity improves your ability to take in, deliver, and use oxygen to create energy for all the activities you want to do. During such activity, the large muscles in your body work for an extended period of time, causing you to breathe faster and deeper and making your heart beat more rapidly.

What Types of Activities Build Stamina?

Activities that build stamina are ones that require you to move large parts of your body, often rhythmically, and that make you breathe deeper and faster. Walking requires moving large muscles in your legs and hips to propel you forward. Cycling requires the rhythmic working of large leg and hip muscles. Rowing and raking leaves use the large muscles of your arms, back, and buttocks. All of these are stamina-building activities. In contrast, think about typing or watching a thriller on TV. When you type you move muscles rhythmically, but only the smaller muscles of the hands and forearms. Unless you're working furiously on a scathing letter to the editor, typing probably doesn't make you breathe any faster or deeper. And while watching a scary movie might make your heart race, it doesn't build stamina, because the increase in your heart rate comes from the release of adrenalin (epinephrine), a stress-related hormone, not from your muscles demanding more oxygen to make energy.

Here is a list of some of the best stamina-building activities:

- Walking (outdoors or on a treadmill)

- Cycling (outdoors or on a stationary bike)

- Swimming

- Jogging or running

- Stair climbing (on actual stairs or a stair-climbing machine)

- Using an elliptical machine

- Hiking

- Cross-country skiing (outdoors or on a ski machine)

- Square dancing, line dancing, or ballroom dancing

- Aerobic dance (in a fitness center or at home)

- Rowing (outdoors or on a rowing machine)

- Racket sports (tennis, squash, racquetball)

- Basketball, soccer, and hockey

- In-line skating or roller-skating

- Jumping rope

Which Activities Should I Choose?

You can't go wrong with walking—it is easy on your joints and when done with others it is a tremendous form of social interaction, providing additional brain benefit. Even if you have exercised for years, walking keeps your muscles and connective tissues strong and your cardiorespiratory system primed and conditioned.

But there are plenty of other options. In terms of health benefits, there is no perfect exercise—only exercises that you like and don't like, or that you can or cannot comfortably do. In choosing your activity, the most important factors to consider are convenience and enjoyment. Pick an activity you like and one you can do easily and often. If you can go to a recreation center or dance studio three times a week for square dancing and you enjoy it, then make that your main activity. If you have ready access to a pool and love the water, then choose swimming. If you love to cross-country ski outdoors and you live in Phoenix, either move or choose a different activity. Just make it enjoyable and convenient.

Another important factor in choosing is ensuring that the condition of your body can meet the demands of the activity without negative consequences. If you have little cartilage left in your knees, running may not be the activity for you. If you have inner-ear troubles, swimming laps will likely leave you queasy and light-headed. If you can't lift your arm over your head, no one will want you on their basketball team. So choose something you are comfortable doing.

It's best to have at least two different stamina-building activities in your brain-enhancing arsenal: a main activity and a supplemental activity. The main activity, the one you do most of the time, should be a weight-bearing activity, or one that requires you to stand up without support. This includes walking, jogging, stair climbing, using an elliptical machine, dancing, racket sports, basketball, skating, jumping rope, or skiing. Weight-bearing activities tend to burn more calories than seated activities or swimming (unless you are doing moderate- to high-intensity laps). They also condition the muscles and connective tissues used in everyday movement and are more likely to enhance bone health. Your supplemental activity or activities may be weight bearing or non-weight bearing, such as swimming, cycling, or rowing. Having at least two regular activities keeps your program interesting and reduces the risk of overuse injuries by distributing stress over different areas of the body.

What Do I Need to Start?

It depends on which stamina-building activities you choose. All you need to begin a walking program is a supportive, comfortable pair of walking shoes, a watch, and a safe and well-lit place to walk. This makes walking a great first choice. Make sure your walking surface is level, with no dangerous surprises such as uneven sidewalks, tree roots, or ice.

How Much Stamina-Building Activity Do I Need?

Significant brain-health benefits have been achieved with as few as 30 minutes of stamina-building activity three times per week. That's the minimum, but we can presume that more activity is better. To garner the maximum points from aerobic activity, you must complete 30 to 60 minutes of stamina-building activity five times per week. If you cannot sustain a certain activity right now for at least 30 minutes, start with bouts of 5 to 10 minutes at a time most days of the week or even multiple times a day, and then gradually work up to at least 30 minutes. You should eventually work up to 30, 45, or 60 minutes, depending on how vigorous the activity is, as shown in the following chart.

ENERGY EXPENDITURE	TYPES OF ACTIVITIES	DURATION	FREQUENCY	WEEKLY POINTS
Mild	Leisurely walking, slow dancing, bowling	60 min.	5x/week	60
Moderate	Brisk walking, water aerobics, leisurely biking	45 min.	5x/week	60
Vigorous	Jogging, playing tennis, fast dancing, swimming laps, jumping rope	30 min.	5x/week	60

There are several factors to consider with respect to amounts of physical activity and how to increase those amounts. First is duration, or how long you exercise in any given session. Second is frequency, or how often (usually days per week) you do the activity. Last is intensity, or how hard you work during the activity (I will explain how to gauge your intensity level below). Your amount of physical activity (work or energy expenditure) is a combination of those three factors, which you can manipulate in order to achieve your goals. For example, if you jog (vigorous energy expenditure) instead of walk (mild or moderate energy expenditure), you can reduce either the duration or the frequency of your exercise, because you will do more work in less time. If you have long exercise sessions three times a week, that is roughly equal to a short session of the same activity six times a week. To summarize, as you work harder and expend more energy, you can exercise less frequently and for less time; as the frequency goes up, the time and intensity can go down; as the length of time you spend exercising goes up, the frequency and intensity can go down.

Determining Your Intensity Level

There are many ways to determine your intensity level, or how hard you are exercising. Some techniques rely on measuring your exercising heart rate and comparing that to your potential maximum heart rate. Other more subjective methods rely on your own perceptions of how hard you are working. The Brain Training Revolution uses the latter approach for several reasons. First, many medications, especially those used to treat high blood pressure or heart disease, can affect your resting heart rate, your maximum heart rate, and your exercising heart rate. In such cases, the heart-rate method becomes unreliable unless you do a maximal exercise test to determine your maximum heart rate on your medications (and that can change when medications or doses change). Second, for the heart-rate method you must be able to accurately measure your heart rate during exercise. This requires either the purchase of a heart-rate monitor or the ability to measure it accurately yourself by placing your fingers on your pulse. Some people find it difficult to take their pulse accurately.

How Hard Am I Exercising? The Perceived Exertion Scale

The method used to gauge exercise intensity in the Brain Training Revolution is perceived exertion. An easy-to-use method, perceived exertion allows you to evaluate how hard you are working by observing how you feel overall rather by than measuring your heart rate. As you exercise, look at the Perceived Exertion Scale below and find the words and corresponding number that best describe your overall sensation of effort, fatigue, or physical stress. Depending on your fitness level and how long you have been engaging in a regular exercise program, you're probably at a perceived exertion level ranging from 3 to 7 (moderate to very hard), with most people remaining between the 4 and 6 (moderately hard to hard-plus) range, which is appropriate for the average healthy adult population.

PERCEIVED EXERTION SCALE

0	Effortless	Can't feel a thing.
1	Very light	A piece of cake.
2	Light	Could do this all day.
3	Moderate	I'm working a bit.
4	Moderately hard	Pretty tough, but I can handle it.
5	Hard	Sure feel this. Got me breathing.
6	Hard-plus	Really tough, but I can press on.
7	Very hard	Hangin' in there, but not for too long.
8	Extremely hard	Exhausting. I'm ready to stop.
9	Near Maximal	Exhausted! Almost stopping.
10	Maximally hard	Unbearable! Olympic athletes only.

Monitoring the ease of your speech while exercising is a simple way to gauge your exertion level. A moderate perceived effort of 3 to 4 allows near normal conversation, a moderately hard 5 to 6 effort allows speaking in labored sentences, while a very hard effort of 7 to 8 restricts speech to only a few words at a time. A perceived exertion of 9 doesn't allow any talking, only breathing.

Keep in mind that at any perceived exertion level, the actual work achieved will increase over time, because you will have built more stamina and will be able to accomplish more work with the same level of exertion. As you get in better shape, you can increase the amount of work you do at a given exertion level and also increase the intensity at which you exercise. Once your musculoskeletal system has become accustomed to the forces placed on it by stamina-building activity and your cardiorespiratory system has adapted to the demands, you can usually safely increase to a higher perceived exertion level. A quicker post-exercise recovery time is one sign that you are ready to exercise at the next intensity level. If you feel like your breathing and heart rate are almost back to normal within a couple of minutes of exercising and you experience no muscle or joint pain the same day or the next day, you're likely prepared to kick up the intensity a notch. However, enjoyment is critical to maintaining a program. If you don't enjoy the feeling of working at a perceived exertion of 6, even if your body can safely do it, then stick with a lower intensity. You can still improve your fitness while exercising at a consistent perceived exertion level. For example, when you first begin to briskly walk you may feel that you are working somewhat hard while going at a 15-minute-mile pace. After four weeks, you may be able to jog at a 14-minute-mile pace while feeling the same level of exertion. You will have improved your fitness without increasing the sensation of how hard you work.

You can choose your own routine based on your needs, preference, and fitness level. The following chart can help guide the progression of your stamina-building program.

WEEK-BY-WEEK GUIDE TO BUILDING YOUR STAMINA

WEEK(S)	FREQUENCY No. of times per week	INTENSITY Perceived exertion level	DURATION No. of minutes per session
1–2	3	4	15–20
3–4	3	4	20–25
5–6	3	4	25–30
7–8	3	4–5	25–30
9–12	3	4–5	30–35
13–16	3–4	4–5	30–35
17–20	3–4	4–5	30–40
21–24	3–4	4–5	30–45
25–28	3–5	4–5	30–45
29–32	3–5	4–6	30–45
33–36	3–5	4–6	30–50
37–40	3–5	4–6	30–55
41–44	3–5	4–6	30–60

Unfit Beginner

If you are not active, begin your workouts at low levels of frequency, duration, and intensity. If you cannot sustain the starting 15-minute exercise time shown in week 1, start with bouts as small as five minutes, three times a day, and gradually increase the time until you can start with week 1, and then follow the program as outlined.

Active Beginner

If you have not been exercising but are active on a daily basis, you can likely begin at weeks 5 to 6. This means that you can begin by walking three days a week for 30 minutes at a modest pace. Within two weeks, you can pick up the pace and push yourself a little harder in terms of the intensity.

89 AND GOING STRONG

My mother has been exercising her whole life and quit playing tennis at the age of 85. Now 89, she takes a senior aerobics class or works out alone at a nearby health and fitness center four or five times a week. On other days she walks on the canal bank near her home for about 30 or 45 minutes. After missing three to four days because of travel, a cold, or because she doesn't feel well, she commonly complains about how tired she feels. Once she starts up again, she notices a renewed sense of energy. Exercise works!

Troubleshooting for Stamina-Building Exercises

What If I Am Overweight?

Most overweight people can still begin with a walking program. If you cannot walk comfortably, begin with a low-intensity, non-weight-bearing exercise such as swimming, water walking, or recumbent biking. Gradually increase the frequency, duration, and intensity in your chosen activity, and then switch to a weight-bearing activity when you can. You may be able to tolerate a weight-bearing exercise because of the increased strength and stamina you gain from the first activity, or you may require some weight loss. After beginning a weight-bearing activity, focus on increasing duration and frequency before increasing your intensity.

What If I Have Arthritis?

Most individuals with arthritis can enjoy a walking program, and exercise usually improves arthritis symptoms. If your arthritis is severe, however, and walking causes pain, try water exercise, such as water aerobics, water walking, or swimming. The Arthritis Foundation states that water temperatures of 83 to 88 degrees Fahrenheit are safe for exercise and usually soothing and comfortable.

If the increased pain you experience from exercise returns to your normal pain level within two hours of the exercise session, the activity is likely fine for you. And don't think that you're limited to walking and swimming. Try any activity you'd like to do and see how it makes your joints feel. If it makes them feel worse for longer than two hours after the activity, choose something else. Do not exercise during an acute flare-up.

What If I Have a Disability?

There are many exercise options for people who have disabilities. Water exercise works well for those with joint issues or balance problems, such as those with multiple sclerosis, cerebral palsy, Parkinson's, or those who are partially paralyzed from a previous stroke. There are also machines, such as recumbent steppers, that have accessible swivel seats and straps for both hands and feet, so that a disabled person can focus on the pushing movement rather than on keeping a good grip or keeping feet on the platforms. Physiatrists, rehabilitation specialists, physical therapists, and personal trainers can assist you in making the best choices. I suggest that you begin by asking your doctor for a recommendation.

What If I Have to Stop Exercising?

If an injury, illness, or other event prevents you from exercising for a period of time, ease back into the workout when you're ready. Your new starting level will depend on why you were out and for how long. If you just had a stomach bug for a day, take it easier with your workout for a week or so, and then you'll be back to your old routine. If you had an injury that kept you out for two months, you'll need to start almost from the beginning, and your doctor or therapist may give you special instructions. If you were still active but not engaging in your regular exercise activity, start back at a lower duration and intensity. Gradually build back up to your prior duration first and then increase your intensity. If you want to play it safe, do not increase the exercise amount or intensity by more than 10 percent per week.

What If I'm Too Busy?

If you can't or won't dedicate five hours a week to exercise, consider increasing the intensity of the exercise and keeping the frequency and duration to the minimum of 30 minutes three times a week. You will still obtain brain-health benefits from this amount of activity, and your fitness level may actually be higher than someone who exercises for longer but at a much lower intensity.

The 10 Percent Rule

Do not increase your duration or intensity by more than 10 percent per week, and do not increase more than one variable (duration, frequency, or intensity) per week.

Use the 10 percent rule to guide both your stamina-building activity and strength training, especially if you participate in more vigorous activities. For the frequency variable, in which going from exercising three days a week to four days is a larger increase than 10 percent, go a little shorter (duration) and easier (intensity) on that extra day for the first few sessions. Within a month, that fourth session can be as long and intense as the other workout sessions.

In terms of duration, you can usually increase by more than 10 percent for low impact activities such as walking. Increasing from 15 minutes one week to walking 20 minutes the next week is more than a 10 percent increase, but fine for most healthy adults. The demand on the joints and connective tissues is not very extreme. However, if you do the same thing with running, you are much more likely to suffer an injury, because the musculoskeletal system needs more time to adjust to the high impact of running.

In following the 10 percent rule, focus on increasing duration and frequency before intensity. Intensity is linked more often to injury than are duration or frequency.

STRENGTH BUILDING

The Brain Training Revolution, just like every well-rounded exercise program, has a strength-building component. Strong muscles allow you to participate in the physical activities of normal daily life, give you the freedom and independence to enjoy recreational activities, and decrease the risk of falls. Even though you are already enhancing your brain with stamina-building activity, the effects of strength building will increase that benefit. Like aerobic exercise, strength training helps keep your arteries open by lowering blood pressure, decreasing stress, and decreasing body fat. What's more, strength building provides benefits that cardiorespiratory activity alone does not, which makes it the second most substantial part of the brain-building pyramid and is the reason it supplies 20 percent of your PQ points.

What are the benefits? Strength building allows you to maintain or even increase your muscle mass and strength. After about the age of 35, for inactive people, the muscles begin to lose mass at a rate of about 5 percent per decade (roughly four to six pounds of muscle per decade). By the time you are 60, you can expect to have lost 10 to 20 percent of your muscle, and with it, a large percentage of your strength. By the age of 80, many people have lost about 50 percent of their muscle mass. Within twelve weeks of engaging in a consistent strength-building program at least twice a week, many individuals will gain muscle mass of 5 to 10 percent. In terms of your muscles, that's the equivalent of being ten to twenty years younger—not bad for a total of twelve to eighteen hours of work.

Bones weaken at a rate about equivalent to that of muscles. The combination of fragile bones and weak muscles puts people at high risk for falls and broken bones. Bone is a living tissue, constantly being broken down and built up (a process called remodeling). After puberty and until you reach about 30, bone is broken down and formed at roughly the same rate, keeping your bone density at its maximum.

After the age of 30, breaking down outpaces bone formation and your bone mass decreases—but high-impact activity and resistance training can restore the balance. When you safely place significant stress on your bones, it activates the cells that lead to bone formation. In this way, resistance training can help maintain and, in some cases, even increase bone mass.

As with aerobic activity, you can manipulate the variables of frequency, duration, and intensity to determine the amount of strength building you do. Frequency is the number of times per week you do strength-building exercises. Duration is the time spent overcoming or resisting a force (in other words, the amount of time your muscles actually work against resistance) and is a combination of the number of repetitions you accomplish with each exercise and the length of each repetition. Intensity is how much weight you lift or how much resistance you overcome.

The Brain Training Revolution features an easy-to-start, progressive strength-training regimen that will benefit both your brain and your body, no matter your fitness level or past experience! No barbells or dumbbells are needed. Each time you complete at least 15 minutes of strength-building exercises twice a week, you earn 20 PQ points toward your goal of 100.

Here are a few general principles and guidelines for strength training:

- Do 8 to 15 repetitions of each exercise. Rest for 30 to 60 seconds. Repeat.

- Exercises should be challenging but not painful. The first 5 repetitions should be relatively easy, and the last 3 repetitions should be quite challenging. As you get stronger, you will have to increase the resistance to keep demanding the appropriate effort from your muscles.

- Each repetition should take about 6 seconds to complete: 3 seconds for the action phase of each repetition and 3 seconds to return to the starting position. You can speed this up to 2 seconds and 2 seconds for one workout per week after eight weeks of training, provided you can control the momentum and maintain good form.

- Breathe naturally throughout the exercises—don't ever hold your breath. Your blood pressure naturally rises when you exercise. Normally, the increase caused by exercise alone is gradual and not dangerous. But if you hold your breath, it can go up suddenly and dramatically, which increases risks to your heart and blood vessels. So keep breathing during all exercises. Don't worry about synchronizing your breaths with the activity. Just breathe in a natural, continuous way.

- Perform the exercises at least twice a week (preferably three times) but not on consecutive days.

Unlike moderate stamina-building activity, which causes metabolic fatigue but does not damage muscle fibers, when you perform strength-training exercises you actually damage the working muscle. The muscle then repairs itself, making the muscle fibers bigger and stronger than they were before. You need to give your muscles at least forty-eight hours to recover from each strength-training session. If you perform the exercises in this book within the given guidelines, one day between workouts should be enough.

Getting Started

If you are new to strength training, use a weight or resistance level that allows you to do 12 to 20 repetitions in a row with proper technique before reaching fatigue. After eight weeks of consistent training, you can increase the resistance to a level that allows you to do only 8 to 15 repetitions. This gradual increase in intensity will give your connective tissues time to adjust to the new demands.

To increase your chances of enjoying your program and remaining injury free, I recommend hiring a personal trainer for at least the first few sessions to ensure that you are doing the exercises properly. The proven method of finding a competent professional is by asking for a recommendation from people you trust. You can read descriptions of the exercise positions and technique, but unless you have acquired heightened body awareness through some sport or exercise, it can be difficult initially to sense your body's position in space and to determine how it is moving. Having a knowledgeable person watch your form and guide you through the exercises a few times with correct body placement will help train your muscles to perform the movements accurately, develop muscle memory, and prevent injury.

Strength-Building Exercises for Brain Health

The following exercises require no special equipment and can be done at home. No need to show off your not-what-it-once-was physique at a health club or to be overwhelmed by the dense forest of specialized equipment. These exercises are designed to train the muscles using the patterns they have to execute every day, thus making your body more efficient in an entire pattern of movement rather than focusing on one muscle at a time. The exercises should make everyday tasks such as unloading the dishwasher, taking out the garbage, doing yard work, carrying groceries, or participating in recreational activities easier and more enjoyable.

For each activity, there is a detailed description of the basic exercise. You can find easier and tougher variations of these exercises on the BrainSavers website. Begin with the basic exercise. If you can perform 15 repetitions of the activity with excellent form and do not experience soreness a day or two afterward, you can move on to more challenging variations. If you cannot complete at least 10 repetitions of a basic activity with good technique, try an easier variation and evolve to more difficult ones when you can do 15 repetitions with excellent form, without pain, and without soreness a day or two later.

Squats

You probably do several squats a day already without realizing it. Any time you sit down, whether to read, rest, eat, go to the bathroom, or get into your car, you have done a squat. You do them during all sorts of daily activities, such as cleaning, gardening, organizing, caring for children (or parents), or participating in any type of sporting activity. Doing multiple squats as part of your exercise program strengthens muscles in your upper legs, hips, and back, making the activities you do on a regular basis easier.

SQUAT OR PARTIAL SQUAT

Starting Position

Stand with your feet about shoulder width apart, knees slightly bent, and toes pointing forward or just slightly out, hands resting on your hips or up by your ears with your elbows out (to help you keep your chest lifted). Maintain proper body alignment: chest up, shoulder blades pulled toward each other and down, abs tight, natural arch in low back, and soft knees (not locked).

Action

While keeping your chest lifted, bend your knees, lowering your hips back behind you and down toward the floor until your thighs are almost parallel to the floor. If that is too difficult, try a partial squat: don't drop your hips down as far, keeping your thighs short of reaching a position parallel to the floor. Push back up to the starting position.

Squat Tips

- Do not allow your knees to move forward past your toes as you squat.

- Take your hips back behind you rather than straight down.

- Keep your knees pointing in the same direction as your toes, not toward the inside of your feet.

- Keep your heels on the floor.

- Keep your chest lifted and do not lean forward too much with your upper body. Chest and head should face forward, not down—think of lowering your hips, not your chest, toward the floor. If you're having trouble keeping your chest lifted try placing your hands behind your head or near your ears, with your elbows out.

Lunges

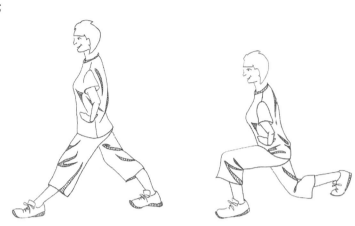

LUNGE

The lunge is another movement you probably do multiple times a day. You may do a lunge when you reach down to pick something up, when you get down on the floor or up from the floor, when you reach forward or to the side for something, or when you vacuum or do yard work. Lunge exercises primarily strengthen the muscles in your upper legs and hips.

STATIONARY BASIC LUNGE

Starting Position

Stand with your feet hip width apart, one leg in front of the other. Point both feet straight forward. Center your body weight between both legs. Maintain proper body alignment.

Action

Keeping your torso upright, bend both knees and lower yourself straight down toward the floor until your back knee is an inch or so from the floor, and your front thigh is roughly parallel to the floor with the knee bent about 90 degrees. Push back up to the starting position.

Option for Knee Pain

Lunge with extended back knee: Place your feet farther apart front to
  back and keep the back leg mostly straight as you lunge. This method
  works better for some individuals with knee pain.

Lunge Tips

- Hold on to a chair, countertop, or doorframe for stability if this
  exercise is new to you or if you have balance concerns.

- If you experience pain in the back knee, shift your weight forward
  for the lunge to keep the back knee straighter.

- Make sure your back foot points straight forward and not out to
  the side.

- Keep your front knee over the ankle or just slightly in front of it.
  Don't allow your knee to extend forward past your toes.

- Maintain proper body alignment: focus your gaze forward, chest
  up, shoulder blades pulled toward each other and down, abs tight,
  natural arch in low back, soft knees.

LATERAL LUNGE

LATERAL LUNGE

Starting Position

Stand with your feet about twice shoulder width apart. Point both feet slightly out to the side. Center your body weight between both legs. Maintain proper body alignment.

Action

Shift your weight to one side, and lean forward from the hips as you bend the support leg. Stop just short of a 90-degree angle at the knee. Your hips should be back behind you as they are in the squat, so that your knee stays over the foot and not in front of it. The end position is much like a lateral squat with the nonsupporting leg extended straight instead of bent. Push back up to the starting position.

Lateral Lunge Tips

- Hold on to a chair, countertop, or doorframe for stability if this exercise is new to you or if you have balance concerns.

- If you experience knee pain, try a shallower lunge (don't go down as far). Do not perform this exercise if you cannot do it without pain.

- Make sure your knees point in the same direction as your toes.

- Keep your bent knee over the ankle or just slightly in front of it. Don't allow your knee to extend forward past your toes.

Heel Raises

The heel raise is simple and straightforward. It's just lifting up onto your toes—what you likely do when you're reaching for something in a high cupboard or putting a carry-on in the overhead bin. Heel raises primarily strengthen the muscles along the back of your lower legs and the stabilizing muscles in your feet, ankles, hips, and thighs.

HEEL RAISE

BASIC HEEL RAISE

Starting Position

Stand with your feet hip width apart, and lift your heels just barely off the floor.

Action

Keeping your knees straight but not locked, use your calf muscles to press yourself up onto your toes as high as possible. Return slowly to the starting position.

Heel-Raise Tips

- Keep your ankles and feet aligned, so your weight remains over the centers of the balls of your feet. Don't let your ankles bend in or out.

- Hold on to a chair, countertop, or doorframe for stability if this exercise is new to you or if you have balance concerns.

- Keep upright with proper spine and hip alignment. Avoid leaning back with your upper body or pressing your hips forward. Keep your knees straight but not locked.

- Lower into the starting position slowly rather than dropping your heels suddenly to avoid a rebounding motion.

Push-Ups

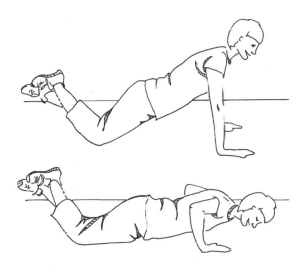

PUSH-UP

You're probably familiar with push-ups. Push-ups strengthen your upper body (mainly the chest, shoulders, and back of the upper arms) and are great for training the stabilizing muscles of your core as well. Almost everyone can do some version of a push-up, and they can be made tough enough even for the very fit. Go to our website to find a variation that is challenging but doable for you.

BASIC KNEE PUSH-UP

Starting Position

Lie on your stomach and place your hands on the floor a few inches to either side of your chest, so that your elbows are bent about 90 degrees. Keeping your knees on the floor and your back straight, push your body up until your elbows are straight but not locked. Your body should form a straight line from the top of your head to your knees.

Action

Keeping your body straight by engaging your abdominal muscles, lower yourself toward the floor until your chest almost touches the floor. Push back up to the starting position.

Push-Up Tips

- Keep your hands and arms even with your chest, not forward toward your face or back toward your ribs.

- Don't let your back or hips sag down or lift up during the exercise.

- Decrease your range of motion if the exercise causes pain or is too difficult. Just lower your body down a few inches and increase the range as you can. Stop the exercise if you cannot do some version of it without pain.

Lean-Backs

LEAN-BACK

Lean-backs strengthen your abdominal muscles and the muscles along the front of the hips and thighs. This exercise conditions stabilizing muscles that you use when getting up out of a chair, reaching while sitting or standing to grab something to the side or behind you, and even walking.

BASIC STANDING LEAN-BACK

Starting Position

Stand with your feet about hip width apart, knees slightly bent, and toes pointing forward. Cross your arms at your chest.

Action

While maintaining proper body alignment, bend your knees and lean back slightly. There should be a straight line from your knees to your head. Keep your abdominal muscles tight, so that your back does not arch. Return to the starting position.

Lean-Back Tips

- Keep your knees pointing in the same direction as your toes.

- Maintain the natural arch in your lower back without allowing an excessive arch.

Opposite Arm-and-Leg Reaches

Opposite arm-and-leg reaches strengthen the back side of your body including your shoulders, back, buttocks, and thighs. This exercise conditions your body for activities that require bending forward, reaching, or a combination of both, such as picking up objects off the floor or ground (like a shoe or a golf ball) or leaning forward to brush your teeth or wash dishes.

OPPOSITE ARM-AND-LEG REACH

OPPOSITE ARM-AND-LEG REACH

Action

From a standing position, reach one arm out in front of you and up over your head while extending the opposite leg back behind you. Bend forward slightly at the hip of your standing leg. Your arm, body, and leg should form a straight line.

Arm-and-Leg Reach Tips

- Hold on to a chair, countertop, or wall if needed for balance.

- Use your abdominal muscles to keep your back from arching excessively.

- Do not lift your leg so high that your back arches beyond its natural position.

- Lengthen your body as much as possible by reaching out from your toes to your fingertips. Think long, not high.

INFORMAL PHYSICAL ACTIVITY AND BRAIN HEALTH

Routine daily activities, referred to in the pyramid as "other physical activities," such as yard work, gardening, playing with children or grandchildren, housework, cleaning out a car or van, or other recreational activities like golf or pool, also contribute to your brain's health. These activities include components of stamina building, muscular conditioning, calorie burning, and, importantly, socialization—all of which are good for the aging brain. Normally, such informal physical activities come automatically as part of an active lifestyle, but if you find that you get no physical exercise outside of your regular routine, you'll need to consciously make it happen. This might mean that you decide to do your yard work or house maintenance yourself rather than hire someone. It might mean that you take your kids or grandkids to the playground once a week. It might mean that you schedule a round of golf or bowling, or whatever else you enjoy that gets you moving.

Spend at least an hour a week engaged in informal physical activity in addition to your structured exercise routine. You can do this any day of the week, regardless of your formal workout schedule. If you meet the goal of getting in at least 30 minutes of informal activity twice a week, you'll earn 5 points per session, or 10 points per week.

BALANCE EXERCISES

Good balance combined with a strong lower body significantly reduces your chances of falling and/or breaking a bone. Most Americans are now familiar with many of the repercussions of breaking a hip—loss of mobility, loss of independence, and sometimes death. But the loss of mobility that comes from such an event also prevents people from being able to engage in many of the important activities necessary for optimal brain function. Your brain cannot afford to have you break a hip. Let's sing a new twist on an old song: "The hip bone's connected to the... hippocampus."

Three key systems in your body contribute to your ability to balance:

your eyesight (or visual system), your inner ear (or vestibular system), and receptors in your muscles and joints (or proprioceptive system). Balance exercises help coordinate the three systems, so that you are stable on your feet, whether you are still or moving. The exercises also sharpen each system individually, so that as one system, such as vision, declines in function, the other systems can pick up the slack.

All three balance systems decrease in sharpness as you age. Visual acuity declines, and is most pronounced after the age of 50. The eyes do not distinguish contrasts as easily, adapt to changes in light as readily, or perceive depth as accurately. Depth perception and contrast sensitivity seem to contribute most to an increased risk of falling. The function of the inner ear also declines. The sensory-hair cells that send messages to your brain about your head's position and movement diminish in number and become less efficient, and the nerve transmission of the signals slows. The nerves that carry impulses from the muscle and joint receptors also deteriorate with age. Connections within the brain itself may slow or be partially lost as well. Nerve endings sometimes lose their ability to generate the chemicals necessary for signal transmission.

Balance training focuses on enhancing the performance of each of the three balance centers, often by removing or diminishing input from one or more centers, thus forcing the others to rise to the new challenge. Even as we move beyond the age of 60, we can improve the performance of our balance systems. For example, exercises that involve closing the eyes force the body to rely on proprioception and input from the inner ear. An exercise in which you turn your head suddenly forces you to rely on proprioception initially while challenging your vision and your inner ear to adjust quickly to the new scene and head movement. An exercise during which you stand on a foam mat diminishes or complicates proprioceptive feedback from your feet and ankles and forces your vision and inner ear to contribute more. With consistent training, you can improve your agility and the function and efficiency of your balance and decrease your risk of injuries and falls.

Each time you exercise, spend 3 to 5 minutes working specifically on balance. Following is a series of progressive exercises grouped in two levels to help you build your balance skills. Begin with the first exercise in level 1, and once you master it, move on to the next exercise and so forth. You may find that the first few exercises are easy for you. If so, continue through the progressions until you're challenged. You may be able to fit four or five exercises into one 5-minute session.

In general, spend your time on the exercises that challenge you. But every few weeks, go back to the more basic exercises to stay proficient in the fundamentals. For safety, always stand near a chair or wall so that you can use it for stability if needed. You can also practice balance exercises outside of working out, such as while brushing your teeth, cooking, or pumping gas.

Mental Images to Help You with Balance and Posture

1. Picture a string extending from the top of your head up to the ceiling. Imagine that you are hanging from the string.
2. Imagine that you are a tall tree, with your head reaching high up into the clouds and your feet planted firmly by roots down into the floor.

Level 1
Exercise No. 1: Practicing Good Posture
Maintain your best standing posture for 60 seconds:

- Focus forward with chin pulled back slightly.

- Lift your chest (imagine a soldier standing at attention).

- Keep your shoulders back and down.

- Keep your palms facing your body (not back).

- Keep a natural curve or arch in your lower back.

- Pull your abdominals in slightly.

- Keep your knees straight but not locked.

- Center your weight evenly over both feet.

- Slightly lift the arches of your feet (put more weight on the outer edges than on the inner edges).

Exercise No. 2: Feet Together

Stand with your feet together and practice the following:

- Look right and hold for 10 seconds.

- Look left and hold for 10 seconds.

- Rock from side to side, shifting your weight from one foot to the other 20 times.

- Rock from front to back, shifting your weight from toes to heels and from heels to toes 20 times.

Exercise No. 3: Tandem Stance (heel to toe)

Stand with one foot directly in front of the other, with the heel of your front foot touching the toes of your back foot. Then practice the following:

- Turn head to the right and hold for 10 seconds.

- Turn head to the left and hold for 10 seconds.

- Rock from front to back, shifting your weight from the front foot to the back foot and from the back foot to front foot 20 times.

- Tandem walk, heel to toe, in a straight line (like the sobriety test) for ten steps, then reverse directions, and do it again.

Exercise No. 4: One Leg

Stand with good posture and lift one foot off the floor. Balance on each leg for at least 30 seconds.

Level 2

Exercise No. 1: Feet Together

Stand with your feet together and practice the following:

- Close your eyes for 30 seconds.

- Lift up on your toes and balance for 10 seconds.

- Lift your toes slightly and balance on your heels for 10 seconds.

Exercise No. 2: Tandem Stance

Stand with one foot directly in front of the other, with the heel of your front foot touching the toes of your back foot.

- Close your eyes for 30 seconds.

- Balance up on your toes for 10 seconds.

- Lift your arms out in front of you and rotate your body and arms to the left and right 5 times each.

- Tandem walk backward for ten steps (make sure you have enough space).

Exercise No. 3: One Leg

Balance on one leg while doing the following (switch sides after each activity):

- Swing your arms (together in the same direction) forward and backward 15 times.

- Swing your arms from side to side 15 times.

- Swing your arms in opposition (one forward and one back at the same time) 15 times.

- Reach your lifted leg out in front, to the side, and behind you 5 times each.

- Look right and left for 10 seconds each.

FLEXIBILITY EXERCISES

End every workout with some stretches or mobility exercises. During the course of your day, and especially when you exercise, your muscles contract, or shorten, many times. Depending on your posture or body position throughout the day and night, some muscles may stay shortened for extended periods of time. Inflexible muscles can make simple tasks such as backing your car out of the driveway or getting dressed a struggle. Flexibility exercises simply lengthen the muscles and stretch the connective tissues to restore balance and harmony to the moving parts of your body. Such exercises are critical for keeping you mobile and pain and injury free.

Mobility exercises don't need to take a long time—just 5 to 10 minutes or so for most people. If you have a physical limitation or issue that requires additional stretching, however, it may take a little more time. Here are some guidelines to follow when stretching:

- Move slowly into each stretch and stop when you feel a gentle pull—don't let yourself get to the point where you feel pain.

- Hold the position for 10 to 20 seconds unless otherwise noted.

- Repeat the stretch 3 to 5 times.

- Stretch at the end of your workout while your muscles are still warm.

- Stop a stretch if it causes pain or if you feel the stretch in a joint rather than in a muscle.

- Continue breathing regularly throughout the stretch.

All of the following stretches may be done while standing or seated in a chair.

Neck Stretches

Side bend: Look straight ahead. Slowly drop your head to one side while lowering the opposite shoulder. Hold for 3 to 5 seconds, and stretch each side twice.

Quarter turn, chin drop: Begin with your focus forward. Turn your head a quarter turn and then drop your chin toward your chest. Keep the opposite shoulder down. Hold for 3 to 5 seconds, and stretch each side twice.

Upper-Back Stretch

Sit upright in a chair or stand with your feet shoulder width apart and your arms straight out in front of you with your fingers interlocked and palms facing away from you. Lower your chin to your chest and press your arms forward until you feel a stretch across your upper back.

Lower-Back and Chest Stretch

Sit upright in a chair with your hands on your thighs. Slowly drop your chin toward your chest and lower your head, then your shoulders and upper back, toward the floor. Hold for 5 seconds. Roll back up to an upright position, and lift your arms up and out to the sides while you also lift your head and chest up toward the ceiling, allowing your upper back to arch back slightly. Hold for 5 seconds. Repeat 3 to 5 times.

You can also do this exercise while standing. Check with your doctor before doing this stretch if you have any back problems.

Side Stretch

Stand with your feet shoulder width apart. Reach up and over your head with one arm and lean to the opposite side until you feel a gentle stretch along the outside edge of your body. Think of lengthening your body upward while you reach.

Trunk Twist

Stand with your feet shoulder width apart. Place both hands on one hip and rotate, or twist, your body in that direction, looking back behind you and pressing your hip forward with your hands. Try to keep your knees facing forward. If you do this exercise while seated, place one hand on the outside of the opposite thigh, and rotate in that direction.

Wrist and Forearm Stretches

Underside of forearm: Lift one arm straight out in front of you with the palm upward. Using your other hand, bend your wrist back so that your fingers point toward the floor.

Top of forearm: Lift your arm straight out in front of you with the palm downward. Bend your wrist down so that your fingers point toward the floor.

For both stretches, stretch each side once unless you feel particularly tight in the wrist or forearms. Decrease the range of motion to a comfortable level if you have arthritis in the wrist.

Hamstring and Calf Stretches

Sit toward the edge of a chair and extend one leg straight out in front of you. Place your hands on the opposite thigh. Keeping your back straight, with a natural arch in your lower back, lean forward at your hips until you feel a stretch along the back of your thigh. Hold for 10 seconds and then slowly pull your toes up toward you while keeping your heel on the floor. Hold for 10 more seconds. Repeat 3 to 5 times on each side.

Quadriceps and Front-of-Hip Stretch

Stand on one leg while keeping your knee slightly bent (use a chair or wall for support if needed). Bend the other leg up behind you and grasp your ankle. Point your knee straight down toward the floor. Your shoulder, hip, and knee should form a straight line. Press your hips forward slightly until you feel a stretch along the front of your thigh. Do not pull your foot to the side or too close to your buttocks.

If you can't grab your ankle behind you, stand with your back to the side of an armchair, couch, or stool (about 2 to 3 feet away) and prop your foot up on the armrest or seat behind you. Tuck your hips under until you feel a stretch along your thigh.

SAMPLE EXERCISE SESSION

We've discussed the various components of your exercise program. Now let's outline what the actual workout sessions might look like, from beginning to end.

1. WATER

Drink a glass of water about an hour or two before you exercise and another glass about a half hour before you exercise.

2. WARM-UP

Begin each workout with a 5- to 7-minute warm-up that prepares your body for the upcoming activities. The warm-up raises your body temperature very slightly and increases the blood flow to your muscles. Warming up makes your muscles more pliable, efficient, and less likely to be injured. Warming up also increases fluid circulation in your joints, thereby creating more mobility.

A warm-up can be any activity that gets you breathing a little harder and faster, elevates the temperature in your exercising muscles, increases your heart rate, and moves all of the muscles and joints that you will use in your workout. If you are doing only the stamina-building activity during your exercise session, you can simply perform that activity at a low intensity as your warm-up. And the warm-up time can count as part of your stamina-building activity. It is simply done at a lower intensity than the rest of your stamina workout. However, if you will also do strength-training exercises during your session, you need to warm up the muscles and joints you'll be using. You can do all of the following warm-up exercises while seated in a chair as well.

The following simple warm-up takes about 6 minutes and will prepare you for working out:

March in place (60 seconds). Lift your feet and pump your arms.

March wide and together (60 seconds). Step out wide to the sides for two steps (right leg then left leg) and back together for two steps. Say, "Out, out, in, in" as you do it until you get the rhythm.

Toe taps with forward arm circles (30 seconds). Lift your right foot and tap the floor in front of you with your right toes. Bring your right foot back in next to your left. Repeat with your left foot. Continue alternating sides. Say, "Step, tap, step, tap" until you get the rhythm. Once you have the footwork down, add forward arm circles. While tapping, lift your arms straight out to the sides and make small forward circles with your arms. Gradually make the circles bigger as your shoulders warm up.

Heel taps with backward arm circles (30 seconds). Lift your right foot and tap the floor in front of you with your heel, and then alternate sides. When you get the footwork down, add small backward arm circles and gradually make them bigger. This is just like the toe taps and arms circles you just did, except that your heels tap the floor and your arms reverse direction.

Step touch with arm curls (60 seconds). Step out to the side with your right foot. Bring your left foot in to meet it and touch your left toes to the inside edge of your right foot. Then step out to the side with your left foot and bring the right foot in to meet it. Continue alternating sides. Say, "Step, touch, step, touch" until you get the rhythm. After you have the footwork down, add arm curls. Keep your arms down at your sides. Each time you touch with the toes, bend your elbows, bringing your hands toward your shoulders. When you step out, drop your arms back to your sides.

Step leg curl with overhead reach (60 seconds). Step out to the side with your right foot. Bend your left knee and kick your heel up behind you. Step out to the side with your left foot, and kick your right heel up behind you. Continue alternating sides. Say, "Step, kick, step, kick" until you get the rhythm. Once you have the footwork down, to add the overhead reach, start by holding your hands slightly above shoulder height with your elbows bent. Every time you kick your heel up, reach your arms up over your head. (If you are performing this warm-up exercise while seated in a chair, instead of kicking your heel up behind you, kick your leg straight out in front of you.)

Step knee lifts with elbow touch (60 seconds). Step out to the side with your right foot. Lift your left knee up in front of you. Step out to the side with your left foot and lift your right knee. Continue alternating sides. Say, "Step, lift, step, lift" until you have the rhythm. Once you have the footwork down, add an elbow touch. With each lift, touch the opposite elbow to the lifted knee. If you can't quite touch, that's fine. Just bring the elbow toward your knee.

Deep breath with overhead reach. Stand with your weight distributed equally between your feet. Take a deep breath in for 3 seconds while reaching your arms out to the sides and up over your head. Breathe out and lower your arms back down to your sides.

3. STAMINA-BUILDING ACTIVITY

This is the 30- to 60-minute walking or other stamina-building exercise of your choice (five times a week).

4. COOL DOWN

Cool down for 5 to 10 minutes at the end of each stamina-building session, even if you will move on to strength training or flexibility activities. Gradually decrease the intensity of the stamina-building activity so that your heart rate and blood pressure can come down. The higher the workout intensity and the longer the workout, the more time you should spend cooling down. As with the warm-up, the cool-down time can count toward your total stamina-building time, but the cool down is at a much lower intensity.

Cooling down reduces your risk of becoming dizzy (due to hypotension) after the workout, facilitates the removal of lactic acid from muscles, and may reduce your risk for heart arrhythmias.

5. BALANCE EXERCISES (five times a week).

6. STRENGTH-TRAINING EXERCISES (two or three times a week).

7. FLEXIBILITY EXERCISES (five times a week).

8. WATER

Drink another glass of water shortly after completing your workout.

Consider this example: If you choose to exercise seven days a week, then you can do stamina-building exercises for five days and strength-training exercises for the other two days. Here's an example of a stamina workout:

- Water

- Warm-up

- Stamina-building activity

- Cool down

- Balance exercises

- Flexibility exercises

- Water

Here's an example of a strength workout:

- Water

- Warm-up

- Strength-training exercises

- Flexibility exercises

- Water

The time that the Brain Training Revolution sets aside for exercise might seem daunting for those of you who have not been exercising regularly. But I promise that you can stay with the program in as few as five hours a week. And while you're building your stamina, you can also be watching TV or talking to friends (bring them on the walk with you!). You will feel the results—in a better mood, better sleep, and even better sex—and the long-term brain and body benefits are real.

The following exercise chart will help you keep track of the exercise portion of the Brain Training Revolution. Keeping a chart helps many people stay motivated, focused, and goal oriented when they embark on a new healthy-lifestyle activity. And watching your Physical Activity Quotient increase will give you a sense of accomplishment. The payoff is not just more points on paper but also being in a better mood, having a more positive outlook on life even in the face of your usual stresses, having a sharper and more focused brain, and having a more energetic and resilient body.

YOUR EXERCISE CHART
Goals for Optimum Brain Health

Stamina-building 5x/week @12 points each = Maximum 60 points

Strength-building 2x/week @ 10 points each = Maximum 20 points

Other activity 2x/week @ 5 points each = Maximum 10 points

Balance exercises 5x/week @ 1 point each = Maximum 5 points

Stretches 5x/week @ 1 point each = Maximum 5 points

	M	T	W	TH	F	SA	SU	TOTAL	RECOM-MENDED
Stamina (12 pts)									60
Strength (10 pts)									20
Other activity (5 pts)									10
Balance (1 pt)									5
Stretch (1 pt)									5
									100

Sample Chart

Julia is an active 60-year-old woman who is just starting her exercise program. On Monday, she went for a 30-minute walk but did not stretch or do balance exercises. On Tuesday, she did strength-training exercises and stretched afterward. On Wednesday, she went for another walk with a friend but did not stretch or work on balance afterward. On Friday, she went for it all. She did her walking, balance, strength-training exercises, and stretches. She and her husband went golfing on Saturday.

Here's what Julia's chart would look like for the week:

	M	T	W	TH	F	SA	SU	TOTAL	RECOM- MENDED
Stamina (12 pts)	12		12		12			36	60
Strength (10 pts)		10			10			20	20
Other activity (5 pts)						5		5	10
Balance (1 pt)					1			1	5
Stretch (1 pt)		1			1			2	5
								64	100

Four months later, Julia's program has somewhat of a new look. Julia's husband bought her a fitness center membership for their thirtieth wedding anniversary, and she's increasingly grateful for it as the weather gets colder and the days shorter. Her exercise program has become quite regular over the past few months.

Monday through Friday, she gets up 45 minutes earlier than she used to and she carved 15 minutes off the time it used to take her to get ready for work so that she would have an hour each workday morning to dedicate to her health. On Mondays and Wednesdays, she walks on the treadmill for 5 minutes to warm up, jogs for two miles at a 12-minute-mile pace, and walks to cool down for 5 minutes. She then works on her balance for 5 minutes and follows that with 15 to 20 minutes of strength-training exercises—on Monday she uses the workout in this book and on Wednesdays she uses weights. She tops off the workout with 5 minutes of stretching.

On Tuesday, Thursday, and Friday mornings, Julia warms up on a recumbent bike for 5 minutes, bikes for 10 minutes more, walks on the treadmill for 30 minutes, and cools down for 5 minutes. On Tuesdays and

Thursdays, she keeps the treadmill set at a level without an incline (zero percent grade) and walks at 4 miles per hour, and Fridays she inclines the treadmill to a 4 percent grade and walks at 3.5 miles per hour. She follows the walking with balance exercises and stretching. Julia and her husband play in a bowling league on Wednesday evenings, and on Saturdays she spends a couple of hours doing work around the house.

Julia's new chart for the week:

	M	T	W	TH	F	SA	SU	TOTAL	RECOM-MENDED
Stamina (12 pts)	12	12	12	12	12			60	60
Strength (10 pts)	10		10					20	20
Other activity (5 pts)			5			5		10	10
Balance (1 pt)	1	1	1	1	1			5	5
Stretch (1 pt)	1	1	1	1	1			5	5
								100	100

The physical activity portion of the Brain Training Revolution indeed involves some sacrifices in terms of time and effort. But trust me—the rewards far outweigh the price. For all the time you put into exercise, you will save even more time—you'll get better-quality sleep, you'll have more energy, and you'll have the ability to get more done in less time. In many ways, you don't have time *not* to exercise. And when you invest in the Brain Training Revolution's exercises, you will see tangible gains in just a few weeks: you will focus better, tackle problems with more energy and direction, feel healthier, and be more positive about every aspect of your life. In the end, your goal of brain-healthy living carries with it so many other valuable fringe benefits.

Chapter 7

BECAUSE GRAY MATTERS: DAILY WORKOUTS IN THE WORLD BRAIN GYM!

"If I had to live my life again I would have made a rule to read some poetry and listen to some music at least once a week; for perhaps the parts of my brain now atrophied could thus have been kept active through use."
—CHARLES DARWIN, IN 1876 AT THE AGE OF 67

"Nor, indeed, are we to give our attention solely to the body; much greater care is due to the mind and soul for they, too, like lamps, grow dim with time, unless we keep them supplied with oil...intellectual activity gives buoyancy to the mind."—CICERO, IN 44 B.C. AT AGE 62

As highlighted in Part 1, the remarkable recent discoveries of the capabilities of aging brains puts on a firm scientific foundation the centuries-old observations and advice of the ancient Greeks and Romans, and more recently Goethe, Charles Darwin, and others. The brain can generate new cells and new connections even in our advanced years, thereby breathing new life into it. What does that mean in our daily lives? It means that we can significantly reduce the "where did I leave my car keys?"; "for the life of me I can't remember her name"; and similar anxiety-provoking moments, as well as the slowing of mental agility and learning ability that normally accompanies aging. Each of us can continue to build brain reserve, our personal brain-health insurance policy. How?

We've already covered the Brain Training Revolution prescriptions for a healthy diet and physical exercise. Now we've come to the third major part of the healthy brain-aging triumvirate: strength-building exercises for your brain. A workout for your brain, along with good nutrition, physical exercise, an active social life, getting enough restful sleep, and keeping stress under control—all of these constitute the Brain Training Revolution—a total brain-fitness program.

It's useful to think of the brain as a powerful muscle, or as a collection of intertwined muscles. Having a fit and sculptured body requires consistent participation in a variety of exercises to strengthen muscle groups of the body and to build stamina.

The same goes for your brain. To create a fit and well-sculptured brain, you should routinely engage in active, challenging exercises that strengthen its many "muscle groups." Languishing in repetitive, unchallenging, mind-numbing, and passive time wasters won't get the job done. As the ancient Roman philosopher Seneca so aptly put it two thousand years ago, "Difficulties strengthen the mind, as labor does the body." It's an easy-to-grasp idea: a few beads of brain sweat lead to better cognitive performance.

YOUR BRAIN MUSCLES

The following is a list of different kinds of brain functions and tasks (see www.BrainSavers.com for a description for each one):

- Alertness and awareness
- Focus and concentration
- Divided attention (multitasking)
- Vision (thinking about what you are seeing)
- Hearing (thinking about what you are listening to)
- Touch (thinking about what you are touching)
- Taste and smell (appreciating nuances of foods and aromas)

- Processing (speed and accuracy)
- Categorizing
- Time estimation
- Motor memories, skills, and habits (eye-hand coordination)
- Working (short-term) memory
- Long-term memory
- Naming (remembering names and objects)
- Learning
- Language
- Analyzing and planning
- Executing and achieving
- Imaginative thinking
- Creativity (everyone has artistic abilities)

Think of the world around you as your brain's private fitness club. Your home, neighborhood, town—the total environment you live in— is your brain's gym, a place teeming with opportunities to explore and thus sharpen your senses, hone your mental processing skills, remember, learn, experiment, and create. The world is your ticket to changing your brain.

Your brain can get all the exercise it needs to grow stronger if you engage it with your surroundings. Interacting with family and friends, especially sharing new brain-boosting activities, is an easy way to start expanding your mental horizons. Social groups or clubs (about books, bridge, chess, religion, outdoors, travel, scrapbooking, and more), art, music, museums, parks, theaters, concerts, continuing education classes, the Internet with its inexhaustible learning resources—the list is endless. And entry into the World Brain Gym (WBG) requires no monthly membership fees—it's free! The benefits you receive depend on your curiosity and motivation to explore, discover, and participate.

CogniByte

David Linden, a neuroscientist at Johns Hopkins University, likens the evolution of the human brain over millions of years to an ice-cream cone being piled up scoop by scoop. The automatic and most primitive reflexes that control our breathing, heartbeat, body temperature, digestion, and basic drives are in the oldest, bottom scoop. As more scoops are added, we next encounter old nooks and crannies where basic emotions like fear and the sensations of vision, hearing, smelling, and others reside. Next come memory and learning functions along with more complex human emotions until we get to the final and newest scoop: the frontal lobes and their massive gray matter cortex. Our executive functions of comparing, planning, decision making, and thoughtful action reside here. At the very top of this last scoop (the prefrontal lobes) is the home of imagination, creativity, and personality.

This chapter provides a complete workout plan for your brain. Practicing the third component of the Brain Training Revolution adds to your brain reserve, which will reduce your risk of Alzheimer's disease. Included are both structured cognitive exercises and what I call unstructured brain exercises. Everything takes place in the WBG.

FIVE SIMPLE RULES FOR MAXIMIZING BRAIN RESERVE THROUGH BRAIN EXERCISE

Apply these rules in your everyday life to enjoy the benefits of a more agile mind. Later in this chapter, you'll find specific cognitive exercises.

1. Start easy and gradually build up to greater mental challenges. If after ten or twenty years of physical inactivity you decided to start physically exercising (a very smart idea!), you would be wise not to begin with a 10K run. Similarly, if you want to learn Spanish, you would take a beginner's class before an advanced one. So don't rush right out for the toughest brainteaser book you can find. Start with activities that moderately challenge you without overwhelming you.

2. Real brain-building benefits come from real cognitive work. Just as there is no magic pill to make your body fit without effort, there is no

magic pill to train your brain. Developing it takes work. Your 6-year-old grandchild builds brain reserve by doing first-grade word puzzles, but this will not work for you. If a mental exercise seems too easy, you're not challenging your gray matter. Effortful but enjoyable cognitive activity is the name of the game. Just as you gradually increase weight resistance to build more arm and leg muscles, increase the difficulty of your cognitive exercises so that you remain challenged. In this way your brain reserve will continue to grow. Be patient. If Rome wasn't built in a day, your brain won't be either. Give yourself time before you expect to become a master bridge or chess player.

3. Exercise all of your brain: Give all the cognitive muscles of your brain in both the left and right hemispheres a regular workout. Don't be a specialist; be a Renaissance person. You can do this by engaging your brain from the bottom of the cognitive pyramid (see page 160) upward in a variety of both structured and unstructured WBG activities.

4. Use each day as an opportunity to grow your brain. Your brain does not have to rest in the same way that a muscle in your arm needs to rest after lifting heavy weights. You can grow your brain even when you are not strenuously challenged, such as by reading a book, playing a game, solving a puzzle, or listening to music. But if you feel mentally fatigued from your brain workout, if the thrill of learning is diminished, take a break.

CogniByte

Your brain can be and should be exercised every day. The neurons in your brain don't suffer the same type of reversible physical trauma that your muscles do from a tough workout. But like your skeletal muscles, your brain cannot function at its peak for hour after hour without becoming fatigued. So after working on a mentally challenging task for 30 to 60 minutes, take a break, even 10 minutes (like a coffee break at work). After a short rest, and perhaps after eating a brain-healthy snack, you will be able to return to the challenge with your brain muscles recharged.

5. Vary your cognitive workout routine, be open to new social opportunities, explore your world, and above all, have fun. Having fun while exercising your brain is crucial. Synapses are firing and wiring! If the activity stresses you out, don't do it. Choose activities that you enjoy and look forward to. Enjoyable, leisure-time social activities have been scientifically documented to build brain reserve.

COGNIBYTE: OBSERVING A FIT BRAIN

Without using expensive technologies like brain scans or sophisticated neuropsychological cognitive testing, we cannot directly observe or measure a brain's fitness level. However, we all know the manifestation of a fit brain: an individual of any age living life to its fullest, with full thinking, language, reasoning, and decision-making powers; being independent; and being smart as a whip. But what does such a brain actually look like?

Cognitive scientists can measure the speed and accuracy with which someone makes a decision, memorizes new information, or executes a series of mental steps. These measurements are the mental analogies of physical fitness attributes such as weight lifting or the time in split seconds it takes to walk, run, or swim a specified distance.

Using modern brain-imaging techniques such as functional MRI and positron emission tomography (PET), various parts of the brain can be seen doing the mental lifting—not of dumbbells and barbells but of myriad sensations from the environment. Scans show involved brain areas processing, analyzing and remembering this information, then planning and executing a response. Scans even have been used to research how emotions influence our decisions.

The good news is that you don't need scans or test scores to document better brain performance. You don't need to need to measure the size of your muscles or your heart rate to feel and experience that you are in better shape after exercising for several months. Your recovery time after exertion is shorter—you feel that you are in better shape, you are in better shape, and you have built physical reserve. Likewise, you will feel and witness the sharper brain function that follows from regularly and repeatedly working your brain.

WHAT ARE BRAIN EXERCISES?

Brain-building exercises, the ones that keep you mentally sharp and build brain reserve, use your eyes, ears, and other senses to transmit sensory signals to that incredible processing apparatus inside your skull. The brain then processes the information—analyzes, dissects, repackages, stores, and learns. The final results can be new thoughts and outputs: creativity in all its manifestations. And just as you perform different strength-training exercises for the various parts of your body, different mental exercises enhance various parts of your brain. Read a stimulating book, look at art, listen to music, discuss the current economic or political situation with a friend, work in your garden, and different areas of your brain do strength training. The brain loves and thrives on this type of workout. It evolved to process endless information coming from your senses, to think, remember, learn, plan, and create.

Thanks to the trillions of connections among brain cells, when you exercise any one part of the brain, there is a spillover effect on other parts. When you swim, your arms and legs are doing most of the work, but your back and abdominal muscles, as well as your heart and lungs are exercising. So it is with the brain. When you specifically exercise vision, for example, you also benefit alertness, focus, memory formation, and other cognitive networks, even if they are not the primary focus of the exercise. Like strengthening the body's muscles, the key to strengthening your brain muscles is repetition and modestly increasing the challenge and adding variation over time.

Structured and Unstructured Types of Brain Exercises

Thinking of your brain as a muscle allows a further analogy to physical fitness. Attending a 30-minute cycling class or running through the workout your trainer designed for you are examples of structured, formal physical exercises. But you can achieve similar results from unstructured, informal physical exercise on your own. A city sidewalk is really just a long, stationary treadmill. Using the stairs instead of an elevator gives you the benefits of a stair stepper, for free! Playing with your grandkids at the playground can rival any structured exercise class. These are examples of unstructured physical exercises.

Similarly, there are both structured and unstructured opportunities for brain exercises in the World Brain Gym as well. Gardening is a nifty example of an activity that can be either structured or unstructured (and it has both fitness and nutritional benefits as well!). You can attend a gardening class or you can plan and grow your own flower and vegetable garden at home using a neighbor's friendly advice, a book or two, or an Internet site. Both are true workouts with real benefits, and both are investments in your brain's long-term reserve.

USING A BRAIN TRAINER: WORLD BRAIN GYM STRUCTURED EXERCISES

Structured brain exercises consist of formal cognitive activities available in specially designed programs that have a fixed beginning and end. Examples include language or other classes at your local community college, craft or hobby workshops, organized and progressive mental games or puzzle books, brain-fitness programs that are increasingly available via home computers or gaming systems, travel-study experiences with lectures by specific experts or historians, or even two weeks in a cooking class in Provence. In short, structured brain exercises have a finite duration, a systematic progression, and often some form of formal instruction.

COMPUTER-BASED COGNITIVE EXERCISES

The DVD enclosed with this book will introduce you to structured interactive memory and other brain-enhancing exercises. Among the benefits of the exercises is their ability to measure your performance level in using specific brain muscles. Some of these programs are able to tailor a training program to fit your specific cognitive needs, much like a personal physical fitness instructor assesses your fitness level and creates a workout program just for you!

SELF-INSTRUCTION IN THE WORLD BRAIN GYM

Specially designed, high-tech, computer-based cognitive exercise software and online training programs certainly provide some brain-training benefits. However, you can obtain truly beneficial cognitive strength through your day-to-day interactions with the world. It is the world we live in that, every day, places in front of us mental challenges and stresses. No matter how much you increase your ability to repeat a string of numbers or a list of objects on the computer screen, it is how well you remember where you left your purse and car keys, your anniversary, your wife's birthday, or that mental grocery list that really matters to you in your daily life. As many cognitive experts have pointed out, it is real-world memory tasks that count. This same world is loaded with brain exercise equipment that will keep your mind busy, challenged, and growing stronger.

Using WBG equipment strengthens your abilities to remember and think while building brain reserve. All you need to do is stretch those brain muscles of attention, focus, sensory input, processing, and outputs. Some of my favorite unstructured WBG activities are spending an hour or two in an art museum, planning a fishing trip or a visit to a new city, working in my garden, reading a novel, listening to classical music, reading the newspaper (especially the opinion columns), discussing news events or politics and global affairs, socializing with family and close friends, playing chess with my son, and discussing my daughter's army experience. Your list of the mentally stimulating activities you participate in will be as long as your sense of exploration allows. When you recognize that there are not enough hours in a day to engage your brain in all the ways you desire, you know you are on the right path. That will be the moment to recruit your executive frontal lobes to prioritize and choose.

There are other advantages of using the world as your personal brain gym. Your day-to-day engagement in your personal corner of the world strengthens those brain muscles (cognitive abilities) important for the unique mental tasks in your daily life. For example, practicing a divided attention task (two or more separate cognitive activities at once) on the computer is beneficial. But practicing multitasking in real-life activities, such as talking on the telephone while simultaneously measuring ingredients from a recipe, directly strengthens your brain to meet everyday challenges. It is real-life functioning. Individuals who combine some structured WBG cognitive exercises along with unstructured brain-training exercise will be creating more brain reserve than someone who engages in only a structured work-out. Remember studying in high school and university and then getting out into the world and trying to put all that book learning to use?

All you need to do is identify the "equipment" of the real world brain gym, along with a positive attitude, motivation, and discipline. Let's try something to get you started. Think of a familiar street or a familiar area of a shopping mall—one that you often travel down when you are shopping. Now close your eyes and try to create a mental picture of the stores and shops in their proper order. Want to build a better memory? If yes, actually go to the street or mall. As you walk down the street, mentally take note of each of the stores that you pass. The brain remembers better when you engage multiple senses. This is a classical memory technique that dates back to Simonides of Ceos, in the fifth century B.C., who invented "the palace of memory." Thus were ancient Greek and Roman orators able to remember and recall vast amounts of knowledge before the printed page was invented.

"A great and beautiful invention is memory, always useful both for learning and for life. This is the first thing: if you pay attention (direct your mind), the judgment will better perceive the things going through it (the mind). Secondly, repeat again what you hear; for by often hearing and saying the same things, what you have learned comes complete into your memory."—DIALEXIS, CIRCA 400 B.C.

So, while you are walking, make mental notes of each storefront's signage and colors; window display; any sounds or music that you hear and can associate with each store; smells from foods, salons, or candle stores; and any other clues that will trigger your memory. As an aid to remembering all these facts, whisper the names to yourself. After you've completed your tour, write down the names of the stores, in order. Then write down what was featured in their respective windows. If you can't recall all of the stores, repeat your walk down the street. When you get home, sit quietly with your eyes closed and re-create your walking tour. Then write it down. You will surprise yourself with the details you remember. Want to improve? Repeat this memory-boosting exercise by walking the same route the next day. You are building a personal palace of memory.

Let's assume that you live in an apartment building. Do you know the name and apartment number of each person living on your floor? How about those on the floor below? Why not create a mental map of the entire building? Put that part of your hippocampus devoted to geographic memory formation to good use, like we learned from the study of London taxi drivers. Take as many trips as you need to form a complete map so that you're able to re-create it from memory. Next, try to draw a mental floor plan of the entire complex, including shared spaces like recreation rooms, storage spaces, and lobbies.

Do you enjoy cooking or baking? If so, why not write down, from memory, the ingredients and the precisely described cooking steps for your favorite recipes. Put them together in a notebook so that you can pass them on to your children.

Do you want to improve manual dexterity and strengthen your eye-hand coordination? How about knitting a sweater for a grandchild or building a model airplane or boat? Given a steady hand and adequate vision (there are some relatively inexpensive magnifying glasses with built-in lights that make the task far easier), this can be fun, and it simultaneously contributes to an important aspect of brain reserve, specifically the strengthening of motor memories, which are critically important for maintaining physical independence.

How about disassembling an old clock, watch, or other mechanical device and trying to figure out what the individual parts are for and how they work together? Use the Internet to assist you. Perhaps you will be further interested to learn the history of the pocket watch's invention during the Renaissance, the mechanical advances contributing to its further development, and even the history of keeping time from sundials to atomic clocks. There is no end to the WBG.

Assuming that your hands are still relatively steady, how about shaving, combing your hair, applying your makeup, and brushing your teeth with your nondominant hand. Do this every day for a month and you will see the result of a Brain Training Revolution experiment. Your brain will have actually rewired itself by building connections between nerve cells in the side of the brain opposite the one you have relied on for years to execute this complex daily motor-memory task.

Can you recall the items of clothing in your closet, the tools in your workshop, the food in your pantry, and how those things are arranged? If you missed some items, repeat the exercise and memorize those that you forgot.

Expose yourself to various types of music, books on different subjects, and new tastes in ethnic cuisines. Think about what you are listening to, reading, or eating. In the case of music, imagine the intent of the composer and identify the instruments. Again, use books or the Internet to assist you. If you have not been to the opera recently, how about attending one? If you live far away from an opera house, many movie theaters now show high-definition broadcasts of operatic performances. Already an opera fan? How about forming some new synapses by listening to jazz, gospel, or rock music?

Some still say, "You can't teach an old dog new tricks." Experience and modern brain science proves they are wrong! Learning is easier than ever, with access to the Internet, books to download, and a plethora of educational and entertaining programs on channels such as Discovery, History, Smithsonian, BBC, and PBS. Not a fan of TV? National Public Radio features a wide range of music and educational programs, free to tune into. We hear stories all the time of older folks completing their education. They not only feel and act smarter but also build brain reserve.

With a little ingenuity, you can easily customize your own WBG. By interacting with the world around you, you will discover endless opportunities to strengthen and grow your mind and build brain reserve.

DO YOU KNOW YOUR CQ?

You know that IQ stands for Intelligence Quotient, a relative measure of the intellectual capacity of a particular person.

CogniByte

The results from numerous published scientific studies, some of which were highlighted earlier, are clear: increased leisure activities and challenging real-life mental activities in midlife and beyond not only increase the quality of life but also can lead to an almost 50 percent lower incidence of Alzheimer's disease and overall dementia. The implications are great for our society and for each of us who is concerned with the aging brain. The scourge of Alzheimer's disease can be tempered through lifestyle changes. No antiaging, unproven, "miracle" supplements—no steroids, testosterone, growth hormones, or other potentially dangerous pills, capsules, or injections are necessary to improve memory and build brain reserve.

But what about your Cognitive Quotient, your CQ? Richard Samuels and I developed the CQ concept as we worked on the Brain Training Revolution. The CQ lets interested people grasp the concept of exercising the brain and the benefits that result. Like the nutritional and physical quotients described in chapters 5 and 6, respectively, are a means to measure and track these brain-building components, the CQ is intended as a means for you to keep track of the daily mental workout you provide to your brain.

Basically, CQ is an estimate of the degree of cognitive activity that a person engages in during a period of time. How much time and how beneficial are the activities to the brain muscles being exercised? We have arbitrarily assigned a numerical value of 100 as an average CQ. Whereas your IQ has a major hereditary component, your CQ is largely influenced by the lifestyle you choose: it is the total of your structured and unstructured brain workout activities. That is, the more time you spend in mentally challenging activities, the higher is your CQ and the greater your brain reserve becomes. It's completely up to you!

There is no test for CQ at present—it can be estimated only by examining the mental activity of your current lifestyle, which is outlined later in this chapter—and it does not matter what your initial score is. The more you exercise your brain, the higher your CQ score will be, just like the PQ score for physical exercise. A person who walks or jogs a couple of miles at least three times a week and goes to the gym several times each week would need little additional exercise to fulfill the physical exercise requirements for a brain-healthy lifestyle. In an analogous way, a person who socializes regularly, solves problems daily, works at a mentally challenging job or volunteer activity, attends continuing education classes, and stimulates his or her mind in a variety of other ways requires less additional cognitive exercise to reach the cognitive exercise requirements for that same brain-healthy lifestyle.

What Your CQ Level Means

Let's begin by looking at some different CQ levels. Using extremes to illustrate the point, our first hypothetical individual, Sluggish Sal, recently retired from a job; seldom reads; and spends the day shopping, gossiping about trivial matters, and watching soap operas or endless sports on TV. In the evenings, Sal watches sitcoms and little else. Although Sal's brain gets plenty of raw sensory stimulation, there is little in the way of brain-strengthening exercises going on. The inputs are not challenging, little new processing is occurring, and the outputs are minimal. Sal's brain gets little cognitive challenge and therefore the CQ is not very high; perhaps 10 or 20, no matter what Sal's IQ may be.

Let's compare Sal's lifestyle to that of Active Annie, who is also retired. Annie reads the newspaper; supplements this with daily forays into her favorite informational websites; has spirited discussions with her husband and friends about current political, economic, and social issues; and relishes the weekly crossword puzzle in her local paper. Each week she plays bridge, studies a foreign language at the local community college, and volunteers for a four-hour shift at the nearby children's hospital. Not only is Annie's brain reserve growing every day, she is also having fun challenging her brain and filling her mind with new information, and serving her community. In essence, Annie is inoculating herself with learning experiences and building brain reserve against age-associated memory loss and the big, bad wolf of Alzheimer's disease. Annie has a high CQ score: perhaps 70 to 80.

Of course, as with physical exercise, most of us fall somewhere in-between these two extremes. Use the chart on page 156 to calculate the CQ score that best reflects your current brain lifestyle. You should be able to approximate your CQ score simply by comparing your cognitive activity level to the hypotheticals of Sal and Annie. Take into account your work, leisure time, and social and other activities that contribute to your level of mental stimulation. Obviously, the higher your CQ is, the more brain reserve you already have and the more it will continue to grow in the future as you continue to strive for brain fitness.

How to Calculate Your Baseline CQ

For many of us, certainly those of us who are not yet retired, our work life encompasses a major portion of our day. Examine your work life as it relates to effortful mental activity. How cognitively challenging is it? Do you work full-time or part-time? Think carefully about this. Often, over time, jobs that were initially mentally challenging become less so with routine. It is not your profession that is so important but the day-to-day mental challenges. We have all had interactions with businesspeople, physicians, teachers, lawyers, librarians, managers, and government employees who have burned out and simply go through the motions. So if you feel truly challenged and excited most days on the job, then give yourself 10 CQ points for each full day you work and 5 CQ points for half a day's work. Assign a value of 7 CQ points per day if you feel moderately challenged on a regular basis. If your job is not cognitively engaging or is largely repetitive with few cognitive challenges, then give yourself just 4 CQ points per day. Don't be shy about asking your supervisor for additional responsibilities or more challenging work assignments!

Regardless of the nature of your work, leisure activities that exercise the brain muscles not specifically exercised during work will round out and further strengthen your brain. Any CQ points earned from a job should be added into the "structured" point column in the chart on page 156.

Retired? Unless you keep up with your field or have begun another, you will have to engage in many more WBG cognitive exercises to keep your brain zipping along, since your baseline CQ level at this time might be low like Sal's. Spend most of your time fishing, knitting, or baking? Experimenting with a truly new recipe is cognitively challenging—worth perhaps 2 or 3 points an hour. Designing a sweater or scarf demands creative thinking and earns you a few points as well. Developing strategies to catch that elusive ten-pound bonefish can be brain work—worth a few points an afternoon depending on how much actual thinking you put into it.

Many retired people devote considerable time to working for charitable and other service organizations. Treat these activities as if they were your job and estimate their CQ point value in the same way you would if you were getting paid for that work. Remember to add these CQ points to the Daily Structured Cognitive Exercise column on the chart.

The following section lists menus of both types of WBG activities and a chart to keep track. Select some from each to create your own personalized cognitive exercise program. These lists contain only a small sampling of structured and unstructured brain exercises that will increase your CQ.

If you are more comfortable following a brain exercise prescription rather than designing your own program, the Brain Training Revolution cognitive exercise program presented in the final sections of this chapter introduces you to a combination of structured and unstructured WBG activities. It is a step-by-step approach to get you started on your way to the recommended weekly CQ level of 100 and a lifetime of brain fitness. What happens if you find yourself in the future with a weekly CQ score of greater than 100? Great! You will be building mega brain reserve!

Getting Down to the Nitty-Gritty: Charting Your CQ

Someday cognitive science will have quantifiable measures for brain strengthening activities, but for now you can estimate and keep score. What's important is knowing that cognitive exercises rewire and strengthen your brain—it's weight lifting for your three-pound universe!

To track your cognitive growth, use the chart on the following page. On a daily basis, record CQ points earned from all of the structured and unstructured WBG activities you engage in.

WEEKLY COGNITIVE QUOTIENT (CQ) CALCULATION CHART

	DAILY WBG STRUCTURED CQ POINTS	DAILY WBG UNSTRUCTURED CQ POINTS	TOTAL CQ POINTS PER DAY
M			
T			
W			
Th			
F			
Sa			
Su			
Weekly total			

WBG Structured Brain Exercises to Increase Your Baseline CQ

Give yourself up to 40 points per week for any of the following activities:

- Taking a continuing education class, including learning a foreign language, philosophy, psychology, art, or music appreciation: 5 CQ points per hour

- Attending adult education classes such as a ceramics, painting with watercolors, home or automotive repair, crafts, or dance: 5 CQ points per hour

- Participating in an ongoing, scientifically valid, computer-based cognitive training program: 5 CQ points per 30-minute session

WBG Unstructured Leisure Activities to Increase Your Baseline CQ

"One ought, every day at least, to hear a little song, read a good poem, see a fine picture, and if it were possible, to speak a few reasonable words."
—JOHANN WOLFGANG VON GOETHE, 1795

Using the lists below as suggestions, you can add an endless number of WBG mental activities to increase your CQ. The more effortful, novel, and varied your mental activities are, the more CQ points you earn.

The following activities earn 10 CQ points for engaging in an activity that results in effortful mental work for approximately two hours:

- Participating in activities at your place of worship, athletic events, and other social gatherings that require mental engagement

- Solving (or giving it your best shot!) the *New York Times* cross-word puzzle weekly on Saturday and one or two other challenging puzzles during the week

- Reading a novel or nonfiction book that requires concentration and thoughtful reflection

- Designing and building models, sewing from a new pattern, creating new recipes

- Learning a foreign language, studying astronomy, art or military history, or music appreciation on your own

- Playing challenging games or doing puzzles on the computer that are not part of a structured brain-game program

- Figuring out a complex route including stops, overnights, and tourist attractions to explore for an extended trip

- Designing, planning, and building a home project such as a kitchen, basement, office, play room, or garden

- Organizing a volunteer group for your place of worship, community activity center, hospital, animal shelter, or other deserving cause

- Modifying and/or revising computer hardware or software

- Creating a slideshow with narrative or editing a movie on your computer

More WBG Unstructured Activities

These are additional brain building pursuits, such as easy reading, introductory brain teasers, and puzzles. Remember, doing simple new things is better than repeating familiar tasks. Give yourself 5 points for:

- Solving challenging Sudoku panels or word or number puzzles for one hour

- Writing with your nondominant hand for 20 minutes five days a week

- Taking alternative driving, cycling, or walking routes to a familiar place such as work, a friend's home, or a favorite eatery for one to two hours total per week

- Reading one hundred pages per week of an easy novel, or a science, political, or craft magazine that does not require deep reflection

- Thoroughly reading a quality daily newspaper for two hours

- Scrapbooking or writing in a journal for one to two hours

- Reading online news or blogs for two hours

- Helping the kids or grandkids with their homework for one hour

- Writing letters or a string of e-mails for two hours

YOUR BRAIN TRAINING REVOLUTION COGNITIVE EXERCISE PROGRAM

The following is an introductory one-week program of cognitive exercise incorporating both structured and unstructured WBG activities. Engaging in one or two structured cognitive exercises at most levels daily, coupled with other WBG activities, will put you on the path to building protective brain reserve. Answers to these puzzles are printed on pages 276 to 291.

Don't worry if some of the exercises seem too challenging, and don't aim to be at levels 6 and 7 immediately. Just as the first day of a physical training program might leave you bushed and wondering whether you can really get into shape, so can a challenging brain-training program. But I assure you, if you stick with it and spend time every day, you will see results within a few weeks. Most of all have fun!

By completing this program, you'll have strengthened your memory and other cognitive functions that I have been talking about throughout this book. When you've mastered the exercises in this book, keep going. Your gray matter needs constant stimulation. Discover other sources and create your own additional cognitive exercises to continue strengthening your brain for the rest of your life!

THE BRAIN PYRAMID

The functions of the twenty brain muscles have been grouped into seven layers on a cognitive pyramid. Approach these exercises as if you are climbing the pyramid, starting at the base and progressing to the top. This is how your brain functions—higher cortical functions depend on underlying evolutionarily older, more basic functions. Recall the ice-cream cone analogy that David Linden suggested. Of course, the pyramid is a schematic and there is considerable overlap between layers. It is intended to make the incredible complexity of the brain understandable.

The Cognitive Pyramid

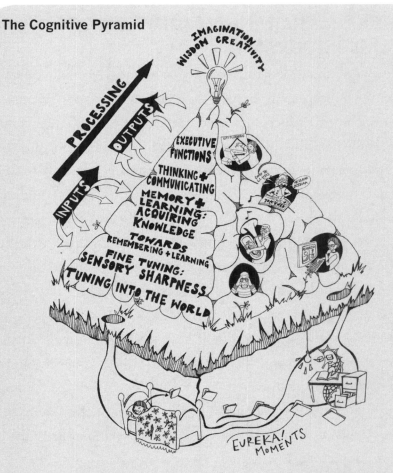

The base of the pyramid, "Tuning into the World," is where our brain perks up to face the world—if it had an underground layer it would be the cognitive processes that occur during sleep (see chapter 9). At this level we become alert, aware, focused, and concentrating so as to enable input signals from eyes, ears, and other primary senses to begin their journey through the complex processing apparatus of the brain on their way up the cognitive pyramid.

The second level, sensory sharpness and perception, involves our brain fine-tuning the inputs by discriminating and establishing priority for selected sensations while filtering out extraneous, unimportant signals—the background noise.

The beginning of working memories and the early stages of learning occur at the third level of the pyramid. Processing occurs to some degree at every level, but here it refers to the brain's interpreting new inputs within the context of what we have experienced and learned before. The brain sorts and categorizes new information. This enhances our ability to focus intently, to really concentrate and organize new inputs on the road to remembering and learning.

The fourth level is where memories are solidified and learning advances on the way to the acquisition of knowledge. Now that processed information has been concentrated into that which is critically important, the hippocampus performs its unique function of creating memories from the highly processed data it receives from widespread areas of the brain. Memories lead to learning and learning leads to knowledge.

The fifth level is where the transition from inputs to outputs begins. Outputs are mentally directed actions that result from what we have remembered and learned. Outputs include thinking and all those brain activities that result in spoken language and other forms of communicating our thoughts to others, as well as the movement of muscles of the arms and legs that result in physical actions.

Nearing the top we get to the sixth level, executive functions. Here higher-level processing results in those human abilities to analyze, judge, make decisions, plan complex goals, and carry out the steps necessary to realize them.

The apex of the cognitive pyramid is imagination and creativity. New ideas expressed in myriad ways only the human brain is capable of occur at this level.

Let's begin with the input side of cognition.

Level 1: Tuning into the World: The Five Senses

The major brain muscles exercised in Level 1 are the following:

- Alertness and awareness

- Focus and concentration

- Vision

- Hearing

- Touch

- Taste and smell

Before memory and learning occur, before taking action, your brain must first receive information from the outside world. It does this via the senses. Being aware of your surroundings, being alert, and being able to concentrate on what is important while ignoring distracting stimuli are skills that the exercises in this section strengthen. How well we are tuned into our surroundings can spell the difference between success and failure in a variety of life's circumstances, even life-or-death situations.

Remember the incredible saga of US Airways Flight 1549 that crash-landed in the Hudson River on January 15, 2009? The heroic Captain Chesley Burnett "Sully" Sullenberger was alert, aware, well focused, and concentrating! First, he relied and made perfect use of his brain's attention and sensory systems to focus on inputs out of the ordinary, ones that signaled danger. His brain processed all this critical information in a few short moments. Then it rapidly created an action plan and ultimately directed the output, truly lifesaving actions. If his brain had taken a misstep at any time during this masterpiece of a climb up the cognitive pyramid, the results would have been catastrophic.

Structured Exercises: 10 points per hour
Answers to these exercises can be found on page 276.

EXERCISE 1

Refer to Level 1, Exercise 1 in the color insert. Focus on the photograph for 15 seconds then answer the questions below.

What color is the vehicle in the background?

What kind of vehicle is in the background?

What color is the dress of the woman in the center of the photo?

What is the woman in the center of the photo carrying?

What color is the handbag of the woman on the right?

How many pedestrians are pictured?

Were any of the pedestrians carrying a suitcase?

EXERCISE 2

Refer to Level 1, Exercise 2 in the color insert. Focus on the photograph for 15 seconds then answer the questions below.

What sport is being played?

What are the colors of the teams?

How many adults are seated with the group in the foreground?

What are the people in the foreground sitting on?

How many kids are in the foreground?

How many kids can be seen lying down?

Are the teams boy, girl, or co-ed?

What structures can be seen in the background?

EXERCISE 3

Refer to Level 1, Exercise 3 in the color insert. Focus on the photograph for 15 seconds then answer the questions below.

How many people are in the photo?

What color are the life vests?

What is the boy holding in his hand?

What color is the man's shirt?

What color is the boy's kayak?

What color is the man's kayak?

EXERCISE 4

Refer to Level 1, Exercise 4 in the color insert. Focus on the photograph for 15 seconds then answer the questions below.

How many people are in the photograph?

How many kids are in the photo?

What is the boy holding in his hand?

How many males and females are in the photo?

Name three items on the table.

What color is the table cloth?

EXERCISE 5

Find the only object that appears in both boxes below.

EXERCISE 6

Find the only object that appears in both boxes below.

LEVEL 1

For each of the two pictures below, focus on the photograph for 15 seconds, then turn to page 163 and answer the questions there.

EXERCISE 1

EXERCISE 2

For each picture below, focus on the photograph for 15 seconds, then to page 164 and answer the questions there.

EXERCISE 3

EXERCISE 4

LEVEL 3

EXERCISE 3

Find the words below in the puzzle; try not to be distracted by the colors:

brain	cognition	capacity
attention	exercise	quick
smart	diet	sharp
thinking	health	clever
perception	fitness	intelligence
stimuli	energy	
senses	response	

```
Q W O B I H G N B X C A C C B Y I O S X
Z P B C R N V B L K T S L J F D I E T O
W H I R U A Y F B T N J E F G H A Z I N
X E X E R C I S E Y H F V P E P Q R M R
P A A S D F X N B T F J E L H E P W U E
U L S M A R T G L I J H R O I R U E L S
T T K S E I S M N C D X B O A C U S I P
H H E E O T I O E A Q L A H S E D H G O
I C X N B N M V B P J K S D F P E N B N
N V M S Z C P Q W A I O R F I T N E S S
K H G E N E R G Y C O G N I T I O N Q E
I E T S B W O R I H G N B X C O N C B Y
N O U X Z P I N T E L L I G E N C E J K
G H F G P E I Q U I C K O A S D F X Z B
```

EXERCISE 10

Step 1: Speak the color of each word aloud.

Step 2: Now speak the color of each word and the word itself.

Blue Green **Orange** Red Pink Yellow **Purple** Grey
White Red Blue **Yellow** Green Grey Orange Pink
Purple **Black Green** Orange Green Orange Red
Purple Yellow Pink Blue Grey **Red** Blue Yellow
Blue Green **Orange** Red Pink Yellow **Purple** Grey
White Red Blue **Yellow** Green Grey Orange Pink
Purple Black **Green** Orange Green Orange Red
Purple Yellow Pink Blue Grey **Red** Blue Yellow
Green Orange Green Orange Red Purple Yellow
Pink Blue Grey **Red** Blue Yellow Blue Green
Orange Red Pink **Yellow** Green Grey Orange Pink
Purple **Black Green** Orange Green Orange Red
Purple Yellow Pink Blue Grey **Red** Blue Yellow
Blue Green **Orange** Pink Blue Grey **Red** Blue
Yellow Blue Green **Orange** Red Pink Yellow
Purple Grey White Red Blue **Yellow** Green **Black**
Green Orange Green Orange Red Purple Yellow
Pink Blue Grey **Red** Blue Yellow Blue Green Blue

How far can you get without making a mistake?

10: Keep working on it.
20: Not bad.
30: Good!
40: Great!
50+: Excellent!

To increase the difficulty, time yourself.

EXERCISE 11

Draw a line to match the name on the top to the color on the bottom.

Blue   **Green**   Orange   Red   **Pink**   Yellow   **Purple**   Grey   Black

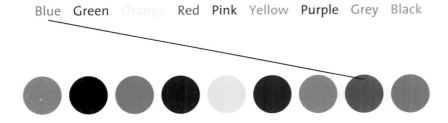

EXERCISE 12

Draw a line to match the name on the top to the color on the bottom.

Blue   **Green**   Orange   Red   **Pink**   Yellow   **Purple**   Grey   Black

Blue   **Green**   Orange   **Red**   **Pink**   Yellow   **Purple**   Grey   Black

EXERCISE 7

Find the only object that appears in both boxes below.

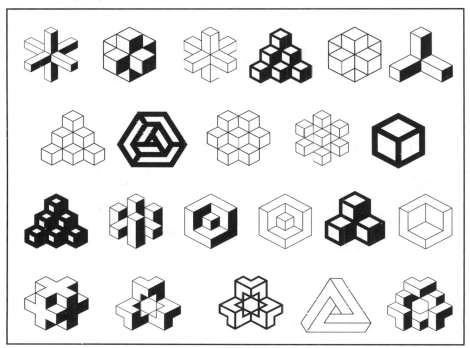

EXERCISE 8

Find the only object that does NOT appear in both boxes below.

EXERCISE 9

Find the only object that does NOT appear in both boxes below.

EXERCISE 10

Find the only object that does NOT appear in both boxes below.

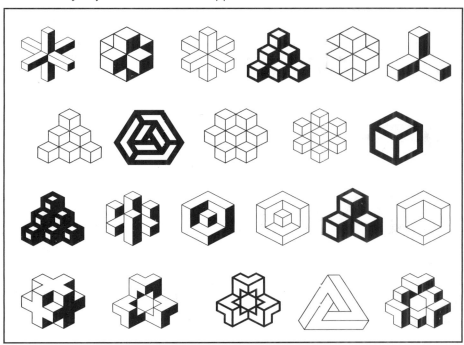

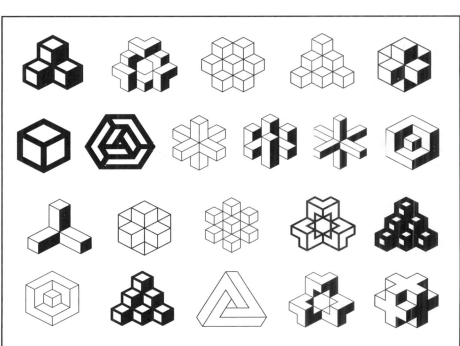

EXERCISE 11

*For each exercise spend 15 seconds reviewing the photos. Then turn to the fol-
lowing page and select the matching set of photos. Hint: use a blank sheet of
paper to cover the other puzzles so you can focus on one puzzle at a time.*

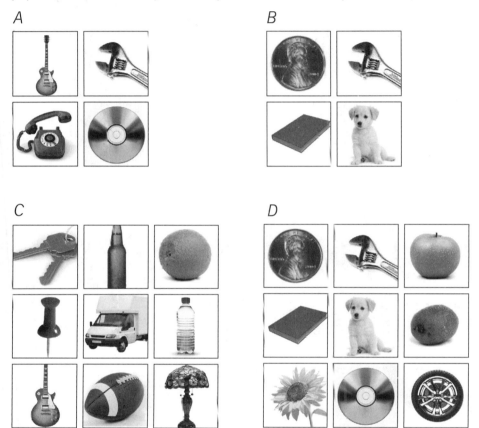

A

B

C

D

Select the matching set of photos from the previous page.

A

B

C

D

Unstructured Activities: 5 points per hour

- Observe a photograph for 5 seconds. How many different objects can you remember immediately? After 3 minutes? After 30 minutes? Repeat several times until you can recall at least ten features of the photograph immediately and seven after three minutes. Repeat with other images.

- Listen to a musical selection for 1 to 2 minutes. How many specific instruments and or voices can you discern?

- While you are walking down the street, observe the types, makes, and models of vehicles passing. If you are observing traffic on a two-way street, simultaneously count cars going in each direction.

- Sit in a quiet area or park and listen to how many different birds and other sounds you can hear. Write them down and then compare this list to your listening experiences in other locations.

- When passing a restaurant or a bakery concentrate on the various aromas. How many specific smells can you identify?

Level 2: Fine-Tuning Sensory Sharpness

The major brain muscles exercised in Level 2 are the following:

- Visual processing

- Auditory processing

- Touch processing

- Taste and odor processing

- Time estimation

- Categorizing

Once the brain has been alerted and is focused, the processing of information begins. The brain prioritizes and orders the entering sensory signals. During this stage, most extraneous information is disregarded while the processing of what is important takes precedence. Exercising these skills can help you to tune out the extraneous and focus on the important. The processes occur so quickly and automatically that we are frequently not at all aware of their occurrence.

What the senses present to our brain becomes a mental representation of the physical world. Our expectations and prior learning alter what we actually perceive mentally. The more accurate our perceptions, the more likely our brain's processing is to result in appropriate responses. Estimating the duration of an event and placing it in the proper mental category or group are important early steps in this process. The finer your brain tunes complex sensations, the more precise your memories will be.

Structured Exercises: 10 points per hour

Answers to these exercises can be found on page 279.

EXERCISE 1

Choose the correct shape from the bottom four that matches the shape on top.

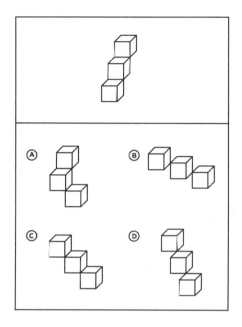

EXERCISE 2

Choose the correct shape from the bottom four that matches the shape on top.

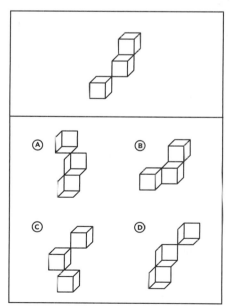

EXERCISE 3

Choose the correct shape from the bottom four that matches the shape on top.

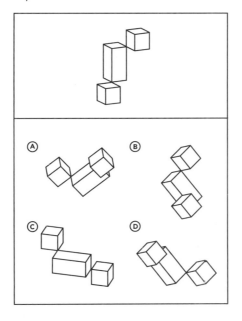

EXERCISE 4

Assuming each shape below is a perfect sphere and all are the same size, which of the bottom figures is NOT an alternate view of the top figure.

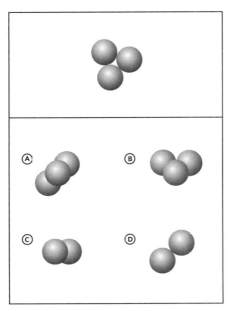

EXERCISE 5

Assuming each shape below is a perfect sphere and all are the same size, which of the bottom figures is NOT an alternate view of the top figure.

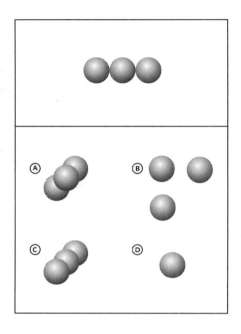

EXERCISE 6

Which shape or letter does not belong?

A

a k m

J d o

f c z

B

A D C

S N F

G H K

C

O a R

q D C

B P g

D

HINT: Pay close attention to the angles

E

HINT: How many sides does each shape have?

F

HINT: Try drawing a vertical line through the middle of each shape.

EXERCISE 7

Which symbol does not belong?

HINT: How do you get from point A to point B?

HINT: What do you call home?

HINT: How do you communicate?

EXERCISE 8

Look at the photograph again from Level 1, Exercise 1 for 15 seconds, paying close attention to details. Then answer the questions below.

How many people appear in the photo?

How many bags are carried by the woman in the light blue dress?

What are the colors of the dresses or skirts worn by the women in the photo?

How many bare legs can be seen?

What kinds of pants are the men in the scene wearing?

EXERCISE 9

Look at the photograph again from Level 1, Exercise 2 for 15 seconds, paying close attention to details. Then answer the questions below.

How many people are in the bleachers?

What are the numbers on any two of the players in the photo?

How many children are standing in the foreground?

How many children are seated on the field?

How many people are standing near the goal?

EXERCISE 10

Look at the photograph again from Level 1, Exercise 3 for 15 seconds, paying close attention to details. Then answer the questions below.

How many kayaks can be seen in the photo?

What color are the oars?

How many oars are in the photos?

What does the man have on his left arm?

What are three of the things that can be seen in the background?

EXERCISE 11

Look at the photograph again from Level 1, Exercise 4 for 15 seconds, paying close attention to details. Then answer the questions below.

What color is the woman's shirt in the background?

How many generations can be seen?

What is the man in the background holding in his hand?

What color are the two glasses on the table?

What does the woman on the right have on her head?

EXERCISE 12

Decode the following puzzles using the key at the top of each.

A

| 11 | 5 | 5 | 16 | | 25 | 15 | 21 | 18 | | 2 | 18 | 1 | 9 | 14 | | 19 | 20 | 9 | 13 | | 21 | 12 | 1 | 20 | 5 | 4 |

k e e p   y o u r   b r a i n   s t i m u l a t e d

| 21 | 19 | 5 | | 9 | 20 | | 15 | 18 | | 12 | 15 | 19 | 5 | | 9 | 20 |

_ _ _   _ _   _ _   _ _ _ _   _ _

B

▶ ✳ ● ▼ ✳□□✳▲ ✳✲✦✳ ▼✳✳ ○□▲▼ ✳✦✳● ✳□□ ▼✳✳ ○□●✳■
WHAT FOODS GIVE THE MOST FUEL FOR THE BRAIN?

✳□✦✳▼▲ ■✦▼▲ ▲✳✳✳▲ ●✳✳✦○✳▲ ✳□●✳■▲
_ _ _ _ _ _ , _ _ _ _ , _ _ _ _ _ , _ _ _ _ _ _ _ , _ _ _ _ _ _ ,
✦✳✳✳▼●○●✳▲ ✳✳▲✳ ●■✳ ▶✳■✳
_ _ _ _ _ _ _ _ _ _ , _ _ _ _ , _ _ _   _ _ _ _ .

C

v c v i x r h v   r h   k f i v   n v w r x r m v
E x e r c i s e   i s   p u r e   m e d i c i n e
u l i   s v z o g s b   y i z r m   z t r m t
f o r   h e a l t h y   b r a i n   a g i n g .

k s b h r x z o   z m w   n v m g z o
_ _ _ _ _ _ _ _   _ _ _   _ _ _ _ _ _

u r g m v h h   h s l f o w   y v   z   k z i g
_ _ _ _ _ _ _   _ _ _ _ _ _   _ _   _   _ _ _ _

l u   b l f i   w z r o b   i l f g r m v
_ _   _ _ _ _   _ _ _ _ _   _ _ _ _ _ _ _

Unstructured Activities: 5 points per hour

- Have a friend play a musical selection, not known to you in advance, for a fixed number of seconds or minutes. Estimate the time. You can do an equivalent visual exercise with a book of photographs or paintings.

- Play a musical selection for 1 to 2 minutes. How many specific instruments or voices can you make out? This is a repetition of the same exercise you did in Level 1, but now replay each selection several times to sharpen your sensory discrimination.

- While in a busy department store, on the subway, or on the bus, how many distinct voices do you hear? You likely will catch snippets of conversations. Identify accents you hear.

- Observe the various types of clothing people wear. Identify the fabrics and observe how many different colors and shades of colors you see. Make mental or written lists of all these various attributes. Become aware of seasonal changes in wardrobes.

- At a park or in a nature preserve, how many different types of plants can you observe and identify by common and scientific names? Get a book on the local flora and fauna and learn both names? How many different birds and their songs can you identify and name? Again, your local library, a bookstore, or the Internet are resources that will help you to identify the birds and match their songs with their names.

- Without looking at them, feel different pieces of fabric and try to identify them on the basis of texture, thickness, and temperature. Start off with fabrics whose textures are clearly different. Do the same with coins.

- Take five spice containers from your kitchen cabinet. Identify the spice from its fragrance. Practice until you can identify all five and then add additional ones. You can do a similar exercise with wines, flowers, leaves, soaps, and candles.

Level 3: Towards Remembering and Learning

The major brain muscles exercised in Level 3 are the following:

- Processing

- Naming

- Categorizing

- Time estimation

- Divided attention

- Working (short-term) memories

Before the brain forms long-term, permanent memories, it needs to further process and categorize new sensory information. By placing stimuli into existing groups and categories, we are better able to mentally manipulate and store this information. This organization into mental categories begins early in life, such as smiling, happy versus unhappy faces, unfriendly facial expressions, friend versus foe, safe versus unsafe, colors and shapes, names of people or of objects, edible versus inedible, food or drink, fruits or vegetables, and so on. Placing sensory inputs into meaningful mental groupings and naming them is part of the processing of information leading to working memories.

CogniByte
Working memory is the scratch pad of the brain. It allows us to retain important information needed to carry out a task over a few minutes. Everyday examples include remembering a telephone number; where you left your car keys, purse, or wallet; directions to a restaurant; or a short list of items to purchase at the supermarket.

Structured Exercises: 10 points per hour

Answers to these exercises can be found on page 282.

EXERCISE 1

Find the words below in the puzzle:

brain	stimuli	exercise
attention	long term	diet
grey matter	short term	health
memory	senses	reserve
smart	cognition	intelligence
think	visual	
perception	auditory	

```
D Y O O G R E Y M A T T E R L P Z A F B
I N T E L L I G E N C E I U Y T R Q P U
E T Y O M E M O R Y M K Q E E P N C B I
T E C Y R A J U A U D I T O R Y P O B S
E X S H O R T T E R M P M O N N B G V M
C E X T X R Z T W S A Q H F O K L N F A
B R A I N A M W E L O S T I M U L I N R
S C K N H V T F A N D S T A P L H T R T
E I Y G T F K U F D T P Q Z T T O I E H
N S T E N N S E E M E I M V L R Q O S V
S E W Y I I W Z I C Q E O A U O G N E L
E Y W H V H G I R I K B E N J U W Z R L
S P T O M N R E W U I H N V Y H F T V H
K U F G T R P U L O N G T E R M X A E O
```

EXERCISE 2

Find the words below in the puzzle:

puzzle

brain cell

perception

coordination

fitness

energy

response

brain twister

left brain

right brain

remember

capacity

quick

sharp

clever

intelligent

wise

cunning

genius

```
D Y O O P U Z Z L E B H E V B A M Q C E
B B O I Y T R E M E M B E R S K G H A L
V R R E S P O N S E S D G A S L N G P S
L A D A N G P I N T E L L I G E N T A R
N I X N I I E O E U U Q W K Y H L Q C I
G N N C M N R W I R H J C L J F N B I G
G T X C V Z C O O R D I N A T I O N T H
E W R A J K E E L Z U C B C K T M N Y T
N I I W U O P T L Q S G L L N N X P O B
I S H A R P T A P L N Q E E N E R G Y R
U T J C X W I S E P X I O V U S X V J A
S E V J H K O J B F K A S E U S V C X I
H R W D C U N N I N G Z N R X C M B V N
J L E F T B R A I N H D G V J K H P U Y
```

EXERCISE 3

Refer to Level 3, Exercise 3 in the color insert.

EXERCISE 4

Identify the photo and fill in the crossword puzzle.

EXERCISE 5

Place the following words into the appropriate space:

brain
exercise
health
memory
nutrition
smart
think

EXERCISE 6

Complete the following crossword puzzle.

ACROSS

3. Mentally fit people have more of this
4. The sea horse–shaped part of the brain
6. Peas are part of this family

DOWN

1. Necessary for a healthy brain and body
2. Debilitating illness of the brain
5. A diet with positive effects on cognitive performance
7. Physical and mental fitness come from this

EXERCISE 7

There are multiple perspectives that can be viewed in the shapes below. How many can you find in each?

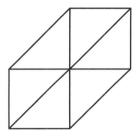 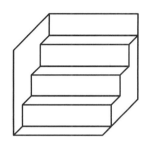 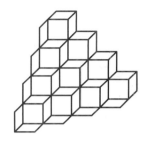

EXERCISE 8

Which of these shapes could be made into tangible objects?

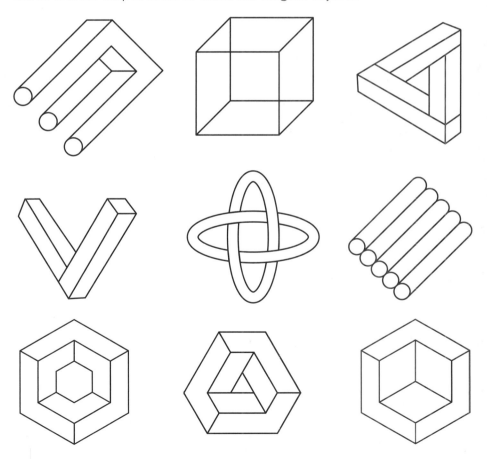

EXERCISE 9

Can you figure out each of these brain twisters?

1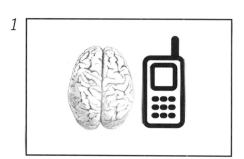

2 | brain   brain |

3 **matter**

4 **memory(x-y²)=z**

5 **memory**
memory

6 **sense**
sense
sense
sense
sense

7 **second**

8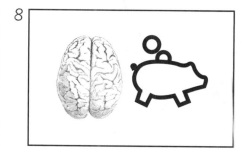

EXERCISE 10

Refer to Level 3, Exercise 10 in the color insert.

EXERCISE 11

Refer to Level 3, Exercise 11 in the color insert.

EXERCISE 12

Refer to Level 3, Exercise 12 in the color insert.

EXERCISE 13

Changing only one letter at a time to form a new word, change the top word into the bottom word. We've solved one of them to show you how.

KEY	FIT	BAD	GET	FIT
H E Y	- - -	- - -	- - -	- - -
H E P	FAN	FAT	FIT	- - -
H I P				- - -
TIP				YOU

MORE	LIVE	HEAD	STAY	GOOD
- - - -	- - - -	- - - -	- - - -	- - - -
- - - -	- - - -	- - - -	- - - -	- - - -
WISE	- - - -	- - - -	- - - -	- - - -
	WELL	- - - -	- - - -	- - - -
		GAME	- - - -	- - - -
			- - - -	- - - -
THINK	BRAIN		WISE	- - - -
- - - - -	- - - - -			IDEA
- - - - -	- - - - -			
- - - - -	- - - - -			
- - - - -	- - - - -			
QUICK	- - - - -			
	- - - - -			
	- - - - -			
	- - - - -			
	SMART			

Level 3. Additional Structured Exercises: 10 points per hour

- Use a structured online or software program that includes time-estimation, naming, categorizing, and short-term working memory exercises.

- Attend a class about medieval history, modern American writing, or any other topic that challenges you to process, organize, and learn new information.

Unstructured Activities: 5 points per hour

- Playing an instrument you already know

- Analyzing optical illusions from a book or online

- Taking a page from a book and categorizing the words according to length, starting letter, conceptual category, and/or part of speech.

- Tackling a messy closet or drawer, removing the items, and replacing them by categories that make sense to you

- Reorganizing your reading and musical libraries, computer documents and files, emails, collections, and magazines into meaningful groups

- Writing down the detailed steps and directions for everyday tasks, such as getting dressed or preparing breakfast

- Attending an art exhibition or viewing paintings and sculpture in a gallery (describe the specific details and attributes of each piece: materials used, technique, subject matter)

Level 4: Memory and Learning: Acquiring Knowledge

The major brain muscles exercised in Level 4 are the following:

- Working (short-term) memory

- Long-term memory

- Motor memory

- Learning

The vast majority of working memories are quickly forgotten. Those important short-term memories destined for long-term storage are integrated with older memories already in the hippocampus and cortex. The repeated processing of information is the basis for learning facts and figures. Repetition is the method for most school-based learning. Learning and memory are intimately linked.

Motor memory refers to our brain's ability to perform simple muscle tasks without focused conscious awareness. The repetition of specific muscle movements controlled and directed by the brain is the basis of motor memory. Your ability to tie your shoelaces without looking is an example of a motor memory. Have you ever tried to explain such a simple physical activity as tying your shoelace to someone just with spoken instructions? It's not easy putting into words a habit that you perform basically without thinking.

Structured Exercises: 10 points per hour

Answers to these exercises can be found on page 287.

EXERCISE 1

For each of the exercises below, look at each character set (numbered 1–10) one at a time for 15 seconds, then write the characters on a separate piece of paper. Hint: use a blank piece of paper to cover the sets you are not focusing on.

1. G27
2. Y6N
3. 4ET
4. HRE94
5. LW21G
6. JLDW5
7. DFG4X
8. 34GHG5W3
9. E4AER684
10. RIG5S34D

*For each of the exercises below, look at each character set (numbered 11–20), one at a time for 15 seconds, then write the characters **backward** on a separate piece of paper. Hint: use a blank piece of paper to cover the sets you are not focusing on.*

11. FG5
12. 2DT
13. E5UG
14. SD5H
15. F35K
16. R5I7
17. FK7S
18. J7F8A3D
19. 6CH56DS
20. D57JU58

For each of the exercises below, have someone read aloud each character set (numbered 21–30). Wait 15 seconds, then write the characters on a separate piece of paper.

21. R54
22. B2J
23. D54
24. S435T
25. C57GV
26. S13YI
27. R6OUI
28. S3H4RYKG
29. 38P7E354
30. QE5YFX76

*For each of the exercises below, have someone read aloud each character set (numbered 31–40). Wait 15 seconds, then write the characters **backward** on a separate piece of paper.*

31. 4R9
32. 4YU
33. 5TY
34. J7FG3
35. BNT3U
36. KM7OU
37. Y4UIK
38. D59Q4ER
39. W2I7D58
40. 2UYAW87

EXERCISE 2, A – H

Using the grid on page 198, look at each horizontal row of objects for 15 seconds, then write the names of each of the objects in order on a separate piece of paper. Hint: cover the extra rows and columns with a blank sheet of paper to focus on one set at a time.

EXERCISES 3, I – P

Using the grid on page 198, look at each vertical column of objects for 15 seconds, then write the names of each of the objects in order on a separate piece of paper. Hint: cover the extra rows and columns with a blank sheet of paper to focus on one set at a time.

EXERCISES 4, Q – U

Using the grid on page 198, look at each diagonal column of objects for 15 seconds, then write the names of each of the objects in order on a separate piece of paper. Hint: cover the extra rows and columns with a blank sheet of paper to focus on one set at a time.

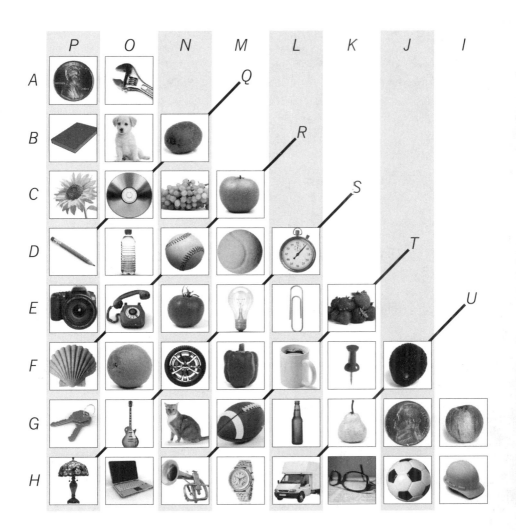

For the exercises below, cover the extra rows and columns with a blank sheet of paper to focus on one set at a time.

EXERCISE 5

For each exercise spend 15 seconds reviewing the photos and their corresponding letter. Then turn the page and write the letter that corresponds to the photo.

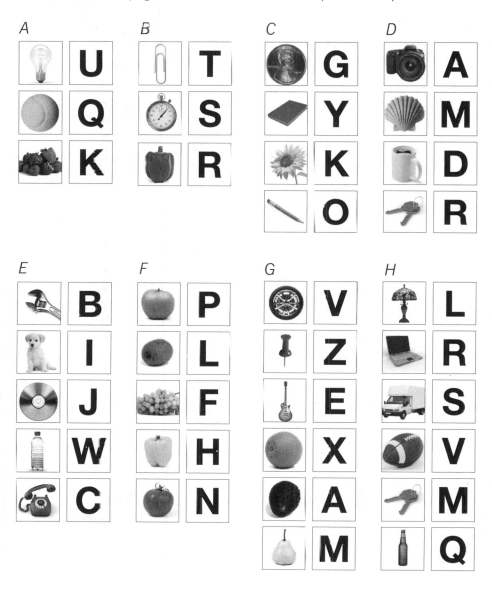

EXERCISE 5

Write the letter that corresponds to the photo from the previous page.

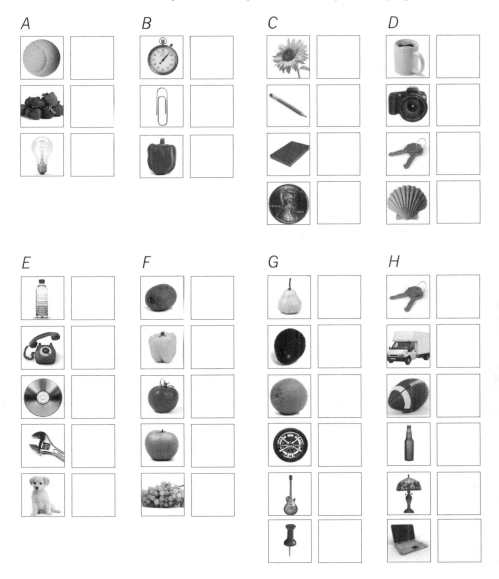

EXERCISE 6

For each of the lists below, remember the number that corresponds to the word, then on the following page write the number next to the corresponding word.

A		B		C		D	
cup	5	dog	2	paper	4	blue	9
friend	3	bowl	6	key	5	bottle	4
book	1	orange	7	bell	1	pencil	2
				rope	0	cat	6

E		F		G		H	
wallet	1	lamp	3	grape	1	cow	8
cord	5	towel	5	sand	6	leaf	6
rug	2	button	9	soap	3	oil	3
coin	4	horn	0	toy	2	shelf	1
phone	7	tea	1	pink	1	door	4
				penny	4	shirt	2

I		J		K		L	
milk	3	coffee	9	cart	2	lamp	4
shoe	5	window	6	chair	8	hat	6
hair	8	pants	4	grass	1	battery	3
clip	7	stand	8	shell	6	cord	1
box	1	tray	5	apple	5	seed	7
basket	6	mug	2	ink	7	tree	8
picture	2	bucket	1	camera	4	rock	2
				nail	3	dime	5

EXERCISE 6

A	*B*	*C*	*D*
friend	bowl	paper	bottle
book	dog	bell	blue
cup	orange	rope	cat
		key	pencil

E	*F*	*G*	*H*
cord	button	pink	shelf
phone	tea	sand	oil
rug	lamp	grape	door
wallet	horn	toy	cow
coin	towel	penny	leaf
		soap	shirt

I	*J*	*K*	*L*
basket	tray	apple	battery
shoe	stand	cart	seed
picture	window	grass	hat
clip	mug	camera	rock
hair	bucket	shell	lamp
milk	coffee	ink	cord
box	pants	chair	dime
		nail	tree

For each of the exercises below, perform the calculations in your head.

EXERCISE 7

A. $(8 \times 3) + (2 \times 5)$

B. $(3 \times 5) - (4 \times 8)$

C. $(6 \times 8) + (3 \times 6)$

D. $(3 \times 8) - (7 \times 4)$

E. $(7 \times 3) + (9 \times 4)$

F. $(9 \times 7) - (6 \times 4)$

G. $(3 \times 6) + (7 \times 4)$

H. $(2 \times 8) - (6 \times 5)$

I. $(8 \times 7) + (3 \times 4)$

J. $(9 \times 7) - (3 \times 3)$

EXERCISE 8

A. $(9 \div 3) + (8 \div 2)$

B. $(9 \div 3) - (8 \div 2)$

C. $(8 \div 4) + (6 \div 2)$

D. $(4 \div 2) - (3 \div 1)$

E. $(2 \div 2) + (6 \div 2)$

F. $(8 \div 4) - (8 \div 2)$

G. $(5 \div 1) + (7 \div 1)$

H. $(6 \div 3) - (8 \div 4)$

I. $(8 \div 2) + (8 \div 2)$

J. $(6 \div 2) - (8 \div 4)$

EXERCISE 9

A. (355×3)

B. (697×2)

C. (447×7)

D. (123×3)

E. (189×8)

F. (258×7)

G. (321×8)

H. (115×2)

I. (451×5)

J. (145×7)

EXERCISE 10

A. $(18 \times 3) + (10 \times 5)$

B. $(13 \times 5) - (41 \times 8)$

C. $(65 \times 8) + (24 \times 6)$

D. $(35 \times 2) - (37 \times 4)$

E. $(94 \times 7) + (16 \times 3)$

F. $(78 \times 30) - (10 \times 45)$

G. $(13 \times 50) + (41 \times 83)$

H. $(65 \times 68) - (24 \times 56)$

I. $(35 \times 18) + (37 \times 24)$

J. $(94 \times 27) - (16 \times 34)$

Level 4. Additional Structured Exercises: 10 points per hour

- Enroll in a memory course at your local college or community education center.

- Attend a music or art appreciation class.

- Under the guidance of an instructor, learn new dances or take up yoga, tennis, golf, or bowling. These all involve forming new motor memories.

Unstructured Activities: 5 points per hour

- Ask a friend to recite a phone number to you slowly, then repeat it back. Once you have mastered the number, recite it backward. Practice this as often as needed to do it correctly. Then start over with a new number.

- Tie your shoelaces without looking. This is an example of a motor memory. Practice other simple physical tasks without using your eyes to build and strengthen motor memories.

- While watching the local weather forecast on TV or after viewing it on your computer, see how well you remember the expected high temperatures for six surrounding towns by writing them down and checking yourself for accuracy; a digital video recorder (DVR) helps.

- Memorize the names of stores sequentially as you walk down your favorite shopping street or section of a mall and write them down in order when you get home.

- Memorize a list of items that you need to buy in the supermarket and go shopping without your list. Start with a few items and lengthen the list as you gain proficiency with practice over time.

- Draw from memory the floor plan of a large store you have

recently visited. Identify the various departments, locations of entrances, and so on. Be as specific as possible. You'll get better with repetition.

- Listen to or watch a newscast and, when it is over, write down summaries of the stories and feature presented. Start with a 10-minute segment of the newscast and extend your observation time by 5 minutes every week or two. Within a few months, you will be able to re-create a complete 30-minute broadcast.

- Memorize the names of books on a shelf in the library or a bookstore. After you leave that area, write down the names of the books in order. Start with a small section of the shelf and build up your ability over time. You can also do this with authors. Then combine the two.

- Learn new vocabulary words; opening a dictionary to a random page is an easy way to begin.

- Listen to an audiobook and write a synopsis of each chapter after listening to the book.

Level 5: Thinking and Communicating

The major brain muscles exercised in Level 5 are the following:

- Motor skills and habits

- Language

- Analyzing and planning

Once the brain forms memories and acquires knowledge, the brain begins to analyze and prioritize, and it starts making plans for the future. All of this is what we call thinking. Thinking leads to actions. Actions are the outputs of the brain expressed by thoughts and as directions to move muscles. The brain directs the muscles of your hands and feet to execute innumerable highly complex motor skills.

Through its control of the muscles involved in the production of speech, the brain expresses itself through spoken language. Language can take many forms, including writing, and conveys your thoughts to others. Dancing, participating in sports, composing music, playing a musical instrument, drawing, and painting are other examples of thinking expressed as complex and expressive motor activities.

Structured Exercises: 10 points per hour

- Enrolling in a course for public speaking

- Learning a new language

- Learning a new musical instrument

- Enrolling in a class for ceramics, needlepoint, woodworking, fly tying, or any other challenging craft or hobby

Answers to the following exercises can be found on page 288:

EXERCISE 1

Step 1:
Using your finger or another pointer, find your way through each maze.

Step 2:
Draw the correct path through the maze without touching the walls.

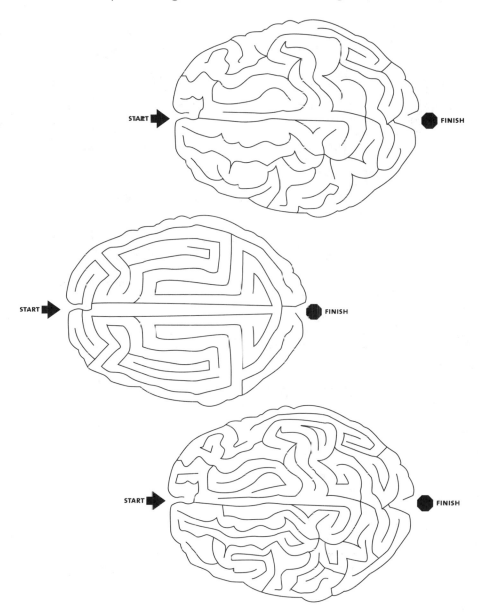

EXERCISE 2

Step 1:

Using your finger or another pointer, find your way through each maze.

Step 2:

Draw the correct path through the maze without touching the walls.

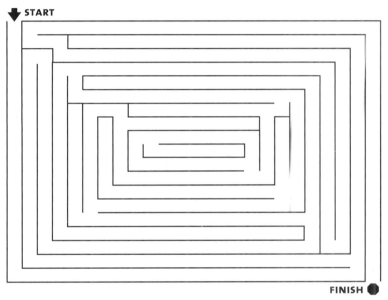

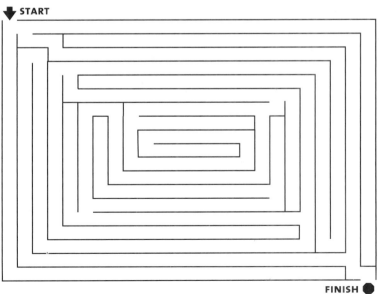

EXERCISE 3

Step 1:

Observe the drawing for 15 seconds, then redraw it from memory on a blank piece of paper.

Step 2:

While looking at the original drawing, copy it onto a blank piece of paper.

Step 3:

Redraw the drawing from memory, again on a blank piece of paper.

EXERCISE 4

Redraw the picture here on a blank sheet of paper. When you finish, turn the page around and see how well you did.

Step 1:

Observe the drawing for 15 seconds, then redraw it from memory on a blank piece of paper.

Step 2:

While looking at the original drawing, copy it onto a blank piece of paper.

Step 3:

Redraw the drawing from memory, again on a blank piece of paper.

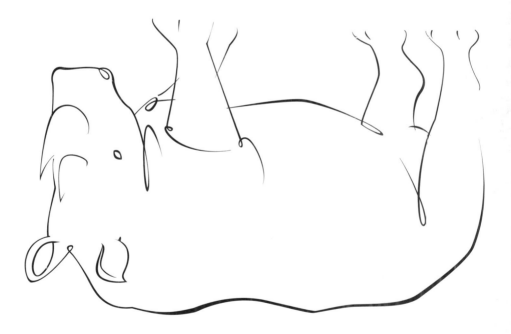

EXERCISE 5

Step 1:

Observe the drawing for 15 seconds, then redraw it from memory on a blank piece of paper.

Step 2:

While looking at the original drawing, copy it onto a blank piece of paper.

Step 3:

Redraw the drawing from memory, again on a blank piece of paper.

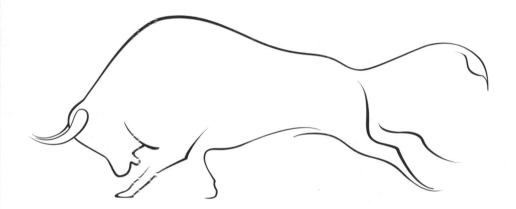

EXERCISE 6

Step 1:

Observe the drawing for 15 seconds, then redraw it from memory on a blank piece of paper.

Step 2:

While looking at the original drawing, copy it onto a blank piece of paper.

Step 3:

Redraw the drawing from memory, again on a blank piece of paper.

*For each of the exercises below, read the paragraph then rewrite the para-
graph, word for word, as best you can from memory on a blank sheet of paper.*

EXERCISE 7

William lives in the suburbs with his wife and their two children. Susie
is eight. Cory is six. They all have brown hair. Cory and his father have
matching eye color. Susie has her mother's green eyes.

EXERCISE 8

Paul and Rich sat down for a meeting with Chris in front of his computer. Paul wore a blue shirt, Rich wore a black shirt, and Chris wore a
green shirt. Each of the three had a cup of coffee. Paul drank his black,
Rich had cream, and Chris had cream and sugar.

EXERCISE 9

Jim drives ten miles east to get to work five days a week. On his way
he first passes a grocery store, then a gas station, and then a hardware
store. For lunch he always drives a mile back toward his home on the
same roads to a restaurant that is just past the gas station.

For each of the exercises below, read the paragraph from the previous exercise and answer the questions.

EXERCISE 10 *(read paragraph from Exercise 7)*

1. What color is William's wife's hair?

2. What color are William's wife's eyes?

3. Where do William and his family live?

4. How old are William's children?

5. Who has the same eye color as William?

EXERCISE 11 *(read paragraph from Exercise 8)*

1. Who was in the meeting?

2. Where was the meeting held?

3. What were the colors of the shirts, and who wore which color?

4. Who owned the computer?

5. How did the owner of the computer drink his coffee?

EXERCISE 12 *(read paragraph from Exercise 9)*

1. How far does Jim drive in a work day?

2. What businesses does Jim drive past on his way to work?

3. How far does Jim drive when he goes to lunch?

4. What direction is Jim's home from his job?

5. How many times a week does Jim pass the hardware store?

Level 5. Unstructured Activities: 5 points per hour

- Tracing a series of drawings or photographs

- Copying simple drawings

- Doing needlepoint work, building models, tying flies for fishing, and engaging in other hobbies that demand eye-hand coordination

- Copying a paragraph from a book or magazine using your non-dominant hand

- Practicing mirror writing by placing a mirror perpendicular to a piece of paper and writing a sentence looking only through the mirror (this can be very challenging)

- Practicing threading a needle, using magnifying lenses if necessary

Level 6: Executive Functions

The major brain muscles exercised in Level 6 are the following:

- Analyzing and planning

- Executing and achieving

- Imaginative thinking

The Level 6 exercises are designed to strengthen the gray matter of your frontal lobes. Higher-level cognitive functions use processed information and stored memories—in other words, knowledge—to plan, make decisions, and execute complex tasks. Success at this level of the cognitive pyramid depends on integration of activities of all your brain muscles.

Structured Exercises: 10 points per hour

Answers to these exercises can be found on page 290.

EXERCISES 1–4

Sudoku puzzles

Fill in the empty boxes with the numbers 1 through 9. Each row, column, and 3x3 box must contain the numbers 1 through 9.

1

9		6				3		
	2	8		5	4	7		
	5		7		9		8	
4	6		2				7	
			1	9	7			
	3				6		2	8
	9		6		5		1	
		2	9	3		8	6	
		7				9		5

2

3	8				6			9
				5	7		3	
7	5	6	1				2	
		7		2		3		5
4			3		1			7
1		3		8		4		
	3				2	1	9	8
	1		9	3				
9			6				5	3

3

			3	5	2			
	7			1			9	
	8	3				5	4	
		5			1			
1		4		7		6		5
		9			7			
	5	2			3	7		
	9			2			1	
			8	6	3			

4

7	2			5		4		3
		3						9
6					3		2	7
		8	7		2			
1				3				6
			5		1	3		
	8		9					1
3						2		
4		5		2			6	8

EXERCISE 5

Place the following in the proper hierarchical order.

A

B

C

D

EXERCISE 6

Rearrange the words below to form a sentence.

1. your exercise mind

2. open an mind keep

3. your lose mind use or it

4. are you you eat what

5. a waste thing is terrible to a mind

6. we the wiser get the older we become

7. active to critical sleep is an brain keep

8. stay every day your mentally challenge brain to fit

9. exercise brain are a way to great your mind twisters

10. healthy a diet good and essential exercise are regular to a brain

EXERCISE 7

Keeping them in a three-by-three layout, arrange the following circles into a more condensed space by only moving four of them.

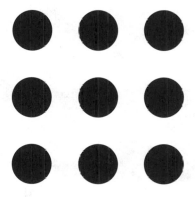

EXERCISE 8

Using as few moves as possible, rearrange the balls so that the triangle pattern points down instead of up.

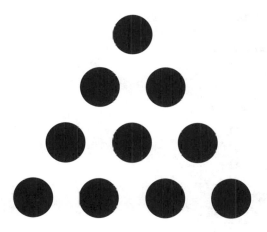

EXERCISE 9

Which box is opened?

1

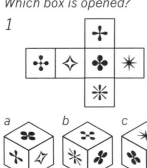

2

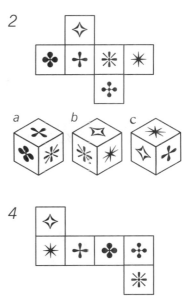

3

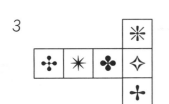
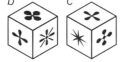
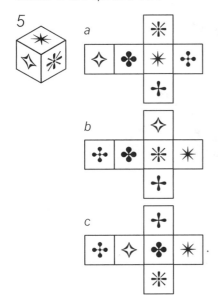

4

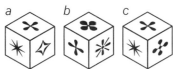
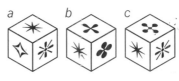

Which is the opened box?

5

6

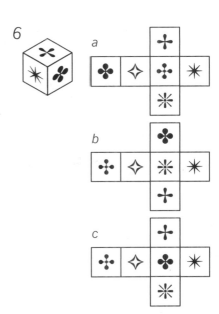

EXERCISE 10

Bill is standing 8th in line with 12 people. There are 2 men to his left, and 4 women to his right. How many men are in line?

EXERCISE 11

You don't want to wake your spouse, nice person that you are, so you are dressing in the dark. You have six shoes of three colors, and 24 socks, black and brown. How many socks and shoes must you take into the light to be certain that you have a matching pair of socks and a matching pair of shoes?

EXERCISE 12

Make the following numbers equal 2 using any mathematical symbols you like:

$$2 \quad 2 \quad 2 \quad 2 = 2$$

Level 6. Additional Structured Activities: 5 points per hour

- Reading a chapter in a novel and after a few days rewriting the chapter from memory. Then comparing your writing with that of the original author (this brain-building exercise was actually done by Benjamin Franklin)

- Taking a class in drama, financial planning, philosophy, comparative religion, the scientific method, or any thought-provoking subjects

- Reading and critically discussing a novel or biography in a group

- Participating in political or foreign affairs discussion groups

- Becoming involved in community, religious, educational, or service organizations

- Getting that high school or college degree you always wanted

Unstructured Activities: 5 points per hour

- In a quiet place, totally redesign your living room in your head and then draw it on graph paper.

- Design your dream home inside of your head. When you are finished, draw it. Add as many details as you can imagine.

- Plan your dream vacation, including destinations, transportation, lodging, and meals. Figure out your budget too!

- Plan and plant a garden.

- Read books that stimulate your imagination: invention and inventors, biographies, science, science fiction, the arts.

- Request an annual report from a company of interest to you as a possible investment. Analyze it and then call the company with specific questions.

- Get into the habit of critically reading news from a variety of sources and of different editorial opinions.

- Reedit a piece of music using computer editing tools.

- Create a lecture about your favorite leisure activity, interest, or work.

- Using only a newspaper headline, speak extemporaneously to create the entire story.

- Learn as much as you can about a famous person you admire. Analyze and describe the personality that led to his or her notoriety.

Level 7: Imagination, Creativity, Wisdom

The major brain muscles exercised in Level 7 are the following:

- Imaginative thinking

- Creativity

From inventing a new practical device to programming software, creating economic models, doing basic research, writing prose or poetry, composing music or choreography, and sculpting, the brain's creative capacity has no limits. It is truly the pinnacle of human endeavor. It is never too late in life to call on the wisdom you have accumulated and use it in novel, creative ways. So, stretch your brain with some of the suggestions here or ideas of your own. You will be amazed at your hidden creative talents.

Structured Exercises: 10 points per hour

- Take an advanced class in a creative area that gets your creative juices flowing: design, music, business, philanthropy, visual arts, mathematics, dance, science.

EXERCISE 1

A. *Complete the drawings by filling in the details.*

B. *Using the same outline, create a drawing with a totally different theme.*

EXERCISE 2

A. *Complete the drawings by filling in the details.*

B. *Using the same outline, create a drawing with a totally different theme.*

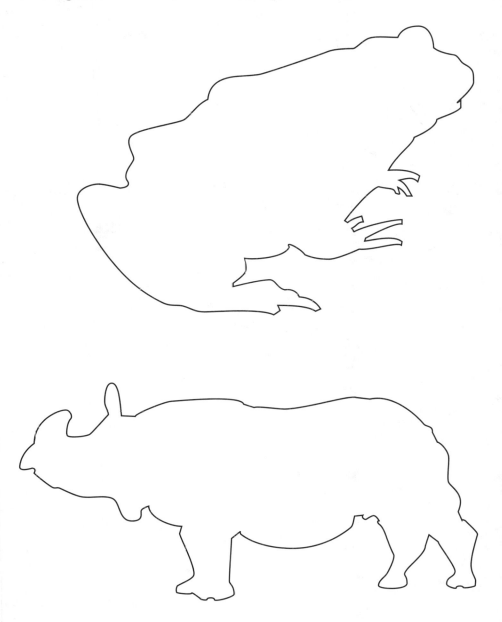

EXERCISE 3

A. *Complete the drawings by filling in the details.*

B. *Using the same outline, create a drawing with a totally different theme.*

For each exercise below, create a composition that tells a story including each of these images. You may resize the images as you like.

EXERCISE 4

EXERCISE 5

EXERCISE 6

EXERCISE 7

EXERCISE 8

EXERCISE 9

Using words for the images you have created in Exercises 1B, 2B, and 3B, write a one-page story.

EXERCISE 10

A. *Complete the drawing using the following suggestions as subject matter: earring, hair, headphones.*

B. *Complete the drawing using the following suggestions as subject matter: surfboard, whale, sunset.*

C. *Now use your own imagination to create a one-paragraph story that describes your drawings.*

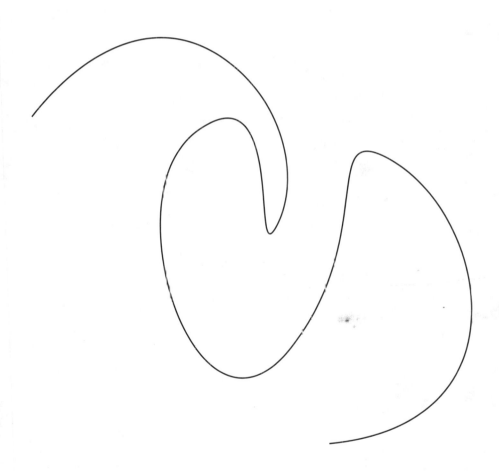

EXERCISE 11

A. *Complete the drawing using the following suggestions as subject matter: comb, man, glasses.*

B. *Complete the drawing using the following suggestions as subject matter: telephone, hair, face.*

C. *Now use your own imagination to create a one-paragraph story that describes your drawings.*

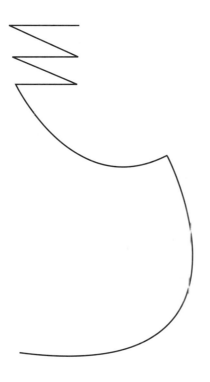

EXERCISE 12

A. Complete the drawing using the following suggestions as subject matter: cacti, building, moon.

B. Complete the drawing using the following suggestions as subject matter: teeth, sound, chin.

C. Now use your own imagination to create a one-paragraph story that describes your drawings.

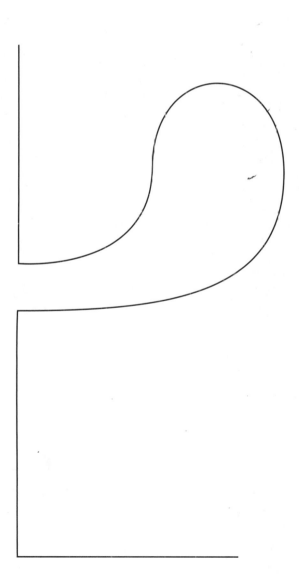

EXERCISE 13

Fill in the conversation between these two people.

EXERCISE 14

Fill in the conversation between these two people.

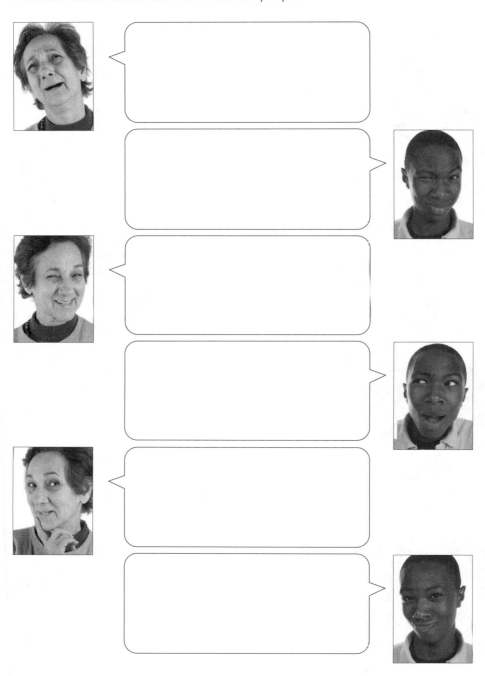

EXERCISE 15

Fill in the conversation between these two people.

Unstructured Activities: 5 points per hour

- Write four short stories using your most vivid imagination from the following elements: (1) A wandering minstrel, a spirited horse, and a family living in rural America at the time of the American Revolution; (2) A swashbuckling space explorer, a young but naive member of royalty, and a distant planet under siege from a villainous alien civilization; (3) A young struggling actor, in the Big Apple, a subway that transports him to September 10, 2001; (4) You, a $30 million lottery jackpot, rules that require you to use $20 million of it for philanthropic purposes.

- Select a recipe from your favorite book or file. Write down the steps it has taken for each ingredient to reach your kitchen, starting with the seed planted by the farmer. You can do the same thing for a household appliance.

- Write your life history.

- Write a personal philosophy for living.

- Create your own crossword puzzle using a list of words that you obtain from a newspaper story.

- Create a Sudoku or other puzzle.

- Create a business plan from a new idea. Don't worry about its practicality.

- Write a movie script or an advertisement for a product you use.

- Create your own movie using your video camera and computer.

- Create lyrics to music that has none.

- Write music, a poem, or a short story.

- Sketch a drawing or paint a picture.

Chapter 8

STRESS BUSTERS

"We are, perhaps, uniquely among the earth's creatures, the worrying animal."—LEWIS THOMAS, MD

In this chapter, you'll learn how to harness the brain-building power of mild stress while reducing the excessive stress that can damage your mind and body.

CAN STRESS BE GOOD FOR YOU?

You may be surprised to know that stress is actually essential to brain health. Neuroscientists have produced groundbreaking work on stress and its impact on the brain, and they've discovered that, in order to learn, we need a certain amount of short-term tolerable stress to stay sharp and grow our brains. But as with nearly all medical science and physiology (and most aspects of life), there is good and bad and everything in between.

STRESS THAT ENHANCES MEMORY (AND OTHER BODY FUNCTIONS)

In the brain, moderate, occasional stress promotes new cell generation in the hippocampus and new connections between existing neurons and neuronal networks. As explained earlier in the book, the enjoyable stress of modest physical exercise may be the best friend your hippocampus has when it comes to growing new cells. Healthy emotions are another type of mild stress—in this case, mental stress. Emotions trigger the amygdala to work with the hippocampus to form memories. It is easier to form permanent memories when an emotional component is part of our experience. Seeing a grandson get his first hit in Little League, attending a son's or a daughter's wedding, or receiving an unexpected promotion at work are good examples of lasting, emotionally triggered memories. The feelings of mild anxiety or eager anticipation, the gentle fluttering of your heart, or the butterflies in your stomach, which we all experience at such important life events are manifestations of mild, tolerable, time-limited, brain-healthy stress.

A certain amount of stress can actually improve your short-term memory. Think of how the pressure and sense of urgency of an impending deadline improves your focus, concentration, and efficiency. Like writing a book! This stress causes the brain to process new information more quickly and with greater efficiency, which translates into better memories.

Stress in moderation is also conducive to health in other systems and organs in your body. As an example, your immune system needs a form of stress to help it stay on guard to protect against serious pathogens and cancer.

Mild physical stress also challenges our bodies to grow stronger. When you exercise, you stress your muscles, heart, lung, bones, and even some of your endocrine system. This stress, if not overwhelming, builds endurance and strength. Imagine our cave-dwelling ancestors, who needed to occasionally escape from a marauding tiger or search for hours on foot for their next meal. That was physical and mental stress! Successfully handling this stress made them not only physically more

CogniByte

The basic stress response, fight or flight, is genetic. It is built into our DNA. If it runs amok, however, or is turned on chronically, stress can impair memory formation and weaken the immune system. Thus, chronic stress impairs the evolutionary purpose of stress—ensuring survival in an acute life-threatening situation.

able but also smarter. They learned from these stressful events and stored this knowledge in their brains, transmitted it via language to family and friends, and passed it on through oral tradition to the next generation.

STRESS THAT DAMAGES MEMORIES

High chronic stress levels are unhealthy and have been shown to damage the hippocampus and thus impair memory and learning. Experimental rats that are kept from moving around freely, a condition that is seriously stressful for them, end up with shrunken hippocampal nerve cells, fewer dendritic branches, and fewer synaptic connections. The result is impaired memory and learning.

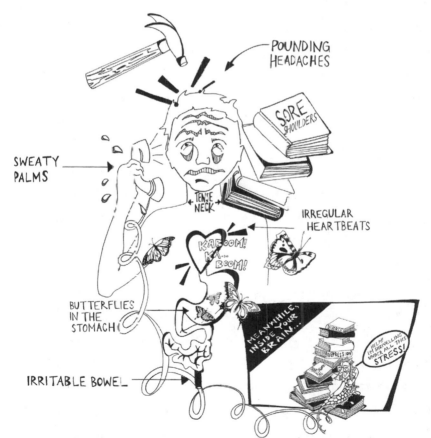

CHRONIC STRESS: BAD FOR BODY AND BRAIN

Chronic stress involves too much of the stress hormone cortisol circulating in the blood. One result is impaired production of brain growth factors, protein molecules that stimulate the growth of nerve cells, axons, dendrites, and synapses. One of the best-studied of the factors is brain-derived neurotrophic factor (BDNF), which has been called a Miracle-Gro fertilizer for the brain. Turn off the stress in the housebound rats by letting them freely exercise, and BDNF levels rise and the hippocampus grows again.

Revealing recent studies that use brain imaging document that the hippocampus shrinks over time in aging folks who are under chronic stress. The results are memory deficits and a brain that ages before its time. Other studies have demonstrated elevated cortisol levels in some depressed patients. With treatment, their cortisol levels decrease, memory improves, and the hippocampus enlarges.

Too much stress also affects the prefrontal cortex of the frontal lobes, the executive center of the brain. No wonder bad decisions at work or in our personal lives correlate with too much stress. Gray matter cells respond to high concentrations of certain neurotransmitters, like dopamine and norepinephrine, that are released in stressful situations, by misfiring while attempting to store long-term memories and to direct complex tasks. Chronic stress is a brain wrecker: it results in shrunken hippocampi, impaired cortical gray matter, poor memories, and bad decisions.

Too much stress affects other brain and body parts as well. If too much stress has weakened your immune system, function is impaired and serious diseases such as cancer may result. Chronic stress can also lead to sleep disorders, incapacitating depression, and panic attacks, as well as other mind-crippling psychological conditions. According to the World Health Organization, depression is the leading cause of disability in the United States and Canada, ahead of heart disease, any given cancer, and AIDS. About one in six American adults experiences depression at some time, and depression has approximately $26 billion in annual costs.

Stress also takes a toll on our intestinal system, resulting in common disorders such as a nervous stomach, dyspepsia, irritable bowel syndrome, and ulcers. Stress can exert an exorbitant price on our cardiovascular system, where it contributes to high blood pressure (hypertension), heart attacks (myocardial infarctions), and even irregular heart rhythms (arrhythmias) that can be felt and are themselves the source of additional stress. The same arrhythmias can lead directly to serious conditions such as stroke and even sudden death.

Dr. Robert Wilson and his colleagues in Chicago at the Rush Alzheimer's Disease Center and Institute for Healthy Aging use stress proneness—a personality trait that reflects a person's tendency to suffer psychological distress in response to unpleasant or negative emotional events in life—in their research. Hardiness, or resistance to psychological stress, is the complementary personality trait. Their study of about eight hundred 75-year-olds found that stress-prone women were more likely than others to have impaired memory for real-life events. Even more frightening was a correlation between stress level and risk of developing Alzheimer's disease. Over the study's period of almost five years, 140 participants were diagnosed with Alzheimer's disease. Those who had high stress proneness had twice the risk of developing Alzheimer's than those with low stress proneness or hardiness personalities.

HOW CAN YOU MAKE STRESS WORK FOR YOU?

Think about how boring life would be without any stress. The rush we feel from the stress of being given a problem to solve and then solving it is positive stress, or the thrill of doing something for the first time, learning a new craft, doing a new job, taking care of a sick grandchild or child. Such positive stressors leave us renewed and invigorated, with the feeling that we have grown. Think of skiing, driving a fast sports car, making a long putt with money on the line, or hiking a difficult trail.

CogniByte

Animals also experience stress, but there is a critical difference between us and them. As Joseph LeDoux explores in his book *Synaptic Self*, the Stanford University stress guru Robert Sapolsky noted that an animal in the wild may be stressed for 30 seconds at a time, such as during a frenzied sprint away from a predator. Urban-dwelling humans, however, have thirty-year mortgages, stock and housing market meltdowns that last years, unemployment, unpaid college tuition bills, job-related hassles, and drawn-out divorces. The seemingly unending nature of human stress, if not managed in a healthy way is what can impair memory formation and recall, and increase our risk of heart disease, depression, infections, cancer, and Alzheimer's disease.

Done correctly, these are positive, mentally stimulating, exciting stressors. They become dangerous and frightening only if done out of control with added unnecessary risk.

Stress builds strength when it is properly handled. It becomes dangerous, impairs function, and contributes to disease susceptibility when it lasts for weeks and months and is not dealt with in a healthy way. So let's figure out how to do that.

> *"Chronic stress isn't the only cause of anxiety and depression, and it doesn't necessarily lead to either of those disorders. But it is clearly at the root of much of our woe, both physiologically and psychologically."*
> —JOHN RATEY, MD, AUTHOR OF *SPARK*

GETTING STARTED

This chapter will arm you with a wealth of weapons to handle and minimize the negative stressors while emphasizing the positive stressors.

Take stock of the daily events that give you stress, and choose the stress-management technique that best suits your individual needs and personality, coping style, and severity of your stress. And don't be timid about experimenting. In this chapter I draw on my own experiences, both personal and professional, and the advice and recommendations of experts in the field to develop the recommendations here and on the accompanying DVD. In addition, in Part 3, you will find some other print and Internet-based resources. At some point, you will realize that you have incorporated what works for you into your lifestyle, and you will recognize that you feel better, are mentally sharper and focused, and are remembering more!

Don't be timid about seeking the help of a psychologist or psychiatrist with professional expertise if you cannot get to a comfortable stress level on your own.

Here's a three-step quick-start guide to managing the stress in your life:

1. First and foremost, listen to your body. Frequent nervous-stomach sensations, recurrent tension headaches, muscle tension and soreness, especially in the neck and shoulders, and chronic fatigue can all be physical manifestations or symptoms of stress.

2. Next, recognize that you are in a stressful situation or that your life has too much chronic stress. Admit that you feel stressed beyond your comfort zone. Each of us has a different threshold for stress and different tolerances. Often your spouse or one of your children will point out that you seem nervous, anxious, or stressed. Listen to them.

3. Finally, and this is usually the most difficult step, adjust your attitude. Give yourself a checkup from the neck up. Listen to your mind, and if tells you it feels stressed, take it seriously and take steps to be your own healer. If you feel you need help, get it from a spouse, friend, doctor, clergy, or other trusted source.

ATTITUDE

Endless research has determined that attitude is key when it comes to stress. It's a mind game, and you control the playing field. How you approach a stressful situation goes a long way in determining your health and well-being, your sense of fulfillment and joy in life, and specifically your chances of avoiding a stress-related illness. Observations over many decades document that folks who handle stress with confidence and recognize that it is a normal part of life have better general health and fewer stress-related illnesses.

People who maintain a commitment toward important professional and personal goals, who accept the reality that they cannot control every facet of life and that not everything works out as we desire, and especially those who see stress as a positive challenge to be dealt with as a learning experience feel better. Change is inevitable, and stress often accompanies it. A positive attitude works. People who approach change-related stress as a learning experience have a better chance of remaining healthy and happy.

TRIED-AND-TRUE STRESS-BUSTING TECHNIQUES
The Four Pillars of Stress Management

1. Keep at it. Believe in your chosen stress management technique and be disciplined. Make a commitment to yourself that you will keep at it for a minimum of a month. Even on days when you do not feel stressed, stick with your regimen. After a month, it is easier to extend the commitment because you are experiencing the benefits.

2. Pay attention and stay focused. Focus intensely on what you are doing, and this will help reduce your feelings of stress. Be in the moment. The mind has mechanisms to control what enters through the gates of perception and consciousness. Relaxation techniques (exercise, meditation, visualization, deep breathing) will help diminish stressful

inputs. If you use controlled breathing as your relaxation technique, the focus is on your breath—count the number of times you inhale and exhale, breathe in for five counts and exhale for five counts. You won't be able to think of anything else! And after several minutes of slowly inhaling and exhaling, your heart rate itself will slow down—a sign that you have less stress.

3. Repeat it. As they say, "Practice makes perfect." Most successful stress relief techniques are repetitious. The best-known example is the mantra, which is central to Far Eastern meditations. A mantra is a word or phrase that is repeated almost endlessly. The so-called zone of mental calmness and focus can be achieved by repeating either mental or physical activity. Try repetitive and focused breathing or visualizing a pleasant image such as a still lake lined with majestic trees, a stanza of a song that brings relaxation, a line or two of poetry, or a bit of familiar classical music. Remember past calming experiences to find a technique that works for you.

4. Combine mental and physical components. Many stress-reduction techniques combine a positive mental effort with a physical component. Take the example of breathing. Deep, slow breathing combined with a mental focus on the repetitive cycle of deep inhaling and slow exhaling is a stress-busting technique used around the world.

Exercise

We've already discussed the lasting and important brain and mental health benefits of a physical exercise program in chapter 6. Exercise is also a proven method of stress relief, a great mood booster, a reducer of anxiety, and even a treatment for some forms of depression. You can use it as a onetime remedy for an acute situation or as a long-term stress manager.

When you exercise, your brain releases endorphins, feel-good chemicals that are related to opiates. That's right, your brain has its own private pharmacy! A surge in production and release of these elixirs of euphoria is responsible for the marathon runner's high, as well as feelings of elation and sublime joy that follow vigorous exercise, sexual orgasm, and other forms of extraordinary excitement.

Building a regular, exercise-based stress-relief program into your daily routine is a kind of preventive maintenance for your hippocampus and overall mental state. Stressed out at home or at work? Simply walking out the door of your home or office and paying attention to nature is a potent way to de-stress. Can't get outdoors? Walk up and down several flights of stairs in your office building or go to your bedroom, close the door, and walk in place for 10 minutes while shadowboxing with your arms.

If your stress is rooted in everyday recurrent stressors like work, finances, or family issues, taking time out for exercise is a wonderful way to de-stress. You will come back with renewed energy, more confidence, and less anxiety. Not only does it release stress, it lowers your risk of memory loss, obesity, heart disease, stroke, diabetes, and perhaps even some types of cancer.

"Motion is a good thing for both soul and body, and immobility is bad."
—SOCRATES, IN PLATO'S *THEAETETUS* (153 B.C.)

Activities for Stress Relief

If you want to exercise, but don't like or cannot afford to join a gym or health and fitness center, walk, dance, jog, garden with some vigor, or find some other regular, moderately taxing physical activity. Choose something you find fun. If not, chances are that you will not continue. Mix it up for variety. Try to do your stress-relieving exercise in a group or with at least another person, not in isolation. The socialization and camaraderie are good for the brain and have been shown to have added benefits beyond stress relief.

Walking, especially outdoors, for 10 or 15 minutes in fresh air will refresh you, decrease stress, lift your mood, and enable you to return to what you were doing with a clearer, more focused mind.

Here are some more stress-busting physical activities to try:

- Yoga or Pilates

- Tennis

- Bicycling

- Rowing

- Golf—walk rather than ride a cart; even hitting a bucket of balls at the driving range is a powerful outlet for stress

- Dancing

- Tai chi

- Swimming pool exercises

- Bowling

- Ping-Pong

- Practicing fly casting

- Gardening

- Pool or billiards

- Gym or exercise activities: treadmill, stationary bicycle, spinning, rowing, jumping rope

- Weight training, stretching and toning exercises, and other forms of nonaerobic activity

Savor Your Food and Drink

The connections between the nerve endings in your nose that convey smell to the brain are among the most ancient parts of the evolutionary brain. They have dense connections with parts of your brain that are critical to your feelings about life and your mood. Savor your food or drink and concentrate on the relaxation and pleasurable sensations it can bring. Spend 15 minutes sipping a fresh glass of fruit juice or slowly eating a tasty snack such as fruit, nuts, or a healthy nutrition bar.

What works for you? That is the recipe. Fresh fruit and tasty vegetables are healthy, stress-reducing foods if you picture them in your mind to be effective. Slowly savor a crisp carrot or a small bunch of cool grapes. Sip fruit juice or a smoothie; eat a cold yogurt or even the occasional ice cream.

Reduce your intake of caffeine from tea, coffee, and colas. Watch out for heavily caffeinated energy drinks, which clearly can raise your stress level. Drink a relaxing tea such as green or chamomile instead. Don't smoke or drink alcohol to relax. A glass or two of red wine in the late afternoon or early evening should be part of socialization and a brain-healthy diet, not a remedy for stress.

Relax and Meditate

It is well documented that meditation and other relaxation techniques can help manage headaches, decrease blood pressure, partially control abnormal heart rhythms, lower cholesterol levels, and provide additional health benefits.

CogniByte

Most of us in the West view meditation as a means of stress reduction. But in other parts of the world, for instance, in India, Nepal, and other population centers of Buddhism, meditation is used as a strict and rigorous routine for mental fitness and training.

Yoga

Yoga is an ancient art, science, and philosophy that combines deep breathing and gentle exercises to improve physical and mental well-being. It is a popular and effective way to reduce stress If you have never participated and hesitate to get started, ask a friend who does yoga to recommend a local yoga studio or health club that offers yoga classes. Many community centers now offer yoga. Some yoga variants include meditation to produce mental relaxation. Many practitioners of yoga attest to developing improved focus, concentration, mental clarity, and memory. Documented studies have shown that yoga can reduce blood pressure, relieve some pain and discomfort associated with arthritis, and reduce the risk of heart and vascular disease.

Breath Control Exercises

Next time you feel stressed, find a quiet place, sit down, and take a few slow deep breaths. Changes in how you breathe affect your mental state and how your mind will interpret and react to an acute stressful situation. When you are feeling worried, anxious, or stressed, a few deep breaths will have a soothing, relaxing effect and will slow down your heart rate and respiration. Even fatigue can be partially compensated for by a deep breath or two—it can make you feel refreshed.

A particularly useful form of deep breathing and relaxation is abdominal breathing, in which you use your diaphragm more than your chest wall muscles. Opera singers and athletes use abdominal breathing not only for efficiency of physiologic air movement but also for stress release. Practice this by concentrating on drawing deep breaths from as low as you can in your abdomen. If you are successful, which you will be with practice, you will see your stomach rise and fall with each cycle.

Another way to practice abdominal breathing is to lie flat on a bed or floor, place one hand on your stomach and one on your heart, and make your breath travel between them. You can observe your hands rising and falling as the breath travels through the body.

Muscle Relaxation

A common physical manifestation of stress is a tightening, uncomfortable feeling in the muscles, especially those of the neck, back, sides of the head, and shoulders. Massage is a terrific way for muscles to relax and for the mind to feel more at ease. Qualified massage therapists can be found in private studios, health and fitness clubs, and community centers. Even many airports now feature 5- to 10-minute massages as a remedy for increasingly stressful air travel.

Another excellent muscle relaxation technique is to immerse yourself in warm water. A warm bath, hot tub, sauna, or warm shower are all relaxing.

Progressive Muscle Relaxation

Progressive muscle relaxation is a proven technique pioneered years ago by the American physician and physiologist Edmund Jacobson. He taught patients to reduce mental anxiety and uncomfortable stress by consciously focusing on the difference experienced between a tense muscle or group of muscles and that same muscle group in a relaxed, noncontracted state. The technique is simple: Sit or recline in a comfortable position with your eyes closed. Starting in one foot, tense or contract the muscles and hold them for about 10 to 15 seconds, and with each contraction concentrate on each muscle group. Then rapidly release the contraction. Now progress to the muscles in your calf and then your thigh; then do the same for the other lower extremity; then the abdomen, followed by the chest, arms one at a time, and neck and head. The idea is to experience the sensation of releasing physical tension, which then affects your mental state.

Mental Visualization

Turning your focus and attention to a soothing, mentally relaxing diversion can be a wondrous stress reliever. With your eyes closed, transport yourself to a place you associate with ultimate relaxation, tranquility, and well-being. It might be a particular location that you have visited or one that you've imagined, or one you've seen in the movies or in a snapshot. For me, it is a small lake high in the San Juan Mountains of Colorado that I have visited and fished. Concentrate on what each of your five senses would experience in your special place, such as the aroma of air after a summer's brief rain, the sound of wind in the pines and water lapping against the shore, the image of clouds with their imagination-stimulating shapes, and the soothing orange, pink, and purple hues of sunset. Or think of your favorite place as a child. After about 5 or 10 minutes, let your mind slowly drift away from this spot and back into your actual physical surroundings.

Music and Art

Another technique for stress relief is to listen with focus and concentration to classical music. Just 10 minutes helps me relax and recharge my mental batteries for another one or two hours of work.

My favorite form of active mental relaxation is to occupy my eyes and my brain by becoming absorbed in a beautiful painting. I do this either by turning my chair around in the office and studying what I have on the wall behind me, or opening a book of art and gazing on the works reproduced within.

Social Activities

There is a time to share and a time to be alone. In my opinion, most stress-relieving activities are best done alone, but this is certainly not a rule. By focusing on yourself and concentrating for 10 to 15 minutes on your breathing or muscle relaxation exercises, you will achieve your goals. Longer sessions such as hour-long exercise, yoga, and some group meditation classes are effectively done with others. Sharing in a group any number of activities is often a potent relaxer and brain protector. Dr. Lisa Berkman at the Harvard School of Public Health and her colleagues determined in a study of more than sixteen thousand retired Americans that social integration—doing activities with others—delays memory loss. Again, go back to what you have found works for you or experiment with some of the suggestions here to find ways to relax your body and mind. Trust your friends for other suggestions.

The Worldwide Stress Reducer

Another mental activity that can produce short-term stress reduction is surfing the Internet. Use your imagination. What is fun for you? If you are an avid shopper but only have a 10-minute break, obviously you are not able to stroll a mall. So "stroll" through the Internet.

PROFESSIONAL STRESS MANAGEMENT

If you've tried all of the activities in this chapter and still feel stressed out, I urge you to consider professional help. Even with the right attitude and approach, your situation may call for more intervention, especially if you find yourself using alcohol, cigarettes, prescription or nonprescription drugs, unsafe sex, or other unhealthy methods to deal with stress. Arrange a brief consultation with a professionally trained and experienced psychiatrist, psychologist, or another practitioner with specific expertise in stress reduction.

ESSENTIAL STEPS FOR A HEALTHY STRESS LEVEL

1. Recognize that stress is part of life. The right amount strengthens your memory but too much weakens it.

2. Make yourself No. 1, and take care of yourself.

3. Set realistic goals.

4. Take regular de-stressing breaks during each day, whether or not you feel stressed.

5. Use relaxation techniques, such as meditation, controlled breathing, muscle relaxation, and mental relaxation.

6. Exercise regularly.

7. Sleep well and long enough.

8. Take mini- or maxi-vacations.

9. Take a day off work periodically.

10. Force yourself, even when you are overloaded, to do social activities.

11. Watch your alcohol, caffeine, and prescription and over-the-counter drug intake.

12. Make meals and snacks relaxing times.

13. If necessary, consult an expert.

The good and bad news of stress depends on how you look at it. Healthy stress has been part of human existence since our ancestors first stood upright, and stress responses have evolved along with all other genetically determined traits. Healthy stress pushes our brains to grow and become more and more adept at handling life's circumstances as we age. In contrast, excessive chronic stress shrinks the hippocampus and impairs our abilities to form memories while also impairing the creative, problem-solving abilities of our gray matter. You can feel when stress has gotten the best of you. Recognizing this is the first step toward discovering the stress-busting techniques that work for you. With our powerful brains, we can train ourselves to find a livable solution and make it part of our daily routine. Your psychological and physical well-being depend on it.

THE NIGHT SHIFT: SLEEP YOUR WAY TO BEDROCK MEMORIES

Weary with toil, I haste me to my bed,
The dear repose for limbs with travel tired;
But then begins a journey in my head,
To work my mind when body's work's expired.
—WILLIAM SHAKESPEARE, SONNET 27

Would you believe that there is a science-based, proven treatment, developed and tested on billions of human subjects in countless clinical trials and free of side effects, that makes your memories stick—and makes you more attentive, improves learning through better concentration and focus, makes you more efficient at work and at play, improves your mood, reduces stress, reduces your risk of injury and death from accidents, and even primes your body's natural defense systems against many types of diseases? And it is free!

Another breakthrough for modern neuroscience! Well, not exactly. This treatment existed long before the disciplines of neurology and brain science saw the light of day. What is it? Sleep.

Working in their white coats among all sorts of high-tech equipment, brain scientists have again proven that your mother was right! Your brain performs better after a good night's sleep.

Sleep makes for easier remembering—whether of a technique you learned in a piano lesson or ceramics class, a new computer-based skill, cooking from a novel recipe, or any activity that requires practice for improvement. Sleep makes us feel better; enhances our capacity to learn, remember, and execute complex goal-oriented tasks; and optimizes us for maximal enjoyment and achievement in life.

In fact, how well someone slept the previous night has a stronger correlation with his or her enjoyment of the day than does household income or marital status. Just an extra hour of sleep improved enjoyment of the next day for 909 women who participated in a "day reconstruction method" study that characterized daily life experiences.

Sleep is also critical for our body's metabolic machinery to operate efficiently, for controlling our internal temperature, for optimizing immune function to protect against infections, for sexual performance, and for many more critical conscious and unconscious life-supporting functions of our brains and bodies.

How many times have you asked yourself, "Since I have only 24 hours in a day, why can't I cut back on sleep so that I will have more time for the critical things in my life?" Why can't you? Because sleep deprivation will eventually take its toll on your performance in all life's activities and in the long run may even shorten your life. An increased risk of death among those who slept less than six hours was one of the findings in a 2004 study of almost eighty-three thousand nurses.

Sleep-deprived individuals use more brain energy and recruit normally uninvolved brain areas to learn the same tasks as folks who are more rested. Researchers at several academic institutions here and abroad have demonstrated that sleep deprivation decreases learning and memory making. Sean Drummond at

CogniByte

"Why all this sleep?—seven, eight, nine, ten hours perhaps—with a living to make, work to be done, thoughts to be thought, obligations to keep, a soul to save, friends to refrain from losing, pleasure to seek, and that prodigious host of activities known as life?"

—Walter de la Mare, *Behold, This Dreamer* (1939)

the University of California, San Diego, concluded that "if you have been awake for 21 hours straight, your abilities are equivalent to someone who is legally drunk."

HOW SLEEP ENRICHES THE MIND

Until recently, our nocturnal sleep was thought of as a physiological state equivalent to short-term hibernation. Scientists thought that during sleep brain activity was turned way down and only those parts of the unconscious brain essential to keep you warm, breathing, and alive were operating, as if you were on autopilot. While it is undoubtedly true that some areas of your brain are powered down while you sleep, other brain areas populated by hardworking, night-shift neurons are firing away over and over again.

There is increasingly solid evidence that sleep actually enhances learning and problem solving in an active way, not just a passive one. While you sleep, the hippocampus and the cortical networks of memory and learning are activated repeatedly. Those same brain cells used during the day, whether you were studying Spanish, practicing the piano, trying out new software on your computer, or even memorizing the twenty-seven member states of the European Union are now repeating the same patterns of firing while you sleep. During these sleep "rehearsals," temporary memories of important newly learned skills and facts are transferred to the gray matter for long-term storage and for recall on demand. A Belgian study found that the same pattern of brain activity displayed while learning a computer task during the day was repeated during sleep. The brain actually practices the newly learned task while the body sleeps, strengthening the synaptic connections between cells. Plasticity in action!

Improving a complex motor skill like hitting a tennis ball involves hours of actual practice. Your brain retains the memory of the complex coordinated muscle activity needed to perform this task. That is why you get better with practice: the brain learns by repetition. But we now know you also practice while you sleep. Under the directorship of the hippocampus, your sleeping brain uses those same cortical gray matter cells that fired while you were in your tennis lesson to solidify the motor memory. Your brain is practicing that forehand volley while you sleep!

As another example of the importance of sleep in making lasting memories, let's consider the huge pasta dinner you ate with a few friends at a local Italian restaurant. That single gustatory experience produced thousands of different sensations and thoughts received in the brain: anticipation of a fine time, ambience of the locale, appearances of foods, dining partners, the hustle and bustle of activity in the restaurant, smells, tastes, sounds, words and thoughts of conversation, and countless other fleeting impressions.

If someone at the table made an outrageous, emotionally laden comment, there is a good chance your amygdala, the emotional sensor sitting alongside the hippocampus, sparked the hippocampus to take special notice. Later, while you sleep, the hippocampus reviews all of the meal's countless sensory inputs and your internal thoughts and decides which "frames" should be bundled together for permanent recording and what should be dumped into the rubbish. It works overtime to make sense of this incredible mass of information, this vast number of the waking brain's experiences. Then during sleep, those synaptic connections between cells involved with this aspect of the pasta dinner are strengthened—a process called memory consolidation. What remains the morning after is a fraction of those sensations bundled into a memory of the evening's meal.

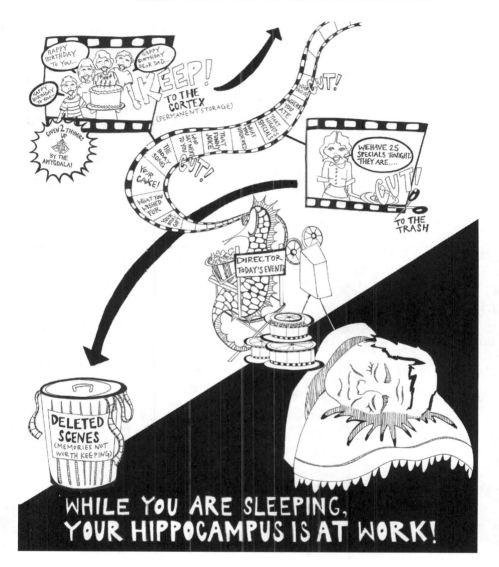

Solid Memories

The influence of the emotionally sensitive amygdala on consolidation deserves emphasis. This is why emotional events in our lives pack such a wallop when it comes to memory formation. They make strong, easily recalled memories. In the case of life's unpleasant emotional events, how often do we wish that these disturbing memories were not so solidly embedded?

A consolidated, solid memory is one that has been moved from its temporary site in the hippocampus to permanent storage in the cortex. A consolidated memory is a strong, easily recallable memory. Consolidation involves plasticity—adding and cementing synaptic connections. Without a good night's sleep, your brain has difficulty consolidating even your most basic memories from the previous day. Subsequently, the more often a memory is recalled or brought into consciousness—the more you practice your forehand volley, the more often you recount the pasta dinner, the more you use a recipe—the stronger or better consolidated is the memory. With each conscious recall during the day, with each practice during wakefulness, the hippocampus is primed again to do its nighttime work.

CogniByte

Even a daytime nap has the power to assist memory formation and learning. The Japanese Ministry of Health, Labor, and Welfare recommends that people nap for 20 to 30 minutes before 3 p.m. to boost health and work efficiency.

Problem Solving

It feels good to solve a problem, no matter how simple or complex it is. When you put your mind to reorganizing a closet or figuring out how to pay for that new home, coming up with a solution is gratifying. It is the unique capacity of our human brain with its large frontal lobe—no other animal has even 1 percent of our problem-solving abilities—to use knowledge stored in the gray matter to figure out solutions.

All the hustle and bustle of replaying newly learned items on your brain's screen during the night can even lead to true moments of brilliant insight. Most of us have occasionally had the feeling on waking of a new insight or even a solution to a problem we had been pondering the day before—eureka dreams, if you will. We now know the brain analyzes, learns, and problem solves during sleep.

In a revealing German study a few years ago, research subjects performed a brain-challenging mathematical task that could be solved by repetition and learning but solved more quickly if a hidden rule was grasped. After initial training in the task, some participants were allowed a good night's sleep while others were not. Eight hours later those who slept were almost three times as likely to recognize the hidden rule for solving the problem than those who were sleep deprived. Those who slept had an insight. While they slept, the hippocampus processed the memory—the learning and knowledge gained from the task. This restructuring and reordering during sleep produced the solution to the problem.

> **CogniByte**
>
> Historically, some well-known sleep facilitated examples of insights and creative breakthroughs are the lockstitch sewing machine patented by Elias Howe, the plot of Robert Louis Stevenson's classic *The Strange Case of Dr. Jekyll and Mr. Hyde,* and the tune for "Yesterday" by Beatle Paul McCartney.

Deirdre Barrett, a psychologist at Harvard Medical School's Behavioral Medicine Program, studies creative problem solving and has found that eureka dreams almost without exception happen after extensive awake-time work has been done. Typically, a stumbling block in a detailed process is then solved in the sleep or dream state.

WHAT'S A GOOD NIGHT'S SLEEP?

Technically, most people need about seven to eight hours of sleep, enough to feel fresh and sharp on waking.

The majority of aging adults need somewhat less sleep. When we are young adults the rule of thumb is one hour of sleep for every two hours of wakeful activities. As we age, the ratio gradually shifts to 45 minutes of sleep for every two hours of wakefulness. So by the time you reach 60 years of age, most of us do well with a six or seven hours of sleep and seventeen to eighteen hours of wakefulness.

As a society, millions of Americans have a considerable sleep debt—on average, we sleep an hour less every night than we should for optimal brain function and optimal health. That's 20 percent less than Americans were sleeping about a hundred years ago. And this has been going on for weeks, months, even years. The 1993 U.S. National Commission on Sleep Disorders Research report *Wake Up America: A National Sleep Alert* found that up to seventy million Americans suffer sleep problems, deprivation being far and away the most common. The report concluded, "By any measuring stick, the deaths, illness, and damage due to sleep deprivation and sleep disorders represent a substantial problem for American society." There is no indication that Americans have paid sufficient heed to this warning over the past sixteen years.

In a study by the National Sleep Foundation, two-thirds of subjects reported that sleepiness interfered with concentration and estimated that the quality of their work was reduced by 30 percent. William Dement, a pioneer sleep researcher, summarized the problem more than a decade ago. "Millions of us are living a less than optimal life and performing at a less than optimal level, impaired by an amount of sleep debt that we're not even aware we carry."

CogniByte

According to the 2009 *Sleep in America* poll, almost two-thirds of women and more than one-half of men report symptoms of insomnia at least a few days a week. In 2008, physicians wrote more than fifty-six million prescriptions for sleeping pills.

HOW TO SLEEP TIGHT FOR BRAIN HEALTH

As we age, we experience the deep, refreshing sleep patterns of youth with decreasing regularity. Waking after a few brief hours of sleep or in the too early morning and having difficulty falling asleep all tend to be bigger issues as we age. Often accompanying these nighttime problems are feelings of tiredness, fatigue, and decreased mental alertness during the day. Napping becomes more frequent.

The good news is that with a concerted effort, many sleep issues can be resolved so that you can wake up in the morning with a feeling of freshness and mental acuity no matter what your age.

Here you will find a list of recommendations designed to help you fall asleep and stay asleep naturally, without the need for sleep medication. Perhaps as important as this list is the list of things I suggest you don't do! Not all recommendations will work for everyone, but they will work for most of us, and they have been developed by the best sleep experts in the country, including the American Academy of Sleep Medicine and the National Sleep Foundation.

If you are not getting a restful night's sleep most nights, pay close attention to the following list, and attempt to identify the culprit:

- Don't drink coffee or other caffeinated drinks four to six hours before you go to bed. This includes some teas, caffeinated sodas, and even chocolate (white chocolate is OK!).

- Don't smoke or use other forms of nicotine within an hour or two of bedtime. And certainly don't smoke during the night if you wake up.

- Don't eat a large meal fewer than four hours or so before your bedtime. This is a tough one for many of us, as we are accustomed to evening dinner as our major meal of the day. If you eat at 6 p.m., do some mild exercise later in the evening around 7 or 7:30, such as taking a 15-minute leisurely walk.

- Don't exercise strenuously within four to six hours of bedtime (a relaxing walk after dinner does not qualify as strenuous exercise, unless you have been a couch potato for years).

- Don't drink more than a glass or two of wine (or the equivalent amount of alcohol) within three to four hours of bedtime. Alcohol is associated with disrupted sleep and especially waking in the middle of the night.

- Don't fall asleep in a chair, on a couch, or any place outside your bedroom.

• Don't use sleeping pills on a regular basis.

CogniByte

Want to have a eureka moment? To increase the chance of having one, think hard with your imagination during the day, stop racking your brains in the evening, relax, and then get your head down on that pillow for a restorative (and productive) night's sleep.

• Don't work or watch TV in bed. No reading business reports or making late work-related phone calls from bed. This will rev up your brain, and the purpose of going to bed is to continue winding down and fall asleep quickly.

The following list has suggestions for getting a good night's sleep:

• Make sure your bed is comfortable and conducive to rest. If you wake up most mornings with lower-back pain, stiffness, or neck pain, you may benefit from a firmer mattress and a pillow that conforms to your head and neck. Numerous choices are available. Search the Internet and talk with your physician, but take your time to find the solution that works for you. Your bed needs to be as comfortable for sleep as your shoes are for an active day on your feet.

• Make your bedroom as dark as possible.

• Leave your work and your worries outside the bedroom.

• Use the time after dinner for stress-free, relaxing activities. This might be non-work-related reading, listening to your favorite music, learning a new language by CD or tape, watching nonviolent television shows, seeing a movie, perusing a relaxing book, knitting, tying flies for fishing, or playing cards.

• Don't go to bed until you are tired enough for sleep.

• If you enjoy reading in bed, read for enjoyment and relaxation.

• If you have trouble falling asleep, leave the room and find another comfortable place in your home where you can engage in a relaxing activity such as reading or listening to soft music. As Dale Carnegie advised, "If you can't sleep, then get up and do something instead of lying there worrying. It's the worry that gets you, not the lack of sleep."

- Maintain a regular wake-up time, even on days off work and on weekends (does not apply to vacations!).

- In your bedroom, play soft background music or use a noise machine that plays nature sounds, such as a gurgling brook or soft breezes in the pines.

- Avoid napping during the daytime, unless you are a regular napper and it does not interfere with your nighttime sleep. If you simply must have a nap because the urge is overwhelming, attempt to nap for only 20 to 30 minutes and not more than an hour. Take your nap no later than 3 p.m. so as not to interfere with crucial nocturnal sleep. Afternoon drowsiness is biologically normal; our brain's clock in the suprachiasmatic nucleus controls it. Better than napping, which most of us cannot do while at work, take a 5 to 10 minute walk outside.

- Review all of your medications with your physician. Are one or more of your medications stimulants?

- Try a warm glass of milk or an herbal tea (chamomile is my favorite).

SLEEP PROFESSIONALS

Specialists in sleep disorders are doctors trained to diagnose and treat those needing professional medical help. Before you consult a sleep expert, try to make some adjustments in your own sleep protocol based on the dos and don'ts here. If you still have trouble getting a consistently good night's sleep, it's time to reach out for help before your sleep debt gets any larger.

The next step is to keep a sleep diary for a week or two. Record the times you go to bed; approximately how long it takes you to fall asleep (you will need to estimate this the next morning); your wake-up time; how you feel in the morning; exercise patterns; the content, size, and time of meals; medications; and anything else you feel might help your physician or a sleep specialist understand your particular sleep issues.

After several weeks of following the advice of your regular physician, if there is still no improvement, consider seeing a physician who specializes in sleep. (Ask your regular physician for a recommendation. Almost without exception every modest-sized city in the United States now has a sleep center.)

I would recommend that you do not simply accept a prescription for a sleeping pill. They are wonderfully effective for the short term and definitely beneficial for acute stressful situations or serious illnesses, but they are not a healthy long-term solution.

WAKING UP WITH CHARGED BATTERIES!

Sleep is a proven remedy for the day's brain-draining activities. Sleep is a form of medicine. In some instances regarding your health, "the delivery of good medical care is to do as much nothing as possible." We often think of sleep as doing nothing, but as noted earlier, while you sleep, parts of your brain are hard at work building stronger, lasting memories and practicing tasks you learned the day before. Sleep improves all other critical brain functions—learning, thinking, planning and executing complex goals, creativity, and problem solving. Restful, restorative sleep is essential for overall health. You will live longer and in better brain and body health if you pay attention to sleep.

YOUR BRAIN'S FUTURE

"The brain is a world consisting of a number of unexplored continents and great stretches of unknown territory."—SANTIAGO RAMON Y CAJAL, 1906 NOBEL PRIZE WINNER

"We need to move row to reinvent and reinforce our fight against Alzheimer's. For the baby-boom generation, this is certainly one of our last chances... We have the nation's future to protect."—NEWT GINGRICH, FORMER SPEAKER OF THE U.S. HOUSE OF REPRESENTATIVES

"The stakes are high. Without a doubt, the future health and well-being of these families—indeed, the health and financial well-being of our entire nation—depends on how swiftly and decisively we act to address this terrible disease."—SANDRA DAY O'CONNOR, FORMER JUSTICE OF THE U.S. SUPREME COURT

What is the future of your brain? My intent has been to provide some understanding of the brain's complexity and enough understanding of the science behind BrainSavers' Brain Training Revolution program to give you the confidence that the future truly belongs to you, no matter your age.

The three major interventions of the Brain Training Revolution program for healthy brain aging—modest aerobic physical exercise, nutritionally sound brain-healthy eating, and the world brain gym exercises and activities—will make you healthier and will help you feel better. This three-part structure, along with an active social life, consistent invigorating sleep, and stress management, results in a total brain- and body-healthy lifestyle. If you follow this prescription, you will go a considerable way toward preserving and optimizing your memory and other cognitive functions as you age, minimizing age-associated memory loss, and reducing your risk for Alzheimer's disease.

As Laura Carstensen, a Stanford University expert in health issues associated with aging posed the question a few years back, "How do we ensure that people come to old age mentally sharp and physically fit?" Aging is a basic biological principle so it does not make sense to speak about defeating aging. But Carstensen correctly predicted, "Eventually, we will figure out how to make people much healthier for much longer." The Brain Training Revolution lifestyle is great for your outlook on life, for your brain, for your heart, and for your overall mental and physical well-being. Activity leads to more exposure to the great adventures life offers. This program is a means to encourage you to explore things that you have not explored in the past and to revisit worthwhile activities that you perhaps ignored in the hustle and bustle of life.

It is gratifying to report that while I was planning and starting work on this book, an early version of the BrainSavers program was tested by my BrainSavers colleagues Richard Samuels and Edward Wein (contributors to this book) on a group of healthy adults between the ages of 58 and 75 (the mean age was 68). These folks used the program for two months. At the conclusion their brains and bodies were in better shape. They reported improved self-image. Improvements in both mental and physical health were quantified. Objective measures of cardiovascular function, strength, and flexibility were higher after two months than at the start. Most noteworthy, they improved their brains by an average of 16 percent in more than a dozen cognitive areas.

Participants commented that the program "was easy to follow"; "it is a very good program, a very good idea—fun and challenging. I became more focused!"; "exercises were great and I enjoyed it all the time"; and finally that it was "valuable, especially for people who aren't doing physical and mental exercises."

Those comments (and the smiles on their faces) are extremely gratifying. After having spent the better part of four years working on the development of the BrainSavers' healthy brain aging program with my colleagues, this sort of reception and results make the entire effort worthwhile. Nevertheless, I am personally committed to updating and improving the program—certainly as new credible scientific results instruct us further about healthy brain aging. But I need your help, too. Please do not hesitate to send your experiences and suggestions to me.

We are in the midst of a true epidemic of Alzheimer's disease, as Justice O'Connor and Newt Gingrich testified on Capitol Hill to a U.S. Senate Committee Hearing on May 14, 2008. As many experts from various disciplines have noted, the Alzheimer's epidemic will reach sky-high proportions if we do not take action now. Just as each of us must contribute to environmental protection, each of us is ultimately responsible for our most treasured internal environment—the activities of our mind.

There is no magic bullet to optimize memory and other brain functions or to prevent Alzheimer's, and there is certainly no effective treatment once the ravages of Alzheimer's are manifest. So, each of us must do our part—for ourselves, for our spouses, for family and friends, and especially for our children and grandchildren and future generations. By taking care of your brain and your memories, at the least you will feel better about yourself. At the most, you will benefit from and enjoy additional years—or decades—of brain-healthy living.

PART 3

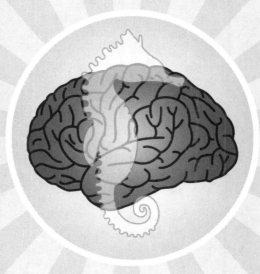

RESOURCES

NUTRITIONAL QUOTIENT SCORECARDS

RECOMMENDATIONS FOR LEVELS 2 AND 3 OF THE JUMP-START METHOD

Notes:

You do not have to adhere to the recommended number of servings for a particular food each day. You may double up one day and not take anything the next day (have two servings of fish one day and none the next). Give yourself the points earned even if it exceeds the expected amount on a given day!

RECOMMENDATIONS FOR LEVEL 2 OF THE JUMP-START METHOD

		Recommended	M	T	W	Th	F	Sa	Su	Total
Whole grain cereals and grains	No. of servings	3								
	1 pt/ 2 servings	1 1/2								
Vegetables	No. of servings	3								
	1 pt/ 2 servings	1 1/2								
Fruit	No. of servings	3								
	1 pt/ 2 servings	1 1/2								
Fish	No. of servings	3 per wk								
	2 pt/ serving	6 per wk								
Beans and legumes	No. of servings	1								
	1 pt/ serving	1								
Nuts and seeds	No. of servings	3 4 per wk								
	1 pt / serving	3 4								
Healthy oils	No. of tsps.: 2	2								
	1 pt/2 tsps.	1								
Low fat dairy	1 2 servings/day	2								
	1 pt/ 2 servings	1								
Total day and week	15 pts/day	15								
	105pts/ week	105								

RECOMMENDATIONS FOR LEVEL 3 OF THE JUMP-START METHOD

		Recom mended	M	T	W	Th	F	Sa	Su	To tal
Whole grain cereals and grains	No. of servings	3								
	1 point/ 2 servings	1 1/2								
Vege tables	No. of servings	3								
	1 point/ 2 servings	1 1/2								
Fruit	No. of Servings	3								
	1 point/ 2 servings	1 1/2								
Fish	No. of servings	3 per wk								
	2 pts/ serving	6 per wk								
Beans and legumes	No. of servings	1								
	1 pt/ serving	1								
Nuts and seeds	No. of servings	3 4 per wk								
	1 pt/ serving	3 4								
Healthy oils	No. of tsps.: 4	2								
	1 pt/2 tsps.	1								
Low fat dairy	2 3 serv ings/day	2								
	1 pt/2 servings	1								
Total day and week	15 pts/day	15								
	105 pts/ week	105								

ANSWERS TO THE EXERCISES

LEVEL 1

EXERCISE 1
What color is the vehicle in the background?
Yellow
What kind of vehicle is in the background?
Taxi
What color is the dress of the woman in the center of the photo?
Blue
What is the woman in the center of the photo carrying?
A grocery bag and a purse/handbag
What color is the handbag of the woman on the right?
Brown
How many pedestrians are pictured?
Six, although five are clearly visible, a sixth can be seen pulling a wheeled bag.
Were any of the pedestrians carrying a suitcase?
No. One is pulling a wheeled bag, not carrying it.

EXERCISE 2
What sport is being played?
Soccer/Football
What are the colors of the teams?
Blue and orange
How many adults are seated with the group in the foreground?
One
What are the people in the foreground sitting on?
Soccer balls and the grass
How many kids are in the foreground?
Five
How many kids can be seen lying down?
One
Are the teams boy, girl, or co-ed?
Co-ed
What structures can be seen in the background?
Goal posts and bleachers

EXERCISE 3

How many people are in the photo?
Two

What color are the life vests?
Blue

What is the boy holding in his hand?
A paddle or oar

What color is the man's shirt?
Yellow

What color is the boy's kayak?
Blue

What color is the man's kayak?
Yellow

EXERCISE 4

How many people are in the photograph?
Six

How many kids are in the photo?
Two

What is the boy holding in his hand?
A cupcake

How many males/females are in the photo?
Three males, three females

Name three items on the table.
cups or glasses, wine glasses, sandwich, rolls. salad, strawberries, picnic basket, cutting board, wine bottle, table cloth, plate with cupcakes

What color is the table cloth?
White

EXERCISE 5

EXERCISE 6

EXERCISE 7

EXERCISE 8

EXERCISE 9

EXERCISE 10

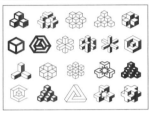

EXERCISE 11

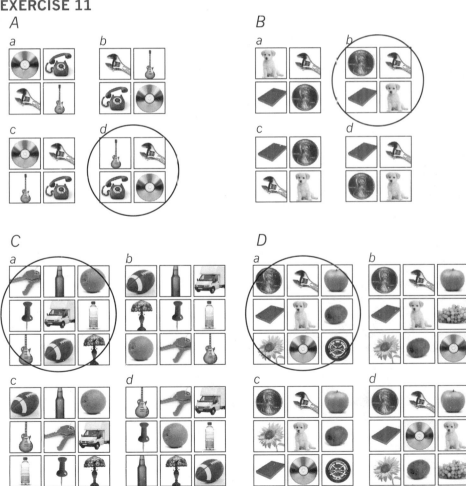

LEVEL 2

EXERCISE 1–5

1 Ⓒ

2 Ⓓ

3 Ⓐ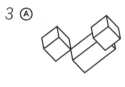

4 Ⓓ

5 Ⓐ

EXERCISE 6–7

A

a k m
Ⓙ d o
f c z
The only uppercase
letter

B
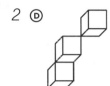
Ⓐ D C
S N F
G H K
The only vowel

C
O a R
q D Ⓒ
B P g
The only letter without
an enclosed space

D

The only shape without
a right angle

E
The only shape with an
uneven number of sices

F

The only shape that cannot
be divided symmetrically

G

The only one unrelated
to music

H

The only one unrelated
to food or eating

I

The only one unrelated
to water

J

The only one that is not a
method of transportation

K

The only one that is
not a home

L

The only one unrelated
to communicaticn

EXERCISE 8

How many people appear in the photo?
Six

How many bags are carried by the woman in the light blue dress?
Two

What are the colors of the dresses or skirts worn by the women in the photo?
One in light blue, another two in dark blue or black (there are three women with dresses/skirts)

How many bare legs can be seen?
Six

What kinds of pants are the men in the scene wearing?
Jeans

EXERCISE 9

How many people are in the bleachers?
None

What are the numbers on any two of the players in the photo?
2, 23, 8, 7, and 5

How many children are standing in the foreground?
None

How many children are seated on the field?
Five

How many people are standing near the goal?
One

EXERCISE 10

How many kayaks can be seen in the photo?
Three

What color are the oars?
Yellow and black

How many oars are in the photo?
Two

What does the man have on his left arm?
Wrist watch

What are three of the things that can be seen in the background?
Water, dirt, trees, clouds, and sky

EXERCISE 11

What color is the woman's shirt in the background?
Pink or magenta

How many generations can be seen?
Three

What is the man in the background holding in his hand?
Wine glass

What color are the two glasses on the table?
Red and yellow

What does the woman on the right have on her head?
Sunglasses and hair

EXERCISE 1

11 5 5 16   25 15 21 18   2 18 1 9 14   19 20 9 13 21 12 1 20 5 4
keep your brain stimulated

21 19 5   9 20   15 18   12 15 19 5   9 20
use it or lose it

❯ ✳◉▼ ✳❑❑✳▲ ✳✳✥✳ ▼✳✳ ○❑▲▼ ✳✦✳● ✳❑❑ ▼✳✳ ◉❑✳✳■
WHAT FOODS GIVE THE MOST FUEL FOR THE BRAIN?

◉❑✦✳▼▲   ■✦▼▲   ▲✳✳✳▲   ●✳✳✦○✳▲   ✳❑✳✳■▲
Fruits, nuts, seeds, legumes, grains,

✦✳✳✳▼◉○●✳▲   ✳✳▲✳ ◉■✳ ❯✳■✳
vegetables, fish, and wine.

---

v c v i x r h v   r h   k f i v   n v w r x r m v
Exercise is pure medicine
u l i   s v z o g s b   y i z r m   z t r m t
for healthy brain aging.

k s b h r x z o   z m w   n v m g z o
Physical and mental
u r g m v h h   h s l f o w   y v   z   k z i g
fitness should be a part
l u   b l f i   w z r o b   i l f g r m v
of your daily routine

LEVEL 3

EXERCISE 1

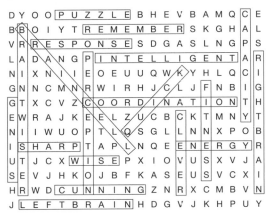

```
D Y O O G R E Y M A T T E R L P Z A F B
I N T E L L I G E N C E I U Y T R Q P U
E T Y O M E M O R Y M K Q E E P N C B I
T E C Y R A J U A U D I T O R Y P O B S
E X S H O R T T E R M P M O N N B G V M
C E X T X R Z T W S A Q H F O K L N F A
B R A I N A M W E L O S T I M U L I N R
S C K N H V T F A N D S T A P L H T R T
E I Y G T F K U F D T P Q Z T T O I E H
N S T E N N S E E M E I M V L R Q O S V
S E W Y I I W Z I C Q E O A U O G N E L
E Y W H V H G I R I K B E N J U W Z R L
S P T O M N R E W U I H N V Y H F T V H
K U F G T R P U L O N G T E R M X A E O
```

EXERCISE 2

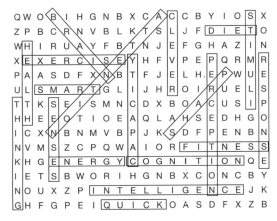

```
D Y O O P U Z Z L E B H E V B A M Q C E
B B O I Y T R E M E M B E R S K G H A L
V R R E S P O N S E S D G A S L N G P S
L A D A N G P I N T E L L I G E N T A R
N I X N I I E O E U U Q W K Y H L Q C I
G N N C M N R W I R H J C L J F N B I G
G T X C V Z C O O R D I N A T I O N T H
E W R A J K E L Z U C B C K T M N Y T
N I I W U O P T L O S G L L N N X P O B
I S H A R P T A P L N Q E E N E R G Y R
U T J C X W I S E P X I O V U S X V J A
S E V J H K O J B F K A S E U S V C X I
H R W D C U N N I N G Z N R X C M B V N
J L E F T B R A I N H D G V J K H P U Y
```

EXERCISE 3 *(from color appendix)*

```
Q W O B I H G N B X C A C C B Y I O S X
Z P B C R N V B L K T S L J F D I E T O
W H I R U A Y F B T N J E F G H A Z I N
X E X E R C I S E Y H F V P E P Q R M R
P A A S D F X N B T F J E L H E P W U E
U L S M A R T G L I J H R O I R U E L S
T T K S E I S M N C D X B O A C U S I P
H H E O T I O E A Q L A H S E D H G O
I C X N B N M V B P J K S D F P E N B N
N V M S Z C P Q W A I O R F I T N E S S
K H G E N E R G Y C O G N I T I O N Q E
I E T S B W O R I H G N B X C O N C B Y
N O U X Z P I N T E L L I G E N C E J K
G H F G P E Q U I C K O A S D F X Z B
```

EXERCISE 4

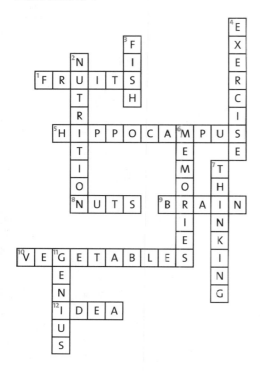

EXERCISE 5

EXERCISE 6

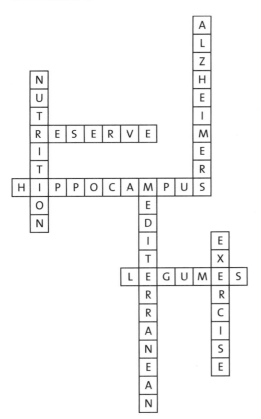

EXERCISE 7

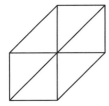

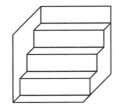

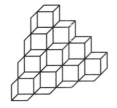

We found a total of 3 perspectives; 2 box shapes and one flat shape.

One perspective looks like stairs leading up. Another looks like the edge of a piece of crown molding.

The trick to this illusion is to focus on each of the three sides of the pyramid. We count three perspectives.

EXERCISE 8

EXERCISE 9
1. Brain Cell
2. Left Brain Right Brain
3. Gray Matter
4. Memory Problem
5. Short-and Long-Term Memory
6. Five Senses
7. Split Second
8. BrainSavers

EXERCISE 11

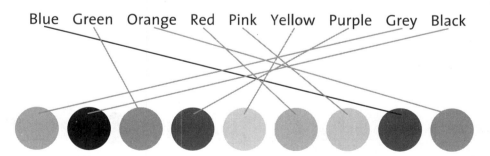

EXERCISE 12

Blue Green Orange Red Pink Yellow Purple Grey Black

Blue Green Orange Red Pink Yellow Purple Grey Black

EXERCISE 13

F I T	B A D	G E T	F I T	M O R E	L I V E
F A T	F A D	G I T	F I N	W O R E	W I V E
F A N	F A T	F I T	Y I N	W I R E	W I L E
			Y O N	W I S E	W I L L
			Y O U		W E L L

H E A D	S T A Y	G O O D	T H I N K	B R A I N
L E A D	S W A Y	W O O D	T H A N K	B L A I N
L E N D	A W A Y	W O O S	S H A N K	S L A I N
L A N D	A W R Y	W O E S	S T A N K	S T A I N
L A N E	A I R Y	W Y E S	S T A R K	S T E I N
L A M E	W I R Y	O Y E S	S T A R T	S T E R N
G A M E	W I R E	O D E S	Q U I C K	S T E R E
	W I S E	I D E S		S T A R E
		I D E A		S T A R T
				S M A R T

LEVEL 4

EXERCISE 7
A. 34
B. -17
C. 66
D. -4
E. 57
F. 39
G. 46
H. -14
I. 68
J. 39

EXERCISE 8
A. 7
B. -1
C. 5
D. -1
E. 4
F. -2
G. 12
H. 0
I. 8
J. 1

EXERCISE 9
A. 1065
B. 1394
C. 3129
D. 369
E. 1512
F. 1806
G. 2568
H. 230
I. 2255
J. 1015

EXERCISE 10
A. 104
B. -263
C. 664
D. -78
E. 706
F. 1890
G. 4053
H. 3076
I. 1518
J. 1994

LEVEL 5

EXERCISE 1

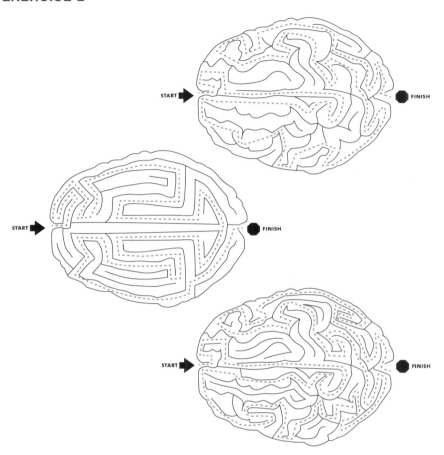

EXERCISE 2

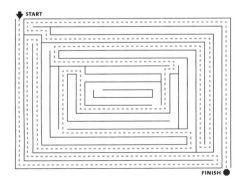

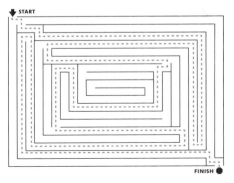

EXERCISE 10 *(paragraph from Exercise 7)*

1. What color is William's wife's hair?
   Brown
2. What color are William's wife's eyes?
   Green
3. Where do William and his family live?
   In the suburbs
4. How old are William's children?
   Six and eight
5. Who has the same eye color as William?
   Cory

EXERCISE 11 *(paragraph from Exercise 8)*

1. Who was in the meeting?
   Paul, Rich, and Chris
2. Where was the meeting held?
   In front of Chris's computer
3. What were the colors of the shirts, and who wore which color?
   Paul wore blue, Rich wore black, and Chris wore green
4. Who owned the computer?
   Chris
5. How did the owner of the computer drink his coffee?
   With cream and sugar

EXERCISE 12 *(paragraph from Exercise 9)*

1. How far does Jim drive in a work day?
   22 miles including round trip to and from work and lunch
2. What businesses does Jim drive past on his way to work?
   Grocery store, gas station, hardware store, and restaurant
3. How far does Jim drive when he goes to lunch?
   2 miles round trip
4. What direction is Jim's home from his job?
   West
5. How many times a week does Jim pass the hardware store?
   20; to and from work, and to and from lunch. 5 days a week

LEVEL 6

EXERCISES 1–4

1

9	7	6	8	1	2	3	5	4
1	2	8	3	5	4	7	9	6
3	5	4	7	6	9	2	8	1
4	6	1	2	8	3	5	7	9
2	8	5	1	9	7	6	4	3
7	3	9	5	4	6	1	2	8
8	9	3	6	7	5	4	1	2
5	4	2	9	3	1	8	6	7
6	1	7	4	2	8	9	3	5

2

3	8	1	2	4	6	5	7	9
2	4	9	8	5	7	6	3	1
7	5	6	1	9	3	8	2	4
8	6	7	4	2	9	3	1	5
4	2	5	3	6	1	9	8	7
1	9	3	7	8	5	4	6	2
6	3	4	5	7	2	1	9	8
5	1	2	9	3	8	7	4	6
9	7	8	6	1	4	2	5	3

3

9	4	1	3	5	2	8	6	7
5	7	6	4	1	8	2	9	3
2	8	3	7	9	6	5	4	1
7	2	5	6	8	4	1	3	9
1	3	4	2	7	9	6	8	5
8	6	9	1	3	5	7	2	4
6	5	2	9	4	1	3	7	8
3	9	8	5	2	7	4	1	6
4	1	7	8	6	3	9	5	2

4

7	2	9	1	5	6	4	8	3
8	5	3	2	7	4	6	1	9
6	4	1	8	9	3	5	2	7
5	3	8	7	6	2	1	9	4
1	7	2	4	3	9	8	5	6
9	6	4	5	8	1	3	7	2
2	8	6	9	4	5	7	3	1
3	9	7	6	1	8	2	4	5
4	1	5	3	2	7	9	6	8

EXERCISE 5

A

In order of food chain

B

In order of invention

C

In order of speed

D

In order of invention

EXERCISE 6

1. Exercise your mind.
2. Keep an open mind.
3. Use your mind or lose it.
4. You are what you eat.
5. A mind is a terrible thing to waste.
6. The older we get the wiser we become.
7. Sleep is critical to keep an active brain.
8. Challenge your brain every day to stay mentally fit.
9. Brain twisters are a great way to exercise your mind.
10. A good diet and regular exercise are essential to a healthy brain.

EXERCISE 9

1. A
2. B
3. C
4. C
5. B
6. A

EXERCISE 10

There are six men in line.

EXERCISE 7

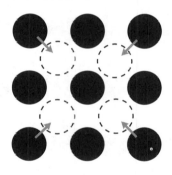

EXERCISE 11

Three socks and four shoes would guarantee that you would have a matching pair of each. Since there are only two colors of socks, as long as you take at least three, you are certain to have two of the same. However, you must pick four shoes, because selecting only three could result in one shoe in each of the three colors!

EXERCISE 8

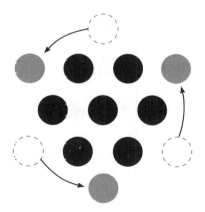

EXERCISE 12

2 / 2 + 2 / 2   2

RECOMMENDED RESOURCES FOR READERS

SUGGESTED READING

Aamodt S., and S.Wang. 2008. *Welcome to your brain: Why you lose your car keys but never forget how to drive and other puzzles of everyday life.* New York: Bloomsbury.

Ackerman D. 2004. *An alchemy of mind: The marvel and mystery of the brain.* New York: Scribner.

Allport, S. 2006. *The queen of fats: Why omega-3s were removed from the Western diet and what we can do to replace them.* Berkeley: Univ. of California Press.

Ancoli-Israel, S. 1996. *All I want is a good night's sleep.* St. Louis: Mosby-Year Book.

Andreasen, N. C. 2005. *The creative brain: The science of genius.* New York: Penguin.

Barrett, D. 2001. *The committee of sleep: How artists, scientists, and athletes use dreams for creative problem-solving—and how you can too.* New York: Crown.

Begley, S. 2007. *Train your mind, change your brain: How a new science reveals our extraordinary potential to transform ourselves.* New York: Ballantine Books.

Blackmore, S. 2006. *Conversations on consciousness: What the best minds think about the brain, free will, and what it means to be human.* New York: Oxford Univ. Press.

Bloom, F. 2007. *Best of the brain from Scientific American.* New York: Dana Press.

Bloom F., M. Beal, and D. Kupfer. 2006. *The Dana guide to brain health.* New York: Dana Press.

Bourtchouladze, R. 2002. *Memories are made of this: How memory works in humans and animals.* New York: Columbia Univ. Press.

Boyer P., and J. V. Wertsch. 2009. *Memory in mind and culture.* New York: Cambridge Univ. Press.

Damasio, A. 1994. *Descartes' error: Emotion, reason, and the human brain.* New York: Penguin.

———. 2003. *Looking for Spinoza: Joy, sorrow, and the feeling brain.* Orlando, FL: Harcourt.

Davis M., E. Eshelman, and M. McKay. 2008. *The relaxation and stress reduction workbook.* 6th ed. Oakland, CA: New Harbinger Publications.

Dement, W. 1999. *The promise of sleep: A pioneer in sleep medicine explores the vital connection between health, happiness, and a good night's sleep.* New York: Dell.

Dennent, D. C. 1996. *Kinds of minds: Toward an understanding of consciousness.* London: Weidenfeld and Nicolson.

Doidge, N. 2007. *The brain that changes itself: Stories of personal triumph from the frontiers of brain science.* New York: Penguin.

Doraiswamy P., L. Gwyther, and T. Adler. 2008. *The Alzheimer's action plan: The experts' guide to the best diagnosis and treatment for memory problems.* New York: St. Martin's Press.

Edelman, G. M. 2006. *Second nature: Brain science and human knowledge.* New Haven, CT: Yale Univ. Press.

Fernandez, A., and E. Goldberg. 2009. *The SharpBrains guide to brain fitness: 18 interviews with scientists, practical advice, and product reviews, to keep your brain sharp.* San Francisco: SharpBrains.

Garland, B. 2004. *Neuroscience and the law.* New York: Dana Press.

Gazzaniga, M. 2008. *Human: The science behind what makes us unique.* New York: HarperCollins.

Glannon, W. 2007. *Defining right and wrong in brain science: Essential readings in neuroethics.* New York: Dana Press.

Glynn, I. 1999. *An anatomy of thought.* New York: Oxford Univ. Press.

Goldberg, E. 2001. *The executive brain: Frontal lobes and the civilized mind*. New York: Oxford Univ. Press.

Gordon, D. 2008. *Your brain on Cubs: Inside the heads of players and fans*. New York: Dana Press.

———, ed. 2009. *Cerebrum 2009: Emerging ideas in brain science*. New York: Dana Press.

Hilts, P. J. 1995. *Memory's ghost: The nature of memory and the strange tale of Mr. M*. New York: Touchstone.

Kandel, E. 2006. *In search of memory: The emergence of a new science of mind*. New York: W. W. Norton and Co.

Kessler, D. A. 2009. *The end of overeating: Taking control of the insatiable American appetite*. New York: Rodale.

Lakoff, G. 2008. *The political mind: Why you can't understand twenty-first-century American politics with an eighteenth-century brain*. New York: Viking.

LeDoux, J. 2002. *Synaptic self: How our brains become who we are*. New York: Penguin.

Lehrer, J. 2007. *Proust was a neuroscientist*. Boston: Houghton Mifflin Harcourt.

Levenstein, H. 2003. *Paradox of plenty*. Rev. ed. Berkeley: Univ. of California Press.

Levitin, D. 2006. *This is your brain on music: The science of a human obsession*. New York: Plume.

———. 2008. *The world in six songs: How the musical brain created human nature*. New York: Dutton.

Linden, D. 2007. *The accidental mind: How brain evolution has given us love, memory, dreams, and God*. Cambridge, MA: Belknap Press of Harvard Univ. Press.

Luria, A. R. 1968. *The mind of a mnemonist: A little book about a vast memory*. New York: Basic Books.

Lynch, G., and R. Granger. 2008. *Big brain: The origins and future of human intelligence*. New York: Palgrave Macmillan.

Martin, P. 2002. *Counting sheep: The science and pleasures of sleep and dreams.* New York: St Martin's Press.

McEwen, B. 2004. *The end of stress as we know it.* Washington, DC: Joseph Henry Press.

McGaugh, J. 2003. *Memory and emotion: The making of lasting memories.* New York: Columbia Univ. Press.

Nestle, M. 2006. *What to eat.* New York: North Point Press.

———. 2007. *Food politics: How the food industry influences nutrition and health.* Rev. ed. Berkeley: Univ. of California Press.

Ornish, D. 2007. *The spectrum: A scientifically proven program to feel better, live longer, lose weight, and gain health.* New York: Ballantine Books.

Pfaff, D. W. 2007. *The neuroscience of fair play: Why we (usually) follow the golden rule.* New York: Dana Press.

Pinker, S. 2007. *The stuff of thought: Language as a window into human nature.* New York: Penguin.

Planck, N. 2006. *Real food: What to eat and why.* New York: Bloomsbury.

Pollan, M. 2006. *The omnivore's dilemma: A natural history of four meals.* New York: Penguin.

———. 2008. *In defense of food: An eater's manifesto.* New York: Penguin.

Posen, D. 2004. *The little book of stress relief.* Buffalo, NY: Firefly Books.

Ramachandran, V. 2004. *A brief tour of human consciousness: From imposter poodles to purple numbers.* New York: Pi Press.

Ramachandran, V., and S. Blakeslee. 1998. *Phantoms in the brain: Probing the mysteries of the human mind.* New York: Quill.

Ratey, J., and E. Hagerman. 2008. *Spark: The revolutionary new science of exercise and the brain.* New York: Little, Brown and Co.

Restak, R. 2001. *Mozart's brain and the fighter pilot: Unleashing your brain's potential.* New York: Three Rivers Press.

———. 2009. *Think smart: A neuroscientist's prescription for improving your brain's performance.* New York: Penguin.

Ridley, M. 2003. *Nature via nurture: Genes, experience, and what makes us human.* New York: HarperCollins.

Rock, A. 2004. *The mind at night: The new science of how and why we dream.* New York: Basic Books.

Sacks, O. 1985. *The man who mistook his wife for a hat.* New York: Summit.

———. 2007. *Musicophilia: Tales of music and the brain.* New York: Alfred A. Knopf.

Sapolsky, R. 2004. *Why zebras don't get ulcers.* 3rd ed. New York: Owl Books.

Schacter, D. 2001. *The seven sins of memory: How the mind forgets and remembers.* New York: Houghton Mifflin.

Searle, J. 2007. *Freedom and neurobiology.* New York: Columbia Univ. Press.

Shenk, D. 2001. *The forgetting: Alzheimer's: Portrait of an epidemic.* New York: Anchor Books.

Squire, L., and E. R. Kandel. 2009. *Memory: From mind to molecules.* Greenwood Village, CO: Roberts and Co.

Taubes, G. 2007. *Good calories, bad calories.* New York: Alfred A. Knopf.

Victoroff, J. 2002. *Saving your brain: The revolutionary plan to boost brain power, improve memory, and protect yourself against aging and Alzheimer's.* New York: Bantam Books.

Wade, N. 2006. *Before the dawn: Recovering the lost history of our ancestors.* New York: Penguin.

Westen, D. 2007. *The political brain: The role of emotion in deciding the fate of the nation.* New York: Public Affairs.

Willett, W. C. 2005. *Eat, drink, and be healthy: The Harvard Medical School guide to healthy eating.* New York: Free Press.

Wolf, M. 2007. *Proust and the squid: The story and science of the reading brain.* New York: HarperCollins.

Yates, F. 1966. *The art of memory.* Chicago: Univ. of Chicago Press.

WEBSITES
Brain Health
Brain Savers
  www.brainsavers.com
The Dana Foundation
  http://www.dana.org/brain.aspx
The Society for Neuroscience
  http://www.sfn.org/index.cfm?pagename=aboutNeuroscience
Centers for Disease Control and Prevention: Healthy Brain Initiative
  http://www.cdc.gov/aging/healthybrain/index.htm
AARP Brain Health
  http://www.aarp.org/health/healthyliving/brain_health/
National Alzheimer's Association: Maintain Your Brain
  http://alz.org/we_can_help_brain_health_maintain_your_brain.asp
Healthy Brain Initiative
  http://alz.org/national/documents/report_healthybraininitiative.pdf

Healthy Aging
National Institute on Aging
  http://www.nia.nih.gov/
American Society on Aging
  http://www.asaging.org/index.cfm
National Council on Aging
  http://www.ncoa.org/
Alliance for Aging Research
  http://www.agingresearch.org/

Physical Exercise
The President's Council on Fitness and Sports
  http://www.fitness.gov/resources_health.htm
American College of Sports Medicine
  http://www.acsm.org//AM/Template.cfm
American Council on Exercise
  http://www.acefitness.org/
National Association for Health and Fitness
  http://www.physicalfitness.org/
Diabetes Exercise and Sports Association
  http://www.diabetes-exercise.org/index.asp

American Heart Association's Physical Activity Calorie Use Chart
http://www.americanheart.org/presenter.jhtml?identifier=756

Nutrition
U.S. Department of Health and Human Services: Dietary Guidelines
http://www.health.gov/DietaryGuidelines/
The Cancer Project: Nutrition Rainbow
http://www.cancerproject.org/resources/pdfs/2006RainbowPoster.pdf
U.S. Department of Agriculture, Nutrient Data Laboratory
http://www.nal.usda.gov/fnic/foodcomp/Data/
U.S. Department of Agriculture, Food and Nutrition Information Center
http://fnic.nal.usda.gov
U.S. Department of Agriculture, Center for Nutrition Policy and Promotion:
MyPyramid Tracker
www.mypyramidtracker.gov
Mediterranean Diet
http://www.mayoclinic.com/health/mediterranean-diet/cl00011
Whole Grains Council
http://www.wholegrainscouncil.org
Discovery Nutrition 365
http://discovernutrition365.com/a-green-wave/
Linus Pauling Institute, Oregon State University
http://lpi.oregonstate.edu/

General Health
National Institutes of Health
http://www.nih.gov/
Institute of Medicine of the National Academies
http://www.iom.edu/
National Center for Complementary and Alternative Medicine, NIH
http://nccam.nih.gov/
Mayo Clinic
http://www.mayoclinic.com/

Alzheimer's Disease
Alzheimer's Association
http://www.alz.org/index.asp
Alzheimer's Foundation of America
http://www.alzfdn.org/

Alzheimer's Disease Education and Referral Center (ADEAR)
http://www.nia.nih.gov/Alzheimers/

Stroke
American Stroke Association
http://www.strokeassociation.org/presenter.jhtml

Sleep
Harvard Medical School, Division of Sleep Medicine
http://healthysleep.med.harvard.edu/.
National Sleep Foundation
http://www.sleepfoundation.org/
American Academy of Sleep Medicine
http://www.aasmnet.org/
American Insomnia Association
http://www.americaninsomniaassociation.org/
National Center on Sleep Disorder Research, NIH
http://www.nhlbi.nih.gov/about/ncsdr/index.htm

Stress
National Institute of Mental Health
http://www.nimh.nih.gov/index.shtml
American Psychological Association
http://www.apahelpcenter.org/
American Psychiatric Association
http://www.psych.org/
Anxiety Disorders Association of America
www.adaa.org
Mental Health America
www.mentalhealthamerica.net
Mayo Clinic
http://www.mayoclinic.com/health/meditation/HQ01070
American Institute of Stress
http://www.stress.org/

NOTES

Introduction

Page xii. "National Alzheimer's Association." http://www.alz.org/we_can_help_brain_health_maintain_your_brain.asp.

Page xii. "The Healthy Brain Initiative." http://www.alz.org/national/documents/report_healthybraininitiative.pdf.

Page xvi. "Current statistics on Alzheimer's disease." See http://www.alz.org/national/documents/topicsheet_alzdisease.pdf, http://www.alz.org/national/documents/report_alzfactsfigures2009.pdf.

Page xvii. Ornish, D. 1990. *Dr. Dean Ornish's program for reversing heart disease*. New York: Random House.

Page xxiv. "Alzheimer's center." The Banner Alzheimer's Institute is located at Banner Good Samaritan Hospital in Phoenix. Eric Reiman, MD, Steve Seiler, former CEO, and Mark Sklar were among the prime movers in establishing this facility.

PART 1: GETTING UP TO SPEED ON YOUR AGING BRAIN

Chapter 1: The Three-Pound Universe

Page 3. "Even though it is common knowledge." Ramachandran, V. 2004. *A brief tour of human consciousness: From imposter poodles to purple numbers*. New York: Pi Press.

Page 3. "1,350 grams." Extensive brain facts and figures can be found online at http://faculty.washington.edu/chudler/facts.html. Additional references are included on this site.

Page 7. *Indusium griseum* means "thin, gray covering," and *amygdala* means "almond-shaped." An engaging and worthwhile mental exercise is to look up the origin and meaning of the parts of the brain and the body.

Page 10. "Phineas Gage." For details of Gage's tragic accident and outcome, see Damasio, A. 1999. *Descartes' error: Emotion, reason, and the human brain.* New York: Penguin, 3–14, and Glynn I. 1999. *An anatomy of thought.* New York: Oxford Univiversity Press, 351–2.

Page 12. "Paul Bach-y-Rita." See Doidge, N. 2007. *The brain that changes itself: Stories of personal triumph from the frontiers of brain science* New York: Penguin, 1–26.

Page 19. "Jackson Pollock." You can create your own at http://jackson-pollock.org/ or view his originals at http://www.artinthepicture.com/artists/Jackson_Pollock/. To see the resemblance to microscopic images of the brain, go to http://micro.magnet.fsu.edu/micro/gallery/brain/brain.html.

Chapter 2: Making Memories

Page 21. "My father leans against." Markham, B. 1982. *West with the Night.* New York: North Point Press, 243.

Page 21. For surveys of American attitudes about brain health, see "Attitudes and Awareness of Brain Health Poll," American Society on Aging/MetLife Foundation, http://www.asaging.org/asav2/mindalert/pdfs/BH.pdf or http://www.drugs.com/clinical_trials/alzheimer-s-foundation-america-survey-americans-memory-concerns-fall-short-talking-doctors-5202.html.

Page 23. "We do not remember." Roach, M. 2003. *Stiff: The curious lives of human cadavers.* New York: W.W. Norton and Co., 183. Background information can also be found in Runes, D. D., ed. 1968. *The Diary and Sunday Observations of Thomas Alva Edison.* Westport, CT: Greenwood Press.

Page 23. "Henry Gustav Molaison." Carey, B. 2008. H.M., an unforgettable amnesiac, dies at 82. *New York Times,* December 5. Available online at: http://www.nytimes.com/2008/12/05/us/05hm.html. For additional background on H.M., see Hils, P. J. 2001. *Memory's ghost: The nature of memory and the strange tale of Mr. M.* New York: Touchstone; Bourtchouladze, R. 2002. *Memories are made of this: How memory works in humans and animals.* New York: Columbia Univ. Press, 43–51; and Shenk, D. 2001. *The forgetting: Alzheimer's: Portrait of an epidemic.* New York: Anchor Books, 46–49.

Page 24. "Landmark 1957 paper." Scoville W.B., and B. Milner. 1957. Loss of recent memory after bilateral hippocampal lesions. *J Neurol Neurosurg Pysch* 20: 11–21. The original paper is reproduced along with an interview with Milner in *Journal of NIH Research* 8 1996, 42–51.

Page 25. Psalm 137 might have originated as an interpretation for what was seen as divine punishment for dementia—"forgetting" Jerusalem. The terms used describe the major findings of a dominant (left) hemisphere stroke: weakness or paralysis ("my right hand forget her cunning"), loss of language and speech abilities ("tongue cleave to the roof of my mouth"), and memory and other cognitive and behavioral problems ("forget thee," "do not remember," "prefer not Jerusalem above my chief joy").

Page 25. "the words 'remember' and 'remembering' occur." Rabbi Albert Plotkin counted 572 usages (pers. comm., 2006).

Page 27. "2000 study." Maguire, E., D. Gadian, I. Johnsrude, et al. 2000. Navigation-related structural change in the hippocampi of taxi drivers. *PNAS.* 97: 4398–4403.

Page 28. "I never noticed part of my brain growing." http://news.bbc.co.uk/2/hi/science/nature/677048.stm.

Page 28. "Mechanism of forgetting." For discussions and descriptions of impaired forgetting, see Bourtchouladze, R. 2002. *Memories are made of this: How memory works in humans and animals.* New York: Columbia Univ. Press, , 105–111; Luria, A. R. 1968. *The mind of a mnemonist: A little book about a vast memory.* New York: Basic Books.

Page 29. "Memory, like a beauty that is always present to hear." Smyth, Lady Robert. 1794? *From the castle in the air to the little corner of the world.* Quoted in Nelson, C. 2006. *Thomas Paine.* New York: Penguin, 258.

Page 30. "a multiplex going on in there." Schroeder, A. 2008. *Snowball: Warren Buffett and the business of life.* New York: Bantam, 757.

Chapter 3: New Thinking on Thinking: The Young Brain, the Old Brain, and the Better Brain

Page 34. "Paul Bach-y-Rita." Adams, M. 2003. Can you see with your tongue? *Discover,* http://discovermagazine.com/2003/jun/feattongue; Fisher, M. 2007. Balancing act. *On Wisconsin,* http://www.uwalumni.com/home/onwisconsin/archives/spring2007/balancingact.aspx.

Page 34. "As the worm turns." Hopkin, K. 2005. I smell a...worm, *The Scientist* 19, (15): 52, http://www.the-scientist.com/article/display/15670.

Page 35. "bloodhound of invertebrates." Beyond recognizing odors, single neuron controls reactions in worm. *Science Daily,* November 2, 2008, http://www.sciencedaily.com/releases/2008/10/081030200636.htm.

Page 35. "model forgetting in mice." Evans, J. 2008. Making mice forget. *The Scientist* (October 22), http://www.the-scientist.com/blog/display/55102/. See also Cao, X., H., Wang, B. Mei, et al. 2008.

Inducible and selective erasure of memories in the mouse brain via chemical-genetic manipulation. *Neuron* 60: 353–366.

Page 36. "rewired mice that respond to a flashing light." Anahtar, M. 2004. Mice rewiring experiments show adult brain plasticity. *MIT Science News in Review*, http://web.mit.edu/murj/www/v11/v11-News/v11-mit.pdf.

Page 36. "Nature determines the initial." Sur, M. 2008. The emerging nature of nurture. *Science* 322: 1636.

Page 36. "as though the brain didn't want to waste." Doidge, N. 2007. *The brain that changes itself: Stories of personal triumph from the frontiers of brain science*. New York: Penguin,, 52.

Page 37. "young birds go through an initial 'babbling.'" Schwarz, J. 1996. Twenty years of bird songs: It's a record filled with scientific high notes. *Univ. of Wash News*, November 20, http://uwnews.org/article.asp?articleid=3056. See also Nottebohm, F. 2005. The neural basis of birdson. *PLOS BIOL* 3 (5): e164. doi:10.1371/journal.pbio.0030164.

Page 38. "Who among us hasn't sat and listened." Levitin, D. 2006. *This is your brain on music: The science of a human obsession*, New York: Plume, 264.

Page 38. "I wonder how many 70-year-olds consider themselves 'old'?" Volhard, J. 2009. Every dog has his day. Room for Debate, *New York Times*, February 11, http://roomfordebate.blogs.nytimes.com/2009/02/11/every-dog-has-his-day/#volhard.

Page 44. "Boskops." For a fascinating evolutionary perspective on human brains and a description of these extinct relatives of ours, see Lynch, G. and R. Granger. 2008. *Big brain: The origins and future of human intelligence*. New York: Palgrave Macmillan.

Page 44. "cultures around the world." For a scholarly treatise on how memory functions in social groups and how cultural influences memory, see Boyer and J. V. Wertsch, eds. 2009. *Memory in mind and culture*. New York: Cambridge Univ. Press.

Page 46. "Both of these studies are exciting." National Institute on Aging. Exercise slows development of alzheimer's-like brain changes in mice, new study finds, http://www.nia.nih.gov/NewsAndEvents/PressReleases/PR20050426Exercise.htm.

PART 2: A BRAIN-HEALTHY LIFESTYLE
Chapter 4: The Brain Training Revolution

Page 52. "Dr. Ralph Paffenbarger." Paffenbarger, R., R. Hyde, A. Wing, C. Hsieh. 1986. Physical activity, all-cause mortality, and longevity of college alumni. *N Engl J Med* 314: 605–613.

Page 54. "study examined healthy but sedentary seniors." Colcombe, S., K. Erickson, P. Scalf, et al. 2006. Aerobic exercise training increases brain volume in aging humans. *J Gerontol Med Sci.* 61A: 1166–1170.

Page 54. "In 2004 two studies." See Abbot, R., L. White, G. Ross, et al. Walking and dementia in physically capable elderly men. *JAMA* 292: 1447–1453, and Weuve, J., J. Kang, J. Manson, et al. 2004. Physical activity, including walking, and cognitive function in older women. *JAMA* 292: 1454–1461.

Page 55. "colleagues in Seattle." See Larson, E., L. Wang, J. Bowen, et al. 2009. Exercise is associated with reduced risk for incident dementia among persons 65 years of age and older. *Ann Intern Med* 144 (2): 73–81.

Page 55. "colleagues in Australia." See Lautenschlager, N., K. Cox, L. Flicker, et al. 2008. Effect of physical activity on cognitive function in older adults at risk for Alzheimer disease: A randomized trial. *JAMA* 300: 1027–1037.

Page 55. "Our results clearly indicate." Erickson, K., R. Prakash, M. Voss, et al. Aerobic fitness is associated with hippocampal volume in elderly humans. (In press) *Hippocampus.* (2009)

Page 55. "Retirement is no excuse" and "You're building a reserve." Fackelmann, K. 2005. Minds in motion stay sharp. *USA Today,* January 25, http://www.usatoday.com/news/health/2005-01-24-alzheimers-cover_x.htm.

Page 56. "Joe Verghese and colleagues." See Verghese, J., R. Lipton, M. Katz, et al. 2003. Leisure activities and risk of dementia in the elderly. *N Engl J Med* 348: 2508–2516.

Page 56. "Advanced Cognitive Training for Independent and Vital Elderly (ACTIVE) study." Ball, K., D. Berch, K. Helmers, et al. 2002. Effects of cognitive training interventions with older adults. A randomized controlled trial. *JAMA* 288: 2271–2281; Willis, S., S. Tennstedt, M. Marsiske, et al. 2006. Long-term effects of cognitive training on everyday functional outcomes in older adults. *JAMA* 296: 2805–2813; Shumaker, S., C. Legault, L. Coker. 2006. Behavior-based interventions to enhance cognitive functioning and independence in older adults. *JAMA* 296: 2852–2854.

Page 56. "Michael Valenzuela and Perminder Sachdev." Valenzuela, M., P. Sachdev. 2005. Brain reserve and dementia: a systematic review. *Psychol Med* 35: 1–14.

Page 57. "As Jean Marx noted in *Science* Magazine." J. Marx. 2005. Preventing Alzheimer's: a lifelong commitment? *Science.* 309: 864–866.

Page 57. "average supermarket stocks." Nestle, M. 2006. *What to eat.* New York: North Point Press, 4.

Page 57. "writer Michael Pollan." Pollan, M. 2008. *In defense of food: An eater's manifesto.* New York: Penguin, 6–11, 17–81.

Page 58. "in Genesis." Gen 1:29.

Page 59. "*Journal of the American Medical Association.*" Engelhart, M., M. Geerlings, A. Ruitenberg, et al. 2002. Dietary intake of antioxidants and risk of Alzheimer disease. *JAMA* 287: 3223–3229; Morris, M., D. Evans, J. Bienias, et al. 2002. Dietary intake of antioxidant nutrients and the risk of incident Alzheimer disease in a biracial community study. *JAMA* 287: 3230–3237.

Page 59. "*Annals of Neurology.*" See Kang, J., A. Ascherio, F. Grodstein. 2005. Fruit and vegetable consumption and cognitive decline in aging women. *Ann Neurol* 57: 713–720.

Page 59. "Mediterranean diet." Scarmeas, N., Y. Stern, M.X. Tang, et al. 2006. Mediterranean diet and risk for Alzheimer's disease. *Ann Neurol* 59: 912–921; Dai, Q., A. Borenstein, Y. Wu, et al. 2006. Fruit and vegetable juices and Alzheimer's disease: the Kame Project. *Am J Med* 119 (2006): 751–759; Willis, L., B. Shukitt-Hale, J. Joseph. 2009. Recent advance in berry supplementation and age related cognitive decline. *Curr Opin Clin Nutr Metab Care* 12: 91–94.

Page 60. "flurry of reviews." Gomez-Pinilla, F. 2008. Brain foods: the effects of nutrients on brain function. *Neuroscience* 9: 568–578. Joseph, J., M. Smith, G. Perry, B. Shukitt-Hale. 2008. Nutrients and food constituents in cognitive decline and neurodegenerative disease. Chapter 17 in Coulston, A. M., C. Boushey, eds. *Nutrition in the prevention and treatment of disease 2nd edition.* New York: Elsevier, 269–287. Scarmeas, N, Y. Stern, R. Mayeux, et al. 2009. Mediterranean diet and mild cognitive impairment. *Arch Neurol* 66: 216–225; Scarmeas, N, J. Luchsinger, N. Schupf, et al. 2009. Physical activity, diet, and risk of Alzheimer disease. *JAMA* 30: 627–637.

Chapter 5: Food for Thinking

Page 61. "Eat right, exercise some. Break free." Victoroff, J. 2002. *Saving your brain: The revolutionary plan to boost brain power, improve memory, and protect yourself against aging and Alzheimer's.* New York: Bantam Books, 237.

Page 62. "adapted from…Michael Pollan." Pollan, M. 2008. *In defense of food: An eater's manifesto.* New York: Penguin, 1.

Page 63. "Mediterranean diet." Serra-Majem, L., B. Roman, R. Estruch. 2006. Scientific evidence of interventions using the Mediterranean diet: a systemic review. *Nutr Rev* 64: Suppl 1: S27–S47. The American Heart Association also provides information: http://www.american-heart.org/presenter.jhtml?identifier=4644.

Page 64. "If it's the choice between a carrot." Sabbagh, M. 2005. *The Alzheimer's answer: Reduce your risk and keep your brain healthy.* Hoboken, NJ: John Wiley and Sons, 150.

Page 66. "glycemic index." For more about this index, see http://lpi.oregonstate.edu/infocenter/foods/grains/gigl.html and http://www.glycemicindex.com/.

Page 68. American Dietetic Association. 2003. Position of the American Dietetic Association and Dietitians of Canada: Vegetarian Diets. *Journal of the American Dietetic Association* 103: 748–65; also in *Can J Diet Pract Res* 64 (2003): 62–81.

Page 69. "Eha Nurk and her Norwegian." Nurk, E., C. Drevon, H. Refsum, et al. 2007. Cognitive performance among the elderly and dietary fish intake: the Hordaland Health Study. *Am J Clin Nutr* 86: 1470–1478.

Page 69. "U.S. Department of Health and Human Services." MacLean, C. H., A. M. Issa, S.J. Newberry, et al. 2005. Effects of omega-3 fatty acids on cognitive function with aging, dementia, and neurological diseases. *Evidence Report/Technology Assessment* No. 114. Prepared by the Southern California Evidence-based Practice Center, under Contract No. 290–02–0003. AHRQ Publication No. 05–E011–2. Rockville, MD. Agency for Healthcare Research and Quality, 2.

Page 71. "A significant number of studies." See Daniels, J. 2009. Antioxidants may "block" benefits of exercise: study. *NutraIngredients.com*, May 12, http://www.nutraingredients-usa.com/Health-condition-categories/Energy-endurance/Antioxidants-may-block-benefits-of-exercise-Study; Ristow, M., K. Zarse, A. Oberbach, et al. 2009. Antioxidants prevent health-promoting effects of physical exercise in humans. *PNAS* 106: 8665–8670.

Page 72. Andrew Weil quote. C. Hallerman. 2007. No scientific evidence diet supplements slow aging. *CNN.com*, May 9, http://www.cnn.com/2007/HEALTH/04/09/chasing.supplements/index.html.

Page 76. "calories from fat." International Food Informational Council. 2006. Dietary Fats and Fat Replacers, http://www.ific.org/nutrition/fats/index.cfm.

Page 76. "*New York Times* writer William Grimes." Grimes, W. 2005. Eating my spinach: Four days on the Uncle Sam diet. *New York Times.* January 23, http://www.nytimes.com/2005/01/23/weekinreview/23grim.html.

Page 76. "2005 USDA diet recommendations." http://www.health.gov/DietaryGuidelines/.

Page 84. "Tommy Thompson." Revised food pyramid to emphasize calories, exercise. *USA Today*, January 12, 2005, http://www.usatoday.com/news/health/2005-01-12-food-pyramid_x.htm.

Chapter 6: Body Moves to Grow and Strengthen Your Brain

Page 93. "physical exercise protects." See Colcombe, S., A. Kramer. 2003. Fitness effects on the cognitive function of older adults: a meta-analytic study. *Psychological Science* 14: 125–130; Hillman, C., K. Erickson, A. Kramer. 2008. Be smart, exercise your heart: exercise effects on brain and cognition. *Nature* 9: 58–65; Erickson, K., A. Kramer. 2009. Aerobic exercise effects on cognitive and neural plasticity in older adults. *BR J Sports Med* 43: 22–24.

Page 95. "Strength training also has brain-health benefits." Cassilhas, R., V. Viana, V. Grassman, et al. 2007. The impact of resistance exercise on the cognitive function of the elderly. *Med Sci Sports Exer* 39: 1401–1407; Lachman, M., S. Neupert, R. Bertrand, et al. 2006. The effects of strength training on memory in older adults. *J Aging Physic Activ* 15: 59–73: Liu-Ambrose, T., M. Donaldson. 2009. Exercise and cognition in older adults: Is there a role for resistance training? *BR J Sports Med.* 43: 25–27.

Page 95. "brain-growth factors." Cotman, C., N. Berchtold. 2002. Exercise: a behavioral intervention to enhance brain health and plasticity. *Trends Neurosci* 25: 295–301; McAuley, E., A. Kramer, S. Colcombe. 2004. Cardiovascular fitness and neurocognitive function in older adults: a brief review. *Brain Behav Immun* 18: 214–220.

Page 102. "Perceived exertion scale." Background available online at http://www.acefitness.org/FITFACTS/pdfs/fitfacts/itemid_2579.pdf. Additional information on monitoring physical activity intensity provided at http://www.cdc.gov/physicalactivity/everyone/measuring/index.html.

Page 103. "the ease of your speech." Hutchinson, A. 2008. Get in the zone. *Runner's World* (February): 32–33.

Page 105. "Arthritis Foundation." http://www.health.state.ok.us/program/apep/AFAP%20FAQ.pdf.

Chapter 7: Because Gray Matters: Daily Workouts in the World Brain Gym!

Page 142. "an ice cream cone." Linden, D. 2007. *The accidental mind: How brain evolution has given us love, memory, dreams, and God.* Cambridge, MA: Belknap Press of Harvard Univ. Press, 21–22.

Page 144. "brain-imaging techniques." For a history of functional neuroimaging, see Cabeza, R. and A. Kingstone, eds. 2007. *Handbook of functional neuroimaging of cognition*, 2nd ed. Cambridge, MA: MIT Press.

Page 148. "the palace of memory." For a detailed, scholarly history of this memory technique, which enabled people to remember vast stores of information before the printed page was invented, see Yates, F. 1966. *The art of memory*. 1966. Chicago: Univ. of Chicago Press, 1–49.

Page 148. "*Dialexis*." Ibid., 29.

Chapter 8: Stress Busters

Page 239. "Stress that damages memories." For a review of stress and the brain by two highly regarded experts, see McEwan, B. 2002. *The end of stress as we know it*. Washington, DC: Joseph Henry Press. 107–134; Sapolsky, R. 2004. *Why zebras don't get ulcers*, 3rd ed. (New York: Owl Books, 215–25.

Page 240. "Miracle-Gro fertilizer." Ratey, J. 2008. *Spark: The revolutionary new science of exercise and the brain*. New York: Little, Brown, and Co. 40; Ramin, C. J. 2007. *Carved in sand*. New York: HarperCollins. 88.

Page 240. "Revealing recent studies." Lupien, S., M. de Leon, S. de Santi, et al. 1998. Cortisol levels during human aging predict hippocampal atrophy and memory deficits. *Nat Neurosci* 1 (1998): 69–77; Bremner, J., M. Narayan, E. Anderson, et al. 2000. Hippocampal volume reduction in major depression. *Am J Psych* 157: 115–118.

Page 240. "depression is the leading cause." Pratt, L. A., and D. J. Brody. 2008. Depression in the United States household population, 2005–2006. *NCHS Data Brief* No. 7, September 2008, http://www.docstoc.com/docs/1926814/Depression-Statistics-in-US-Households; also Lopez, A. D., and C. C. J. L. Murray. 1998. The global burden of disease, 1990–2020. *Nature Med* 4: 1241–1243.

Page 241. "stress proneness." See Wilson, R., D. Evans, J. Bienias, et al. 2003. Proneness to psychological distress is associated to risk of Alzheimer's disease." *Neurol* 61: 1479–1485; Wilson, R., J. Schneider, P. Boyle, et al. 2007. Chronic distress and incidence of mild cognitive impairment. *Neurol* 68: 2085–2092.

Page 242. "book *Synaptic Self*." LeDoux, J. 2002. *Synaptic self: How our brains become who we are*. New York: Penguin. 279–80.

Page 242. "Robert Sapolsky noted." Sapolsky, Robert. 1999. The physiology and pathophysiology of unhappiness. In *Well-Being*, ed. D. Kahneman. New York: Russell Sage Foundation, 453–69.

Page 242. "Chronic stress isn't." Ratey, J. 2008. *Spark: The revolutionary new science of exercise and the brain.* New York: Little, Brown, and Co., 77.

Page 252. "social integration." Ertel, K., M. Glymour, L. Berkman. 2008. Effects of social integration on preserving memory function in a nationally representative U.S. elderly population. *Am J Pub Health* 98: 1215–1220.

Chapter 9: The Night Shift: Sleep Your Way to Bedrock Memories

Page 256. "day reconstruction method." Kahneman, D., A. Krueger, D. Schkade, et al. 2004. A survey method for characterizing daily life experience: The day reconstruction method. *Science* 306: 1776–1780.

Page 256. "2004 study of almost eighty-three thousand nurses." Patel, S., N. Ayas, M. Malhotra, et al. 2004. A prospective study of sleep duration and mortality risk in women. *Sleep* 27: 440–4.

Page 256. "Why all this sleep?" de la Mare, W. 1939. *Behold, this dreamer.* Quoted in Martin, P. 2002. *Counting sheep: The science and pleasures of sleep and dreams.* New York: St Martin's Press, 26.

Page 257. "if you have been awake." Douglas, K., et al, 2005. 11 steps to a better brain. *New Scientist* 2501(May 28): 28, http://www.newscientist.com/article/mg18625011.900-11-steps-to-a-better-brain.html?full=true.

Page 257. "Belgian study." Maquet, P., S. Laureys, P. Peigneux, et al. 2000. Experience-dependent changes in cerebral activation during human REM sleep. *Nat. Neurosci* 3: 831–836; Maquet, P., S. Schwartz, R. Passingham, et al. 2003. Sleep-related consolidation of a visuomotor skill: Brain mechanims as assessed by functional magnetic resonance imaging. *J. Neurosci* 23: 1432–1440.

Page 260. "Japanese Ministry of Health." Ramin, C. J. 2007. Carved in sand. New York: HarperCollins, 153.

Page 260. "eureka dreams." See Barrett, D. 2001. *The committee of sleep: How artists, scientists, and athletes use dreams for creative problem-solving—and how you can too.* New York: Crown; and Mills, G. 2001. Stumped on a problem…sleep on it! *ipFrontline.com,* http://www.ipfrontcom/printtemplate.asp?id=471.

Page 260. "German study." Wagner, J., S. Gais, H. Haider, et al. 2003. Sleep inspires insight. *Nature* 427: 352–355.

Page 261. "sleep facilitated examples of insights." See Maquet, P., P. Ruby. 2004. Insight and the sleep committee. *Nature* 427: 304–305. Also, "Sleep and Innovation," Enterprise Resilience

Management blog, http://enterpriseresilienceblog.typepad.com/enterresilience_man/2008/10/sleep-and-innov.html.

Page 262. "1993 U.S. National Commission. National Commission on Sleep Disorders Research (U.S. Department of Health and Human Services). 1993. *Wake up America: A national sleep alert; a report of the National Commission on Sleep Disorders Research*, vol. 1. Bethesda, MD: National Institutes of Health.

Page 262. "study by the National Sleep Foundation." 2009 Sleep in America Poll, http://www.sleepfoundation.org/sites/default/files/2009%20Sleep%20in%20America%20SOF%20EMBARGOED.pdf.

Page 262. "Millions of us are living." Dement, W. 1999. *The promise of sleep: A pioneer in sleep medicine explores the vital connection between health, happiness, and a good night's sleep.* New York: Delacorte Press. 72.

Page 262. "fifty-six million prescriptions." Gallene, D. 2009. Sleeping pill use grows as economy keeps people up at night. *Los Angeles Times*, March 30, http://www.latimes.com/features/health/la-he-sleep30-2009mar30,0,1418832.story.

Page 263. Recommendations of the American Academy of Sleep Medicine and the National Sleep Foundation are available online at http://www.aasmnet.org/ and http://www.sleepfoundation.org/.

Page 265. "Specialists in sleep disorders." http://www.sleepcenters.org/.

Page 266. "the delivery of good medical." Shem, S. *The house of God.* 1978. New York: Bantam Dell, 381.

Conclusion: Your Brain's Future

Page 267. "We need to move." Comer, M. 2008. The "tipping point" in the Alzheimer's dialogue: it's all about the messenger. *Alzheimer's & Dementia* 4: 300–304.

Page 267. "The stakes are high." Ibid.

Page 268. "How do we ensure." Laura Carstensen, quoted in Cook, K. New age thinking. 2004. *Stanford Magazine*, July/August, 49–54, http://www-psych.stanford.edu/~lifespan/articles/StanfordMagazine.pdf.

REFERENCES

"No one but the author is interested in a long list of references stuck onto the end of an article like barnacles on a ship's bottom."—NEW ENGLAND JOURNAL OF MEDICINE, 1964

Brain, neurology, neuroscience, health, and aging are enormous subjects. Scholarly peer-reviewed references from the past twenty years on memory, aging brains, and Alzheimer's disease alone would number in the tens of thousands. A recent Google search for "Alzheimer's" resulted in more than 17 million hits—1.24 million for "memory peer-reviewed articles"! Thus, this bibliography is highly selective. It can be found on my website www.brainsavers.com. Included there are books and an extensive list of academic journals and articles that I researched. I hope this will be useful for those seeking further scholarly reading. I would be remiss if I did not acknowledge the tens of thousands of brain researchers and thinkers whose tireless and often underappreciated work over the past few decades resulted in the scientific discoveries upon which both BrainSavers and *The Brain Training Revolution* are based.

RECIPES

BREAKFASTS

Whole-Wheat Fruit Pancakes

By Jim Perko

Serving size: 2 pancakes; makes 12–14 pancakes

1 1/3 cups whole-wheat pastry flour

1 tablespoon baking powder

3/4 teaspoon salt

1/2 teaspoon cinnamon

1 tablespoon ground chia seeds

1 1/3 cups water

1 tablespoon vanilla extract

1/2 cup toasted walnuts

1 apple, freshly grated

1 pear, freshly grated

1 banana, peeled, halved, and thinly sliced

1. In a large bowl, combine the dry ingredients—flour, baking powder, salt, cinnamon, and ground chia seeds—mixing well with a wire whisk.
2. In a separate measuring cup, combine the water and vanilla extract. Add the water and vanilla mixture to the dry ingredients, mixing well with the wire whisk.
3. Mix the walnuts into the pancake batter mixture. Then, add the grated apple and pear to the mixture, immediately followed by the banana.

Mix well. If the batter seems a little thick (depending on the ripeness and juiciness of the fruit), add two more tablespoons of water.

4. Spoon the batter into a preheated nonstick pan that has been wiped with a light film of vegetable oil. Cook each pancake over medium heat until golden brown.

Berry Nutty Oatmeal

By Dorothy Turner
Serving size: 1/2 cup; serves 4

2 cups rolled oats
1/8 cup cranberries, raisins, or goji berries
2 tablespoons shredded coconut
2 tablespoons ground flaxseed
1/8 cup chopped nuts (pecans or walnuts)

1. Combine all ingredients with 4 cups of water in a large pot. Bring the mixture to a boil and then simmer until all the water is absorbed.

SALADS

Apple-Pear-Jicama Waldorf Salad

By Jim Perko
Serving size: 1 cup; serves 12

3 pears (any variety)
2 cups unsweetened pineapple juice (to prevent jicama, pears, and apples from browning)
3 Fuji apples
1 pound jicama
2 cups red grapes

1/2 cup brown or golden raisins
1/2 cup sliced almonds, toasted
1/2 cup chopped walnuts, toasted
1/2 cup unsalted sunflower seeds
16 ounces grapeseed oil vegenaise
3 ounces agave nectar

1. Wash and dice the pears into 1/4-inch squares. Place the pieces of pear in a bowl with the pineapple juice. Let the pears sit in the juice for 5 minutes; then, using a slotted spoon, move the pears to a large serving bowl. Reserve the pineapple juice and set aside.
2. Wash and dice the apples into 1/4-inch squares. Place the pieces of apple in the bowl containing the pineapple juice. Let the apples sit in the juice for 2 minutes; then, using a slotted spoon, move the apples to the bowl containing the pears. Reserve the pineapple juice and set aside.
3. Peel and dice the jicama into 1/4-inch squares. Place the pieces of jicama in the large bowl containing the pineapple juice. Let the jicama sit in the juice for 2 minutes; then, using a slotted spoon, move the jicama to the bowl containing the pears and apples. Reserve the pineapple juice and set aside.
4. Wash and cut the grapes in half, placing them in the bowl containing the jicama and other fruit. Add the raisins, almonds, walnuts, and sunflower seeds to the serving bowl, and mix thoroughly.
5. In a separate bowl, mix together the vegenaise and agave nectar, making a dressing. Toss the salad with the dressing thoroughly and serve.

Note: The reserved pineapple juice can be frozen for later use; be sure to label it before freezing. In order to prevent browning, pears need to be soaked for the longest period of time; jicama requires significantly less time.

Chicken Salad Veronique

By Jim Perko

Serving size: 1 cup; serves 4

1/2 cup vegenaise

2 tablespoons Dijon mustard

1 tablespoon fresh chopped parsley

1/2 teaspoon kosher salt or table salt

1/4 teaspoon freshly ground black pepper

1 pound chicken breast, cooked through and diced

1 cup red seedless grapes, halved

1/3 cup walnuts, toasted and crumbled

1/3 cup celery, diced

1/3 cup white onion, diced

1/3 cup hardboiled egg white, diced

1. Combine the vegenaise, mustard, parsley, salt, and pepper and in a
   large bowl. Mix well with a whisk.
2. Add the remaining ingredients, mix, and serve.

Note: You may cover, label, date, and refrigerate the salad for several
days before serving.

SOUPS

Chia Gazpacho

By Jim Perko

Serving size: 1 cup; serves 8

2 cups diced (1/4-inch pieces) peeled and seeded cucumber

1 cup diced (1/4-inch pieces) red pepper

1 cup diced (1/4-inch pieces) orange pepper

2 cups diced (1/4-inch pieces) seeded ripe tomatoes

1/2 cup finely minced red onion

2 cups tomato juice

1 tablespoon chia seed

3 tablespoons red wine vinegar

3 tablespoons lemon juice

2 tablespoons minced fresh garlic

4 tablespoons extra-virgin olive oil

4 dashes Cholula Mexican hot pepper sauce

3 tablespoons fresh chopped cilantro or parsley

Salt, to taste

1. Place all the ingredients in a large bowl and mix together well. Pour half of the mixture into a food processor or blender, and pulse the mixture to a coarse consistency.
2. Return the puréed portion to the bowl containing the remaining ingredients. Mix well, cover, and refrigerate for at least 2 hours before serving. Serve chilled.

LUNCHES

Quick and Easy Quinoa, Golden Beets, and Sunflower Seeds
By Melanie Albert
Serving size: 1 cup; serves 2 to 4

1 cup quinoa

2 cups water

2 golden beets, sliced into small pieces

1/4 cup sunflower seeds

1/4 teaspoon turmeric

1/8 teaspoon fresh ginger

1. Add all the ingredients to a rice cooker and turn the rice cooker on.
2. When the rice cooker's cycle stops, remove the mixture and serve.

Mexican Cabbage Dip with Fish Tacos

By Dorothy Turner

Serving size: 1 to 2 tacos; serves 4 to 6

Dip

2 avocados

1 lemon

1/2 cup green salsa

1/8 teaspoon cumin

1/4 cup chopped cilantro

1–2 medium cloves garlic, minced

1/2 cup vegenaise

Salt, to taste

Freshly ground black pepper, to taste

1 medium head raw cabbage, shredded, for garnish

Chips, for garnish

1. Blend all ingredients, except the cabbage and chips, in a large bowl. Mix thoroughly. Chill for 1 to 2 hours before serving.
2. Spread the cabbage on a platter and place the dip on top. Serve with the chips and the Fish Tacos.

Tacos

Extra-virgin olive oil

1 large onion, chopped

1 pound white fish (halibut or cod)

1 large green pepper, chopped

Fresh chopped parsley, to taste

Flour taco shells

1. Pour the olive oil into a large sauté pan and sauté the onions until transparent, about 3–4 minutes.
2. Add the fish and sauté until the fish is opaque, about 3 to 4 minutes.
3. Add the green peppers and sauté another 2 minutes. Sprinkle the parsley over the mixture and remove from heat.
4. Fill the taco shells with the cooked fish mixture. Serve warm with the Mexican Cabbage Dip.

DINNERS

Hearty Veggie and Garlic Roast

By Sarah Cahill

Serving size: 1 cup; serves 4 to 6

3 red onions, quartered

3 yellow peppers, quartered

3 red peppers, quartered

3 orange peppers, quartered

2 zucchinis, diced

1 eggplant, diced

10 cloves garlic, unpeeled

4 tablespoons olive oil

1 tablespoon chopped fresh thyme

1 tablespoon chopped fresh rosemary

1 tablespoon chopped fresh oregano

1 tablespoon chopped fresh marjoram

1 pinch freshly ground black pepper

1 avocado, sliced

1. Preheat the oven to 350°F.
2. Place the onions, peppers, zucchinis, eggplant, and garlic on a large baking sheet (or 2 sheets, if necessary). Sprinkle the vegetables with the olive oil, herbs, and black pepper. Mix well. Bake at 350°F for 40 to 50 minutes.
3. Remove the tray from the oven and transfer the vegetables to a serving platter. Top with the avocado. Serve with a salad or with a fish or chicken entrée.

Wild Sockeye Salmon with Dill

By Melanie Albert
Serving size: $1/2$ fillet; serves 4

3–4 tablespoons Dijon mustard
3 stalks fresh dill
Juice of 1 lemon
2 wild sockeye salmon fillets

1. Preheat the oven to 425°F.
2. In a mixing bowl, mix together the Dijon mustard, dill, and lemon juice.
3. Place the salmon fillets in a baking dish. Pour the mustard-lemon juice mixture over the salmon fillets.
4. Bake at 425°F for 15 minutes. Remove from the oven and serve.

DESSERTS

Baked Pears with Walnuts

By Sarah Cahill

Serving size: 1 pear; serves 4 to 6

4–6 pears, washed and cut in half

1/2 cup maple syrup

1/2 cup raw walnuts

1 dash cardamom

1. Preheat the oven to 350°F.
2. Lightly oil a large baking dish and arrange the pears inside. Drizzle the maple syrup over the pears, and sprinkle the walnuts and cardamom on top.
3. Bake, covered, at 350°F for 20 minutes. Remove from the oven and serve.

Apple Pie

By Theresa Healy

Makes 1 9-inch pie; serves 8

Pie Crust

2 cups almonds, soaked for 12 hours, rinsed, and dehydrated until crunchy (about 12 more hours)

1/2 cup dates, soaked for 20 minutes

1. Combine the almonds and dates in a food processor and pulse until evenly ground and mixed.
2. Press the mixture into a 9-inch pie dish.

Pie Filling

7 Gala or Fuji apples, peeled and chopped

1 banana, peeled and chopped

1 cup dates, soaked for 20 minutes

1/2 cup raisins, soaked for 30 minutes

1 teaspoon cinnamon

Juice of 1 lemon

1. Combine all the ingredients in a food processor and purée.

2. Spoon the filling into the pie crust and serve.

INDEX

ABOUT THE AUTHOR

Paul E. Bendheim, MD, has dedicated his career to researching Alzheimer's disease and other neurodegenerative disorders. He is an internationally recognized neurologist and an authority on Alzheimer's and other dementias, with twenty-five years of academic neuroscience research and industry-related drug development in Alzheimer's and other brain degenerative diseases. He is a member of the American Neurological Association, American Academy of Neurology, Scientific Review Board, and Institute for the Study of Aging. He was the Max Varon Visiting Professor of Neurobiology, Weizmann Institute of Science, Israel; and the medical director of development and research neurologist at the Banner Alzheimer's Institute in Phoenix. As a passionate advocate for brain health, he serves as CEO and chief medical officer of BrainSavers, a company he founded and whose mission is to help maintain healthy minds, reducing the impact of age-related memory impairment and the risk of developing Alzheimer's disease. He also currently serves as chairman of the Clinical Advisory Board, Intellect Neurosciences. A graduate of Pomona College and the University of Arizona College of Medicine, Dr. Bendheim is the father of two and lives with his wife in Arizona.

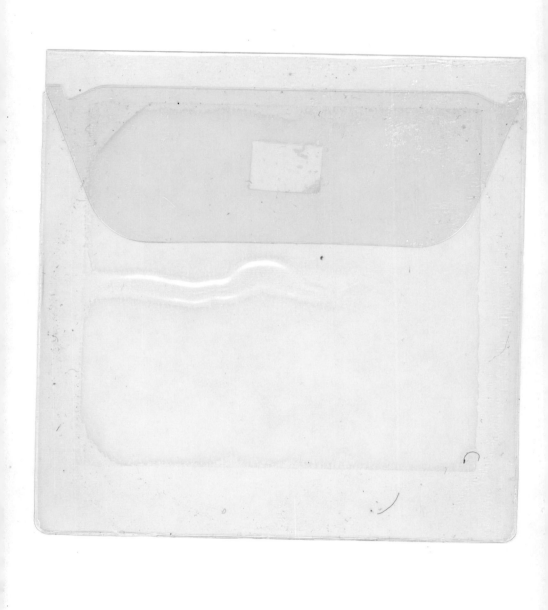